ROTATION

Yreka
~~1/5/15~~

Ft. Jones
~~6/14/15~~

Dorris
~~9/19/15~~

Happy
Camp
~~1/29/16~~

Yreka
5 29/16

The Art of Freedom

Also by Earl Shorris

FICTION

Ofay

The Boots of the Virgin

Under the Fifth Sun: A Novel of Pancho Villa

In the Yucatán

NONFICTION

The Death of the Great Spirit: An Elegy for the American Indian

The Oppressed Middle: Scenes from Corporate Life

Jews Without Mercy: A Lament

Power Sits at Another Table: Aphorisms

While Someone Else Is Eating (EDITOR)

Latinos: A Biography of the People

A Nation of Salesmen: The Tyranny of the Market and the Subversion of Culture

New American Blues: A Journey Through Poverty to Democracy

Riches for the Poor: The Clemente Course in the Humanities

In the Language of Kings: An Anthology of Mesoamerican Literature—
Pre-Columbian to the Present (EDITOR, WITH MIGUEL LEÓN-PORTILLA)

The Life and Times of Mexico

The Politics of Heaven: America in Fearful Times

The Art
of Freedom

TEACHING THE HUMANITIES
TO THE POOR

Earl Shorris

W. W. Norton & Company

NEW YORK   LONDON

For information about permission to reproduce selections from this book,
write to Permissions, W. W. Norton & Company, Inc.,
500 Fifth Avenue, New York, NY 10110

For information about special discounts for bulk purchases, please contact
W. W. Norton Special Sales at specialsales@wwnorton.com or 800-233-4830

Manufacturing by RR Donnelley, Harrisonburg
Book design by Fearn Cutler de Vicq
Production manager: Devon Zahn

Library of Congress Cataloging-in-Publication Data

Shorris, Earl, 1936–2012.
The art of freedom : teaching the humanities to the poor / Earl Shorris. — 1st ed.
        p. cm.
ISBN 978-0-393-08127-5 (hardcover)
1. Humanities—Study and teaching—United States. 2. Education, Humanistic—
United States. 3. Poor—Education—United States. 4. Adult education—Study and
teaching—United States. I. Title.
AZ183.U5S56 2013
001.3071'073—dc23
                                2012034389

W. W. Norton & Company, Inc.
500 Fifth Avenue, New York, N.Y. 10110
www.wwnorton.com

W. W. Norton & Company Ltd.
Castle House, 75/76 Wells Street, London W1T 3QT

1 2 3 4 5 6 7 8 9 0

For Michael

Contents

Contents

In 1995, having been unable to answer the most important question about poverty in the United States, I went to the Bedford Hills prison north of New York City to observe its Family Violence Program. I had a book to write, and I could not find an ending for it. For years I had looked everywhere, interviewed hundreds of people, and while I had developed a theory about poverty and its causes, no solution presented itself. I hoped I would find one there in the prison. Like most of what one learns about the poor, the surface life of the prison revealed less than I had expected and the emotional and intellectual depths were greater than I could have imagined. The next seventeen years would be governed by that afternoon at Bedford Hills. I would struggle to continue my work as a writer while the ideas engendered that afternoon threatened to engulf me.

I have written elsewhere about some of the people who partici-pated in the program that came to be called, in much of the world, the Clemente Course in the Humanities and also the Odyssey Course or Venture or Alta Cultura Maya–Hunab Ku or Yaaveskaniryaraq, or simply Humanities 101. The effort, until now, was always to pres-ent the theory, with the people no more than illustrative of the work.

This is a book about the people, about the founders of some of the many courses, their struggles, their generosity, and their extraordi-nary intelligence.

1

The center of every course is now, in every language and culture, as it has always been, the students who come heroically out of a surround of force, at the edge of hopelessness, to the beauty and clarity of reflective thinking. They and their children are proof that poverty is not a necessary condition of human life.

We teach freedom.

A Prison Romance

I was wrong, not entirely wrong, but wrong. And it took almost seventeen years to uncover the errors.

She was the cause of it all; about that I have no doubt. She was there at the beginning, she and her freckles and opaque eyes. You might say that she was the beginning, and you wouldn't be far off the mark, although it didn't happen quite the way it sounds. It was a series of accidents. I had not gone up to the prison to find romance or a plot line or a character for a novel; my interest was sociological: I went with a cold eye. That much is true. It is also true that a maximum security prison is a writer's dream, for writers are romantics, and I am no exception. Had it been otherwise there would have been no mistake and I would have wandered the world with different intellectual goods in my salesman's kit. I first wrote about the woman in the prison and the work she engendered a long time ago, before I could say what I knew about her or the effect she would have on me and the work I was to do.

The Bedford Hills prison—an hour and a half north of New York City on a good day—was almost a hundred years old when I first saw it. In summer, the road off the freeway curls around and down through stands of tall, spindly trees and runs on beside summer fields. Half a mile in, there is a hint of what lies ahead: a dead and stony field where yellow buses and cars frosted with gray dust sit parked in the sun, waiting. Nothing moves outside the prison unless the shifts change or the visitors come and go on the yellow buses. The brick buildings beyond the dead square set among the old, heavy trees give off an air of patience. It is a maximum security prison. Every woman there has been sentenced to at least six years, and more than a few will be there for life.

At Bedford Hills I would learn that prison is more violent than the streets. She would teach me. She would be my professor, as I would soon be hers.

On that first afternoon, the prisoners and two social workers and I sat in a circle of metal chairs in a large room somewhere in the center of the prison; I do not know where. The social worker directed me to sit next to a small, slightly chubby young woman. The woman and I shook hands and introduced ourselves in the formal manner I thought appropriate to a prison visit. When she looked at me, her eyes were perfectly opaque—hostile, prison eyes—and her mouth was set in the beginning of a sneer.

We listened to presentations about the abuse of women and heard their stories, saw them weeping as they spoke. There was a videotape of some of the women, more intimate than what they said in the room. After the videotape had played, a tall woman with yellow hair strode to the center of the circle. She stood very straight, her hands at her sides, and spoke plainly in a flat, unaccented voice. She said that she had taken part in the robbery of a convenience store. Her role was to hold a knife to the throat of the store clerk. She did not intend to harm him, she said, but when he struggled to free himself from her grasp, she did not know what to do. She told him to be still, and when he continued to struggle, she slit his throat.

The tall woman spoke without expression. She made only one gesture: she raised her right hand and drew it across her neck as if it was the throat of the remembered man. Then she dropped her hand to her side, paused, and said she was going home soon. She did not say anything more about the murder, nor did she speculate on the life she would have at home. As she passed close by me, returning to her chair, I saw that she had been weeping.

I did not look over at the woman next to me while the tall woman with yellow hair told her story. I was more interested in the reactions of the circle. No one shuddered, no one shrank away from the woman who confessed the bloody act. Perhaps they had heard the story before, perhaps they had heard it ten times, a hundred. Prison is about repetition; that is the essence of the punishment. The great Argentine writer Jorge Luis Borges said that repetition is death, but it is not that. I do not know exactly what it is, but repetition is something different; it is the reason why people who know prison life call it "doing time."

In the respite from stories of violence and redemption on the videotape, I turned again to the woman who sat beside me. Because I did not know what to say and because I had not forgotten why I was there, I asked: "Why do you think people are poor?"

"Because they don't have the moral life of downtown."

"What do you mean by the moral life?" I thought she must be talking about religion.

"You got to begin with the children," she said, speaking rapidly, clipping out the street sounds as they came into her speech. She paused long enough to let the change of direction take effect, then resumed the rapid, rhythmless speech. "You've got to teach the moral life of downtown to the children. And the way you do that, Earl, is by taking them downtown to plays, museums, concerts, lectures, where they can learn the moral life of downtown."

"What you mean is the humanities."

She looked at me as if I were the stupidest man on earth. "Yes, Earl, the humanities."

I was surprised by her use of my name. Hers was not an ordinary name; I did not remember it. I smiled at her, misunderstanding, thinking I was indulging her, not realizing that it was the other way round. I said, "And then they won't be poor anymore?"

She read every nuance of my response, and answered with the sneer now in her voice too, "And they won't be po no more."

"What you mean is—"

"What I mean is what I said—a moral alternative to the street."

She did not speak of jobs or money. In that, she was like the others I had listened to. No one, in all the places where I had been, had spoken of jobs or money. I saw people in every part of America who lived in what I had come to think of as a surround of force— ugliness, violence, hunger, abuse, poor schools, drugs, bad housing, vermin, crowding, brutal police, the nightmare of television and billboards constantly driving home the humiliation of relative poverty—this last perhaps the worst, the least bearable, especially for the children, to have less by comparison, to live in a country where billboards and television commercials constantly remind them that they are the have-nots. It went on and on so that there was never a moment's respite, a time for reflection, nothing was left for them but to react. I appreciated what she said, her solution to the problem of poverty, but how could the "moral life of downtown" lead anyone out of the surround of force? How could a museum push poverty away? Who could dress in statues or eat the past? And what of the political life? The way out of poverty was politics, I thought, not the moral life of downtown. But to enter the public world, to practice the political life, the poor had first to learn to reflect. Was that what she meant by the "moral life of downtown"? I looked at her for a moment, then turned away without speaking. Contempt does not require an answer.

On the drive back to the city from the prison I thought of my own education and of what she had said. If there was a way to give the poor the moral life of downtown, perhaps they would emerge from poverty, or if not from economic deprivation at least from the surround of force that bound them to a busy and fruitless life of reaction. I put the question aside, and followed her lead. It occurred to me then that she had set the agenda for my thoughts, but I did not dwell on it, for my mind was on writer's work and I thought I had found my way home.

What you mean is the humanities.

Yes, Earl, the humanities.

No one really knows what is meant by "the humanities." The Oxford English Dictionary does not attempt to offer an article about the word. Fowler's *Modern English Usage* says that a person reading the word "humanities" in a newspaper could assign any of four meanings to it, and be correct in every instance. I had accepted the meaning implied by a woman in a maximum security prison. And partly as a result of her definition, I was to spend the next seventeen years slightly but significantly off the mark. She did not mention Petrarch or his definition of the humanities, but I thought that was what she meant, and I accepted what she said. Petrarch had defined the humanities during the Renaissance, and he had left no wiggle room: The humanities consisted of classical works in moral philosophy, art history, history, literature, and logic. No more, no less. If that was not what she meant, she did not tell me so. She controlled by acquiescence, not by dispute or even suggestion. She was by then an accomplished prisoner.

I have one photograph of her, which appears in a book—*Breaking the Walls of Silence: AIDS and Women in a New York State Maximum Security Prison*—that was given to me by the prisoners who wrote it. She is one of the people in a group photograph. The photograph is undated; I do not know if it was made before or after I had begun to teach the humanities in the city and the prison. She is almost unrecognizable—a small, round-faced woman with a child's smile. Of all the women whose pictures appear in the book, she is the only one who wears the face of innocence. Over the years I have searched the face in the photograph many times looking for the controlling irony, and I have never found it. Perhaps the secret is the secret itself—and the irony is so perfect I cannot see it.

The origins of her ironic self were never entirely clear to me. She said very little about herself, following the informal rule of silence about crimes and sentences that prevailed in prison life. In a women's prison there are families, and only the families know. The confession by the tall woman with yellow hair that had been my introduction to the prison was an anomaly, a woman willing to sacrifice her privacy to bring her closer to home. When I sought to learn what was behind the opaque eyes and contemptuous tone of the prisoner I knew best and least, my questions were quickly rebuffed. Whatever I learned about her came from other prisoners and the staff of the prison. Slowly, bits of detail, terrors, shards of a life, tales and imaginings of a bloody and brutal existence became a narrative.

I saw her again at the end of August in a small prison room. We sat on hardback chairs facing each other. She wore dark red shorts and a green top and carried something in her hand. The end of summer heat lay thickly on our skin. The air in the room was close; the windows had been closed and the shades drawn to keep out the heat. The sun made ochre lamps of the window shades. It was not a good visit. The entrance to the prison, the search, the metal detector, the sliding steel bars that locked one or more persons into a small cabinet had unnerved me. A guard behind bulletproof glass inspected the people inside the cabinet. It was the place in which liberty was surrendered and prison began. Although I always knew I would be leaving in a few hours, passing through the cabinet again on my way out of the prison, I found it an almost unbearable moment.

I told her about the progress we had made in the city and in

the prison, recruiting teachers, and students, developing a curriculum in each discipline. She asked what I would be teaching, and I
recited the reading list. "There's something missing," she said.

It was the flat drawl of contempt again.

"What?"

"The Allegory of the Cave."

She opened her hand and I saw two large white pills. She put
the pills in her mouth one-at-a-time, and swallowed them. I recognized the medicine, the insufficient dose the prison provided.
I formed the question in my mind, "HIV?" But she had already
answered with the slow blink of her eyes. The end of the narrative
had been foreordained. "Yes," I said, meek in the presence of death.
"We will begin with the Allegory of the Cave."

And we did.

In the prison classroom the women sat in rows. Not one was
unkempt, not one was angry. One sat apart from the rest. She had
assembled the class, she managed the class; for a long time I did
not know how. I spoke to her as I spoke to the others, but I did not
engage her, she did not participate in the dialogue. She sat apart
from the others, in her own place. She made herself different as the
social worker was different. She rarely spoke. Her eyes were not like
the eyes of the other women. I looked at her often, thinking I might
catch the meaning of her eyes in a yearning glance, a wistful stare,
focus lost in thought or dreaming. I knew and I did not want to
know. I no longer heard contempt when she spoke.

The classes were dialogues, a kind of education none of the
women had ever known. Only Judy Clark, who had, like me,
been a student at the University of Chicago, was at ease with the
Socratic method. She was unlike the others, but not as I expected;
they loved and pitied her, perhaps because she had been a tracked
prisoner, watched day and night, set to doing the most menial
work, denied the few privileges of prison life. Although she was

something like a teaching assistant, she did not distance herself from the class. Only one woman sat in a separate place: Viniece Walker, "Niecie" to those who knew her. She was not the teaching assistant nor was she the teacher, yet the other women permitted her this distance in the classroom. While the others struggled with ideas, tried to embrace Keats in a prison classroom, looked desperately for a distinction between Greek and Roman art, she sat without speaking.

I found her name in the newspapers. There was a picture of her under a headline in enormous type on the front page of the *New York Daily News*:

CRACK BACK KILLERS

The print on the page was too dark and too thick with ink to show details in the photograph. A tiny woman stood before a high bench or perhaps a wall. Her hair hung down straight, uncombed and heavily greased. Her clothes were colorless and seemed unclean. She looked like a fallen child.

The photograph had been made the day of the arrest or perhaps the next day. I could not find the story inside the paper. I did not know what she had done. Whatever it was, it was not a common killing; she had merited the front page of the tabloid. Yet she looked meek, sickly, weary, worse than disheveled, unclean. I did not ask her about the killing or the arrest. She would not have told me. The revelations came out in chapters, like a novel.

Meanwhile the class went on in the city and the prison.

"Why we studying philosophy?" one of the women asked.

"Why *are* we studying philosophy; sentences need verbs unless they are interjections. However, I understand your concern, and I will bring you a book written in a prison cell in the sixth century by a man named Boethius. Philosophy, his childhood nurse, comes to visit him and helps him to escape."

A voice in the back of the room, hidden somewhere among the others, said, "We don't use that word around here." And everyone laughed.

The Consolation of Philosophy did not affect them as I had intended. They preferred history to ideas. They lived in wards or unheated cells. Ice formed on the inside of their cell walls in winter. The students examined the life of the man who had once been a Roman consul, they read the work each in her own way: the thief, the drug dealer, the killer, the embezzler, the weightlifter, the mules, the one who took revenge and the one who could not. They had read the beginning of the book, the page that gave the lie to all the rest. The Boethius whom they knew before they read a word he wrote had been tortured, bludgeoned, and died. They did not think of him freed in his prison cell, but they could envision his death.

As the year went on, I saw the change in them, especially in her. We held a graduation party in a small room in the prison. I managed to arrange for a lunch to be smuggled in from a Chinese restaurant in the nearest town. It was against prison rules, which pleased the women more than the food. We all thought I had done something heroic until the warden came to congratulate the women, whom she spoke of that afternoon as students rather than inmates. Niecie and another of the women talked about an argument they had had the night before the Chinese lunch. They had fought over opposing views of Blake's poem "*Black Boy*." Was it a racist poem or did Blake believe the black boy's skin was dark because he was closer to God? Niecie said it was racist.

I saw her now and again. Years passed. We found a way to speak by telephone, although it was not permitted. People thought we had secrets. I did not even know her middle name. Whenever I spoke to an audience or to a newspaper about the work of teaching the humanities to the poor, I spoke of her. And when people asked why she was in prison, what crime she had committed, I did not answer. I sent her newspaper clippings that mentioned her name. She gathered them into a folder along with a letter from the former mayor of New York City and another from the editor of *Harper's* magazine. Every two years she assembled a dossier to send to the parole board. When the day for her hearing came, she went alone, for no advocate was permitted. The first time she was still in her twenties, and when she was thirty she went again, and again after she was thirty, and each time the hearing lasted less than a minute. The parole board did not read the material she had prepared. "Denied," the parole board said. "Nature of the crime."

She was born and raised in Harlem, and she had never been poor. I do not know when she met the man who was with her that day. I do not know his name or the name of the prison where he served his time. She did not write to him and he did not write to her. She spoke of him ruefully, if she spoke of him at all. Silence, of course, is not the same as forgetting. There were the white pills that she took every day, and because the pills were not effective and the state did not allow a woman to go home to die, she thought of him when she saw the coffins and when she prayed for the dead.

Of all the memories she had of him, the one she could not erase from consciousness was of him and the bird. He reached into the cage and grabbed her pet bird and while she watched he took it out of the cage and broke its neck. He showed her the dead bird so that she would not forget. After that she did what he required of her. She walked the streets and brought the money home to him. They smoked crack cocaine, and the more they smoked, the more she worked. Theirs was a common story, a New York uptown tragedy.

It was the strangled bird that made it operatic and terrible. The bird was the fulcrum. It revealed a life the girl's mother could not bear to see, for she knew what the death of the bird symbolized. And then the mother died and left her pension and insurance money to her daughter, but because she did not trust her only child, she left it all with the girl's grandmother. The old woman doled out the money slowly, week by week.

They went to the old woman's apartment to get it all. When she would not give it to them, he beat the old woman. Her granddaughter went to the window and looked out on the city and was not there while he beat the old woman. The beating made sounds of crushing and cracking of bones and flesh and the sphere of the skull. Outside the window there was the city, and she passed through the window into the distant city. She was not there in the room, she did not hear the sounds of the bludgeoning of the old woman, and she did not see death or catch the smell of butchery.

Suddenly they fled. Had he finished the old woman by then? Why had they left without taking the bank card or the old woman's credit cards? Was someone screaming? I did not ask her, she would not have told me. Abused women absent themselves from pain; they have no other means of surviving the moment. I do not know when she came aware again or what she saw outside the window. I do not know who was screaming.

Without the bank card they demanded from the old woman, afraid that someone had heard the sounds of killing, they fled. They did not go back to the place where they lived. They were sure the police were waiting for them there. For three days they moved through the uptown slums, afraid to go where they were known. They thought the police were hunting them. They did not eat or bathe or sleep. They smoked rock cocaine and kept moving. At the end of the third day, they had no money and no place to sleep and they were exhausted. They were sick, eaten by desire, withdrawing from crack.

The police did not bother to look for them. They had found the bank card still hidden in the old woman's apartment. It did not require the mind of the philosophers of outlaws, François Villon and Michel Foucault, to know what would happen next. When she opened the door to the old woman's apartment, the police were waiting there. She did not protest. When the newspaper photographer took her picture, she no longer had the strength to cover her face.

I spoke to her through most of her years in the prison, less often as her study of the humanities diminished the need to talk with me. She earned an advanced degree in English. In the last years before completing her sentence she became quieter, reading more, an unofficial but effective social worker, counselor to the people she called "inmates."

When she passed through the cabinet into the outside world, she left no forwarding address. Terri McNair, the social worker who had been so close to Niecie, could not find her. By then the HIV infection had become acquired immunodeficiency syndrome (AIDS). She had needed the "cocktail" of antiretroviral drugs used to slow the progress of the infection. The single drug the prison provided each day was cheap and ineffective.

She died. I do not know where Viniece Walker died or which of the opportunistic diseases finally killed her. She had never known sweet social life amidst the beneficiaries of liberty, but the humanities had given her the excitement of freedom Boethius had found when Philosophy came to visit him in his cell. She understood. She died free.

All but one of other women who attended the Clemente Course in the Humanities in 1995 have been released from prison, and not one has returned. The recidivism rate of women prisoners with some college education, including those released from maximum security prisons, is very low, but zero is extraordinary.

Only Judy Clark, whose confusion about social justice led her to murder, is still in prison, serving a sentence that amounts to life without parole. I am one of the many people who wrote to the courts asking that she be given a new trial.

Since Viniece Walker first told me about "the moral life of downtown," more than ten thousand people around the world have attended the Clemente Course that began in the prison and in the city at the Roberto Clemente Family Guidance Center. For a long time, the course adhered rigidly to a curriculum based on the Western classics. It was exactly what Boethius and Petrarch and Robert Maynard Hutchins and Viniece Walker and I thought was the only possible curriculum. I approached the world like an eighteenth-century British schoolmaster besotted with Greeks and tea. As I traveled the world, I carried my rigid response to life in the surround in my knapsack to one city, one country, one continent after the next. And the world redefined the humanities. Beauty answered to many names, wisdom spoke many languages, the menu of history was beyond the comprehension of one mind, poetry was impervious to translation. I had declared war on the surround of force, the life of reaction, but the varieties of reflection had not occurred to me, not then, not in the beginning. In a freezing village near the Bering Sea and in the Náhuatl-speaking heights above Mexico City, among the homeless of Seoul and the varieties of Chicago, in Africa and Argentina, I would come to understand the democracy of the humanities. By the time I went to San Antonio Sihó, a tiny village in Yucatán, Mexico, I had learned that I was wrong, but not entirely wrong. There was something to be done, and there was a way.

CHAPTER 1

In the Beginning—1995[1]

On September 8, 2006, in a small Texas town not far from the Gulf of Mexico, a tall, slim young woman wrote a letter that finally brought to a close the first year of the humanities course at the Roberto Clemente Family Guidance Center. It had been a long time since I last saw her, but I remembered her. I had interviewed her almost ten years earlier when she came to the center to apply for entrance to the course. She had a good mind and as I recall a stronger academic background than many of the people who asked to be admitted. After talking with her for twenty minutes, however, I decided to turn down her application. There was something wrong. I did not know what; perhaps it was only that a pretty blonde from Texas seemed so out of place on the Lower East Side of New York.

The view from the front door of the Clemente Center in 1995 was one of the best known sights in America. The three buildings directly across the street were used as the opening of the popular television program *NYPD Blue*. Apparently, the producers thought the dilapidated tenements, abandoned by landlords, now occupied by squatters and drug dealers, represented the ugliest, most violent

---

1 Much of this chapter and a portion of the preceding section in a different form appeared in *Riches for the Poor: The Clemente Course in the Humanities* (New York: W. W. Norton, 2000).

police precinct in America. Dr. Jaime Inclán, perhaps in an act of defiance, had chosen the site to establish the only clinic in the city offering psychological counseling to Spanish speakers. Earlier that summer I had asked him if he would listen to an idea for an experiment in education for the poor.

I explained to him that after nearly three years of interviewing poor people across the country I had seen that numerous forces—hunger, isolation, illness, landlords, police, abuse, neighbors, drugs, criminals, and racism, among many others—exert themselves on the poor at all times and enclose them, making up a "surround of force" from which, it seems, they cannot escape. I had come to understand that this was what kept the poor from being political and that the absence of politics in their lives was what kept them poor. I don't mean "political" in the sense of voting in an election but in the way Pericles[2] used the word: to mean activity with other people at every level, from the family to the neighborhood to the broader community to the city-state.

By the time I presented the idea to Dr. Inclán, I had listened to more than six hundred people, some of them over the course of two or three years. Although my method is that of the brico-leur, the tinkerer who assembles a thesis of the bric-à-brac he finds in the world, I did not think there would be any more surprises. Of course, that was before I met Viniece Walker in the Bedford Hills Prison. I did not know her well when I sat in Jaime Inclán's office that day, yet it had already become clear to me that when she spoke of "the moral life of downtown" she meant the humanities, the study of human constructs and concerns, which has been the source of reflection for the secular world since the Greeks first stepped back from nature to experience wonder at what they beheld. If the political life was the way out of poverty, the humanities provided an entrance to reflection and the political life. The

---

2   Pericles' Funeral Oration in Thucydides, *The Peloponnesian War.*

poor did not need anyone to release them; an escape route existed. But to open this avenue to reflection and politics, a major distinction between the preparation for the life of the rich and the life of the poor had to be eliminated.

Once Niecie had challenged me with her theory, the comforts of tinkering came to an end; I could no longer make an homage to the happenstance world, and rest. To test Niecie's theory outside the confines of the prison, students, faculty, and facilities were required. And the ethics of the experiment had to be considered: I resolved to do no harm. There was no need for the course to have a "sink or swim" character; it could aim to keep as many afloat as possible.

Dr. Inclán offered the center's conference room for a classroom. We would put three metal tables end to end to approximate the boat-shaped tables used in discussion sections at the University of Chicago of the Hutchins era, which I used as a model for the course. A card table in the back of the room would hold a coffeemaker and a few cookies. The setting was not elegant, but it would do.

Now the course lacked only students and teachers. With no funds and a budget that grew every time a new idea for the course crossed my mind, I would have to ask the faculty to donate its time and effort. Moreover, when Hutchins said, "The best education for the best is the best education for us all," he meant it: he insisted that full professors teach discussion sections in the college.[3] If the Clemente Course in the Humanities was to follow the same pattern, it would require a faculty with the knowledge and prestige that students might encounter in their first year at Harvard, Yale, Princeton, or Chicago.

I turned first to the novelist Charles Simmons. He had been

---

3   Under the guidance of Robert Maynard Hutchins (1929–1951), the University of Chicago required year-long courses in the humanities, social sciences, and natural sciences for the bachelor of arts degree. Hutchins developed the curriculum with the help of Mortimer Adler, among others; the Hutchins courses later influenced Adler's Great Books program.

assistant editor of the *New York Times Book Review* and had taught at Columbia University. He volunteered to teach poetry, beginning with simple poems, Housman, and ending with Latin poetry. Grace Glueck, who wrote art news and criticism for the *New York Times*, planned a course that began with cave paintings and ended in the late twentieth century. Timothy Koranda, who did his graduate work at MIT, had published journal articles on mathematical logic, but he had been away from his field for some years and looked forward to getting back to it. I planned to teach the American history course through documents, beginning with the Magna Carta, moving on to the second of Locke's *Two Treatises of Government*, the Declaration of Independence, and so on through the documents of the Civil War. I would also teach the political philosophy class.

Since I was a *naïf* in this endeavor, it did not immediately occur to me that recruiting students would present a problem. I didn't know how many I needed. All I had were criteria for selection:

Age: 18–35.

Household income: Less than 150 percent of the Census Bureau's Official Poverty Threshold (though this was to change slightly).

Educational level: Ability to read a tabloid newspaper (this would also change, to reading a page of a good translation of the *Apology* of Socrates, because the prose in the tabloids was sometimes incomprehensible).

Educational goals: An expression of intent to complete the course.

Inclán arranged a meeting of community activists who could help recruit students. Lynette Lauretig of The Door, a program that provides medical and educational services to adolescents, and Angel Roman of the Grand Street Settlement, which offers work and training and GED programs, were both willing to give us access to prospective students. They also pointed out some practical considerations. The course had to provide bus and subway tokens, because fares ranged between $3 and $6 per class per student, and the students could not afford $60 or even $30 a month for transportation. We also had to offer dinner or a snack, because the classes were to be held from 6 to 7:30 p.m. (later extended to 8 p.m.).

A few days later Lynette Lauretig arranged a meeting with some of her staff at The Door. We disagreed about the course. They thought it should be taught at a much lower level. Although I could not change their views, they agreed to assemble a group of Door members who might be interested in the humanities.

On an early evening that same week, about twenty prospective students were scheduled to meet in a classroom at The Door. Most of them came late. Those who arrived first slumped in their chairs, staring at the floor or greeting me with sullen glances. A few ate candy or what appeared to be the remnants of a meal. The students were mostly black and Latino, one was Asian, and five were white; two of the whites were immigrants who had severe problems with English. When I introduced myself, several of the students would not shake my hand, two or three refused even to look at me, one girl giggled, and the last person to volunteer his name, a young man dressed in a Tommy Hilfiger sweatshirt and wearing a cap turned sideways, drawled, "Henry Jones, but they call me Sleepy, because I got these sleepy eyes—"

"In our class, we'll call you Mr. Jones."

He smiled and slid down in his chair so that his back was parallel to the floor.

Before I finished attempting to shake hands with the prospective students, a waiflike Asian girl with her mouth halffull of cake said, "Can we get on with it? I'm bored."

I liked the group immediately. Perhaps it was the challenge they presented, or the willingness to engage. In retrospect, it was that this was still the beginning, the experiment. In the beginning, there is no responsibility. The burden of lives does not come until much later. If it all went down, if the project collapsed, no one would have been wounded. And this lightness that accompanied the start is what enabled the project to go forward. It did not occur to me that anyone could be hurt by the failure of the still nameless project, not even me. The book that I had planned would not end as Starling Lawrence and I had hoped it would, but books often do not meet their promise. There would be another kind of ending, talk instead of action. Talk was a form of action. I was loosed, if not freed, by the nature of beginning. There were still limitless options. The group gathered in the small room at The Door was an option; they interested me, and I thought they could be recruited to the experiment, at least for a little while, long enough to see if the humanities could win them.

My first effort to recruit students, in the South Bronx, had been a disaster. An African woman, a social work administrator now living in the United States, had invited me to speak to a group of her clients. She had left two white social workers in the room with me and many black women, all poor, most of them single mothers. Everything had gone well until a white social worker asked if I was going to teach African history.

"No," I said. "We will teach American history. Of course, the history of black people is very important in the development of the United States."

The white woman demanded African history. The black women said nothing. The white social workers were in charge. They were the grim employees of goodness, intense. The African woman,

Ms. Nabakaba, who presided over the entire program, had left the room. I had no allies. I soldiered on: American history, I told her.

It was hopeless. The social worker who spoke—the other one was silent—sat in her place in the back of the room, as big as Gertrude Stein and as stony as the famous sculpture of her, and said that the women should not come to the course. And when I asked how many of the women wanted to take this free college course, not one raised her hand.

I resolved to approach these prospective students at The Door differently. "You've been cheated," I said. "Rich people learn the humanities; you didn't. The humanities are a foundation for getting along in the world, for thinking, for learning to reflect on the world instead of just reacting to whatever force is turned against you. I think the humanities are one of the ways to become political, and I don't mean political in the sense of voting in an election but in the broad sense." I told them Pericles' definition of politics.

"Rich people know politics in that sense. They know how to negotiate instead of using force. They know how to use politics to get along, to get power. It doesn't mean that rich people are good and poor people are bad. It simply means that rich people know a more effective method for living in this society.

"Do all rich people, or people who are in the middle, know the humanities? Not a chance. But some do. And it helps. It helps to live better and enjoy life more. Will the humanities make you rich? Yes. Absolutely. But not in terms of money. In terms of life.

"Rich people learn the humanities in private schools and expensive universities. And that's one of the ways in which they learn the political life. I think that is the real difference between the haves and have-nots in this country. If you want real power, legitimate power, the kind that comes from the people and belongs to the people, you must understand politics. The humanities will help.

23

"Here's how it works: We'll pay your subway fare; take care of your children, if you have them; give you a snack or a sandwich; provide you with books and any other materials you need. But we'll make you think harder, use your mind more fully, than you ever have before. You'll have to read and think about the same kinds of ideas you would encounter in a first-year course at Harvard or Yale or Oxford.

"You'll have to come to class in the snow and the rain and the cold and the dark. No one will coddle you, no one will slow down for you. There will be tests to take, papers to write. And I can't promise you anything but a certificate of completion at the end of the course. I'll be talking to colleges about giving credit for the course, but I can't promise anything. If you come to the Clemente Course, you must do it because you want to study the humanities, because you want a certain kind of life, a richness of mind and spirit. That's all I offer you: philosophy, poetry, art history, logic, rhetoric, and American history.

"Your teachers will all be people of accomplishment in their fields," I said, and I spoke a little about each teacher. "That's the course. October through May, with a two-week break at Christmas. It is generally accepted in America that the liberal arts and the humanities in particular belong to the elites. I think you're the elites."

The young Asian woman said, "What are you getting out of this?" That is what I had liked about the class; not the hostility, but the willingness to engage.

"This is a demonstration project. I'm writing a book. This will be proof, I hope, of my idea about the humanities. Whether it succeeds or fails will be up to the teachers and you."

All but one of the prospective students applied for admission.

I repeated the new presentation at the Grand Street Settlement and at other places around the city. There were about fifty candidates for the thirty positions in the course. Personal interviews began in early September.

Meanwhile, almost all of my attempts to raise money had failed. Only the novelist and editor Starling Lawrence at W. W. Norton, which had contracted to publish the book; the publishing house itself; and a small, private family foundation supported the experiment. We were far short of our budgeted expenses, but my wife, Sylvia, and I agreed that the cost was still very low, and we decided to go ahead.

Of the fifty prospective students who showed up at the Clemente Center for personal interviews, a few were too rich (a postal supervisor's son, a fellow who claimed his father owned a factory in Nigeria that employed sixty people) and more than a few could not read. Some of the applicants were too young: a thirteen-year-old and two who had just turned sixteen. Lucia Medina, a woman with five children who told me that she often answered the door at the single-room occupancy hotel where she lived with a butcher knife in her hand, was the oldest person accepted into the course. Carmen Quinones, a recovering addict who had spent time in prison, was the next eldest. Both were in their early thirties. The interviews went on for days.

Abel Lomas[4] shared an apartment and worked part time wrapping packages at Macy's. His father had abandoned the family when Abel was born. He had seen his mother murdered by his stepfather when Abel was thirteen. With no one to turn to and no place to stay, he lived on the streets, first in Florida, then back in New York City. He used the tiny stipend from his mother's Social Security to keep himself alive.

After the recruiting session at The Door, I drove up Sixth

---

4 Not his real name, although the person I am speaking about has been one of the grandest successes of the course. His drive and the quality of his mind are exceptional.

Avenue from Canal Street with Abel, and we talked about ethics. He had a street tough's delivery, spitting out his ideas in crudely formed sentences of four, five, eight words, strings of blunt declarations, with never a dependent clause to qualify his thoughts. He did not clear his throat with badinage, as timidity teaches us to do, nor did he waste his breath with tact.

"What do you think about drugs?" he asked, the strangely breathless delivery further coarsened by his Dominican accent. "My cousin is a dealer."

"I've seen a lot of people hurt by drugs."

"Your family has nothing to eat. You sell drugs. What's worse? Let your family starve or sell drugs?"

"Starvation and drug addiction are both bad, aren't they?"

"Yes," he said, not "yeah" or "uh-huh" but a precise, almost formal "yes."

"So it's a question of the worse of two evils? How shall we decide?"

The question came up near Thirty-fourth Street, where Sixth Avenue remains hellishly traffic-jammed well into the night. Horns honked, people flooded into the street against the light. Buses and trucks and taxicabs threatened their way from one lane to the next where the overcrowded avenue crosses the equally crowded Broadway. As we passed Herald Square and made our way north again, I said, "There are a couple of ways to look at it. One comes from Immanuel Kant, who said that you should not do anything unless you want it to become a universal law; that is, unless you think it's what everybody should do. So Kant wouldn't agree to selling drugs or letting your family starve."

Again he answered with a formal "Yes."

"There's another way to look at it, which is to ask what is the greatest good for the greatest number: in this case, keeping your family from starvation or keeping tens, perhaps hundreds of people from losing their lives to drugs. So which is the greatest good for the greatest number?"

"That's what I think," he said.

"What?"

"You shouldn't sell drugs. You can always get food to eat. Welfare. Something."

"You're a Kantian," imputing his answer to the categorical imperative.

"Yes."

"You know who Kant is?"

"I think so."

We had arrived at Seventy-seventh Street, where he got out of the car to catch the subway before I turned east. As he opened the car door and the light came on, the almost military neatness of him struck me. He had the newly cropped hair of a cadet. His clothes were clean, without a wrinkle. He was an orphan, a street kid, an immaculate urchin. Within a few weeks he would be nineteen years old, the Social Security payments would end, and he would have to move into a shelter.

Some of those who came for interviews were too poor. I did not think that was possible when we began, and I would like not to believe it now, but it was true. There is a point at which the level of forces that surround the poor can become insurmountable, when there is no time or energy left to be anything but poor. Most often I could not recruit such people for the course; when I did, they soon dropped out.

Over the days of interviewing, a class slowly assembled. I could not then imagine who would last the year and who would not. One young woman submitted a neatly typed essay that said: "I was homeless once, then I lived for some time in a shelter. Right now, I have got my own space granted by the Partnership for the Homeless. Right now, I am living alone, with very limited means. Financially I am overwhelmed by debts. I cannot afford all the food I need. . . ."

A brother and sister, refugees from Tashkent, lived with their parents in the farthest reaches of Queens, far beyond the end of the subway line. They had no money, and they had been refused admission by every school to which they had applied. I had not intended to accept immigrants or people who had difficulty with the English language, but I took them into the class.

I also took four who had been in prison, three who were homeless, three who were pregnant, one who lived in a drugged dream state in which she was abused, and one whom I had known for a long time and who was dying of AIDS. I had met her at Young Mothers, a center for recovering addicts in the South Bronx, while I was interviewing people about poverty. She had leapt into a group discussion to attack what I had said about someone who was no longer an addict. She backed off her argument when I said that the person was dead. She spoke more openly after that. All the other women in the group looked at her with wonder. She was, by any standard, beautiful, with skin that looked like black velvet. I had never seen a woman of any race with such skin. Her husband, too, had admired it, and he put it to use to pay for his drug habit and hers, sending her out into the street to work as a prostitute. I did not know then that she had AIDS. There were no signs of it. She was simply beautiful. When she said she would come to the course, I did not ask her to read a newspaper. I had listened to her in many of the group sessions at Young Mothers. She would do well.

As I listened to the prospective students, I wondered how the course would affect them. They had no public life, no place; they lived within the surround of force, moving as fast as they could, driven by necessity, without a moment to reflect. Why should they care about fourteenth-century Italian painting or truth tables or the death of Socrates?

Between the end of recruiting and the orientation session that would open the course, I made a visit to Bedford Hills to talk with Niecie Walker. That was when she asked me what I intended to teach in the moral philosophy section. I said, "We'll begin with Plato: the *Apology*, a little of the *Crito*, a few pages of the *Phaedo* so that they'll know what happened to Socrates. Then we'll read Aristotle's *Nicomachean Ethics*. I also want them to read Thucydides, particularly Pericles' Funeral Oration in order to make the connection between ethics and politics, to lead them in the direction I hope the course will take them. Then we'll end with *Antigone*, but read as moral and political philosophy as well as drama."

That was when she said, "There's something missing."

At the beginning of the orientation at the Clemente Center a week later, I gave out the first assignment: "In preparation for our next meeting, I would like you to read a brief selection from Plato's *Republic*: the Allegory of the Cave."

I tried to guess how many students would return for the first class. I hoped for twenty, expected fifteen, and feared ten. Sylvia, who had agreed to share the administrative tasks of the course, and I prepared coffee and cookies for twenty-five. We had a plastic container filled with subway tokens. Thanks to W. W. Norton, we had thirty copies of Bernard Knox's *Norton Book of Classical Literature*, which contained all of the texts for the philosophy section except the *Republic* and the *Nicomachean Ethics*.

At six o'clock there were only ten students seated around the long table, but by six fifteen the number had doubled, and a few minutes later two more straggled in out of the dusk. I had written a time line on the blackboard, showing them the temporal progress of thinking—from the role of myth in Neolithic societies to the Gilgamesh Epic and forward to the Old Testament, Confucius, the Greeks, the New Testament, the Koran, the Epic of Son-Jara, and ending with Náhuatl and Maya poems, which took us up to the contact between Europe and America, where the history course began. The time line served as context and geography as well as history: no race, no major culture was ignored. "Let's agree," I told them, "that we are all human, whatever our origins. And now let's go into Plato's cave."

I told them that there would be no lectures in the philosophy section of the course; we would use the Socratic method, which is called maieutic dialogue. "'Maieutic' comes from the Greek word for midwifery. I'll take the role of midwife in our dialogue. Now, what do I mean by that? What does a midwife do?"

It was the beginning of a love affair, the first moment of their infatuation with Socrates. Later, Abel Lomas would characterize that moment in his no-nonsense fashion, saying that it was the first time anyone had ever paid attention to their opinions.

Grace Glueck began the art history class in a darkened room lit with slides of the Lascaux caves and next turned the students' attention to Egypt, arranging for them to visit the Metropolitan Museum of Art to see the Temple of Dendur and the Egyptian Galleries. They arrived at the museum on a Friday evening. Darlene Codd brought her two-year-old son. Pearl Lau was late, as usual. One of the students, who had told me how much he was looking forward to the museum visit, didn't show up, which surprised me. Later I learned that he had been arrested for jumping a turnstile in a subway station on his way to the museum and was being held in a prison cell under the Brooklyn criminal courthouse.

In the Temple of Dendur, Samantha Smoot asked questions of Felicia Blum, a museum lecturer. Samantha was the student who had burst out with the news, in one of the first sessions of the course, that people in her neighborhood believed it "wasn't no use goin' to school because the white man wouldn't let you up no matter what." But in a hall where the statuary was of half-human, half-animal female figures, it was Samantha who asked what the glyphs meant, encouraging Felicia Blum to read them aloud, to translate them into English. Toward the end of the evening, Grace led the students out of the halls of antiquities into the Rockefeller Wing, where she told them of the connections of culture and art in Mali, Benin, and the Pacific Islands. When the students had collected their coats and stood together near the entrance to the museum, preparing to leave, Samantha stood apart, a tall, slim young woman, dressed in a deerstalker cap and a dark blue pea-coat. She made an exaggerated farewell wave at us and returned to Egypt—her ancient mirror.

I had asked Charles Simmons to teach literature, giving him a brief idea of a reading list. He agreed, but when it came time to teach, he had decided he would teach only poetry. He was a fine teacher of poetry and a better teacher about the nature of volunteers. Simmons began the poetry class with poems as puzzles and laughs. His plan was to surprise the class, and he did. At first he read the poems aloud to them, interrupting himself with footnotes to bring them along. He showed them poems of love and of seduction, and satiric commentaries on those poems by later poets. "Let us read," the students demanded, but Charles refused. He tantalized them with the opportunity to read poems aloud. A tug-of-war began between him and the students, and the standoff was ended not by Charles directly but by Hector Anderson. When Charles asked if anyone in the class wrote poetry, Hector raised his hand.

"Can you recite one of your poems for us?" Charles said.

Until that moment, Hector had never volunteered a comment, though he had spoken well and intelligently when asked. He preferred to slouch in his chair, dressed in full camouflage gear, wearing a nylon stocking over his hair and eating slices of fresh cantaloupe or honeydew melon.

Hector stood and recited verse after verse of a poem that belonged somewhere in the triangle formed by Ginsberg's *Howl*, the Book of Lamentations, and hip-hop. When Charles and the students finished applauding, they asked Hector to say the poem again, and he did. Later Charles told me, "That kid is the real thing." Hector's discomfort with Sylvia and me turned to ease. He came to our house for a small Christmas party and at other times. We talked on the telephone about a scholarship program and about what steps he should take next in his education. I came to know his parents. As a student, he began quietly, almost secretly, to surpass many of his classmates.

Timothy Koranda was the most professorial of the professors. He arrived precisely on time, wearing a hat of many styles—part Borsalino, part Stetson, and at least one half World War I campaign hat. He taught logic during class hours, filling the blackboard from floor to ceiling, wall to wall, drawing the intersections of sets here and truth tables there and a great square of oppositions in the middle of it all. After class, he walked with students to the subway, chatting about Zen or logic or Heisenberg.

On one of the coldest nights of the winter, he introduced the students to logic problems stated in ordinary language that they could solve by reducing the phrases to symbols. He passed out copies of a problem, two pages long, then wrote out some of the key phrases on the blackboard. "Take this home with you," he said, "and at our next meeting we shall see who has solved it. I shall also attempt to find the answer."

By the time he finished writing out the key phrases, however, David Iskhakov raised his hand. Although they listened attentively, neither David nor his sister Susana spoke often in class. She was shy, and he was embarrassed at his inability to speak perfect English.

"May I go to blackboard?" David said. "And will see if I have found correct answer to zis problem."

Together Tim and David erased the blackboard, then David

began covering it with signs and symbols. "If first man is earning this money, and second man is closer to this town . . . ," he said, carefully laying out the conditions. After five minutes or so, he said, "And the answer is: B will get first to Cleveland!"

Samantha Smoot shouted, "That's not the answer. The mistake you made is in the first part there, where it says who earns more money."

Tim folded his arms across his chest, happy. "I shall let you all take the problem home," he said.

When Sylvia and I left the Clemente Center that night, a knot of students was gathered outside, huddled against the wind. Snow had begun to fall, a slippery powder on the gray ice that covered all but a narrow space down the center of the sidewalk. Samantha and David stood in the middle of the group, still arguing over the answer to the problem. I leaned in for a moment to catch the character of the argument. It was even more polite than it had been in the classroom, because now they governed themselves.

The question that Jaime Inclán had thought would give some indication of the effect of the course on the students was whether they had progressed from reaction to reflection. It was, we agreed, a key to knowing if a person had defeated the surround of force. A proof of our progress came on a Saturday morning in January. David Howell telephoned me at home. "Mr. Shores," he said, anglicizing my name, as many of the students did.

"Mr. Howell," I responded, recognizing his voice.

"How you doin', Mr. Shores?"

"I'm fine. How are you?"

"I had a little problem at work."

Uh-oh, I thought, bad news was coming. David is a big man, generally good-humored but with a quick temper. According to his mother, he had a history of violent behavior. In the classroom he had been one of the best students, a steady man, twenty-four years old, who always did the reading assignments and who often made interesting connections between the humanities and daily life. "What happened?"

"Mr. Shores, there's a woman at my job, she said some things to me and I said some things to her. And she told my supervisor I had said things to her, and he called me in about it. She's forty years old and she don't have no social life, and I have a good social life, and she's jealous of me."

"And then what happened?" The tone of his voice and the timing of the call did not portend good news.

"Mr. Shores, she made me so mad, I wanted to smack her up against the wall. I tried to talk to some friends to calm myself down a little, but nobody was around."

"And what did you do?" I asked, fearing this was his one telephone call from the city jail.

"Mr. Shores, I asked myself, 'What would Socrates do?'"

The blond girl from Texas had joined the class after all. I had told Dr. Inclán about her, saying that the way she was living in a homeless shelter, and the serious family problems she discussed, were bound to cause trouble for her and the class. I thought it would be best not to accept her, but I wanted his opinion, for he was the professional. He smiled, the grand Spanish mustache signaling the irony to come: "I think you are prejudiced against white people."

I laughed and admitted the young woman, whom we can call Laura, to the class. At first, she was an ideal student; not only smart but well spoken. During the one moment of aggression in the entire year, she made a statement in a philosophy class that so upset

Henry Jones that he rose from his chair, pointed his finger at her as if it were a weapon, and said, in a lethal voice: "Define your terms!"

And she did.

But later in the year she asked me if she could bring her roommate to class. I told her that we did not permit spectators, because I feared that their presence would be disruptive. The group had begun to coalesce, the dialogues were more open, the students no longer feared making a mistake. At the next meeting of the class Laura's roommate appeared. The two young women were living together at a homeless shelter in the northern part of the city. The roommate, a young black woman, could easily have been a film star. She was slim, almost thin, immaculately groomed, with elegant, extremely defined features, and so tense she seemed about to shatter. I told her that she could never return. Neither she nor Laura appeared for the next class, or the next. I phoned the shelter where they had been staying. After many refusals to tell me what had happened to Laura, a woman at the shelter said that she had been badly beaten by her roommate and that she did not want anyone in the class to see her. Later, her roommate barricaded Laura in her room and set it on fire. I did not know what to believe. Laura did not return to class, nor did she attend the graduation ceremony to applaud her classmates.

While Laura was coming to class, I had spoken to an admissions officer at New York University about her. I thought Laura was so bright that she could easily manage the classes at NYU or any university. The admissions officer agreed. The next fall, apparently having overcome her troubles, Laura entered New York University, and that was the last I heard from her until the letter arrived in 2006. The class went on. Laura's contributions were missed, but the group had become so integrated and the humanities were beginning to have such a powerful effect that no one student, no matter how bright, could dissuade the others from exciting conversation.

The class grew smaller as the year passed. The woman with the velvet skin whom I had met at Young Mothers in the South Bronx had always brought her tiny daughter to class with her. And sometimes the tiny girl cried for her mother when we left her with the other children in the room we had devoted to child care. If I was not teaching on those days, I often carried the child in my arms and stood at the door to the classroom where she could see her mother. It came to an end one evening before the start of class. There was a phone call for me at the front desk of the Clemente Center. What I heard was a woman's voice struggling to speak. It was the most beautiful of students, the mother of the little girl. She apologized for not coming to class. She was in the hospital, suffering from pneumonia. I told her not to worry about it. "I'll ask your friend, Carmen, to bring the assignments to you, and when you feel better, my wife and I will help you to catch up with the class." And then I asked about her daughter. She said that the child had not been infected. A few days later, Carmen told the class her friend had died.

Near the end of the year I took the students to a quasi-Italian restaurant in Greenwich Village. We all sat together at a long table. I told them to order whatever they liked from the menu, but I did say there was a limit of one glass of wine or bottle of beer. They all ordered soft drinks. Most of them were careful to order the cheapest thing on the menu: a dinner salad, a cup of soup. Only after a little coaxing were they willing to ask for a plate of pasta or a cutlet of breaded veal or chicken. Some had difficulty deciding which utensils to use. Others were baffled by the menu. One young woman asked the waiter if he needed help in the kitchen. When dinner was over, the students began gathering up the plates, scraping them, and preparing to carry them into the kitchen. I asked the students to put the plates back onto the table. "The waiters get paid to do that," I explained. "If you carry the plates into the kitchen, the

waiter won't have anything to do, and he will probably lose his job."
A discussion of manners might have been just as effective and perhaps more appropriate, but the brutal economics of people struggling to earn a living made sense to them in the same immediate,
stunning way that Emily Dickinson revealed the meaning of death
to them through the buzz of a fly.

One evening, in the American history section, I was telling
the students about Gordon Wood's ideas in *The Radicalism of the
American Revolution*. We were talking about the revolt by some
intellectuals against classical learning at the turn of the eighteenth
century, including Benjamin Franklin's late-life change of heart,
when Henry Jones raised his hand.

"If the founders loved the humanities so much, how come they
treated the natives so badly?"

I didn't know how to answer this question. There were con-
founding explanations to offer about changing attitudes toward
Native Americans, vaguely useful references to views of Rousseau
and James Fenimore Cooper. Then I saw Abel Lomas's raised hand
at the far end of the table. "Mr. Lomas," I said.

Abel said, "That's what Aristotle means by incontinence, when
you know what's morally right but you don't do it, because you're
overcome by your passions."

Lomas, a man gifted with the ability to understand contemporary philosophy, had endured and overcome cruel injustice more
than once in his life, and he was to suffer once more near the end
of the year. On Mother's Day, he was spotted by the police sitting
outside the homeless shelter where he stayed, drinking beer from a
can wrapped in a paper bag. The police arrested him for drinking
in public, sent his name to the central computer, and were told that
there was a federal warrant for Abel Lomas.

He was charged with distributing and selling illegal drugs, the
family business he had told me about the first time I met him, the

life he had chosen not to lead. It was ridiculous: a person dealing in large quantities of illegal drugs was not likely to live in a homeless shelter. Nonetheless, Lomas was charged and held for trial. Peter Neufeld, a young lawyer in one of the city's leading firms, agreed to take on Lomas's case pro bono. He arranged a meeting with Assistant U.S. Attorney Patrick Smith in which several people, including Lynette Lauretig, spoke about the quality of Lomas's mind and gave examples of his good character. The character references had no effect. Only when I asked Lomas to speak about the *Crito* and *Antigone* did the young assistant U.S. attorney take notice. Lomas spoke unhurriedly about the decision of Socrates to obey the law at the cost of his life. The stronger display, however, was his knowledge of *Antigone*, for he had been accused of choosing the drug-dealing life of his family. One of the people arrested in a major case had said Lomas was the kingpin in the drug ring. And then the others had taken the same position. It would have worked had Lomas not made the case for choosing to obey the law over loyalty to the family.

The assistant U.S. attorney asked Neufeld and me to step out into the hall. While Lomas waited in the interview room, Smith confessed that he knew very little of the classics, even though he had graduated with high honors from a fine university. He was astonished by Lomas's knowledge. Even so, he told us, a federal warrant could not be dropped; Lomas would have to go before a judge. The government would ask for the lightest possible sentence, but there would be a sentence. Abel Lomas was sentenced to a brief period on probation, and set free.

When Lomas spoke of incontinence in the classroom, the other students nodded. Perhaps some of them were aware of his ordeal in the federal system, and they understood the profound meaning of his argument for Aristotle's view of human foible. They were all inheritors of wounds caused by the incontinence of educated men;

now they had an ally in Aristotle, who had given them a way to analyze the actions of their antagonists.

Those who appreciate ancient history understand the radical character of the humanities. They know that politics did not begin in a perfect world but in a society even more flawed than ours: one that embraced slavery, denied the rights of women, practiced a form of homosexuality that verged on pedophilia, and endured the intrigues and corruption of its leaders. The genius of that society originated in man's re-creation of himself through the recognition of his humanness as expressed in art, literature, rhetoric, philosophy, and the unique notion of freedom. At that moment, the isolation of the private life ended and politics began.

The winners in the game of modern society, and even those whose fortune falls in the middle, have other means to power: they are included at birth. They know this. And they know exactly what to do to protect their place in the economic and social hierarchy. As Allan Bloom, author of the best-selling tract in defense of elitism *The Closing of the American Mind*, put it, they direct the study of the humanities exclusively at those young people who "have been raised in comfort and with the expectation of ever increasing comfort."

In the last meeting before graduation, the Clemente students answered the same set of questions they had answered at orientation. Between October and May, students had fallen to AIDS, pregnancy, job opportunities, pernicious anemia, clinical depression, a schizophrenic child, and other forces, but of the thirty students admitted to the course, sixteen had completed it, and fourteen had earned credit from Bard College. Dr. Inclán found that the students' self-esteem and their abilities to divine and solve problems had significantly increased; their use of verbal aggression as a tactic for resolving conflicts had significantly decreased. And they all had notably more appreciation for the concepts of benevolence, spirituality, universalism, and collectivism.

It cost about $2,000 for a student to attend the Clemente Course. Compared with unemployment, welfare, or prison, the humanities are a bargain. But coming into possession of the faculty of reflection and the skills of politics leads to a choice for the poor—and whatever they choose, they will be dangerous. They may use politics to get along in an unfair society, that is, to escape from the surround of force into a gentler life, where they will exercise the right to vote, perhaps participate in community activities. Or they may choose to seek a more just society by joining a union or a political party, or even organizations that work toward radical change.

On the night of the first Clemente Course graduation, the students and their families filled the eighty-five chairs we crammed into the conference room where classes had been held. Robert Martin, associate dean of Bard College, read the graduates' names. David Dinkins, the former mayor of New York City, handed out the diplomas. There were speeches and presentations. The students gave me a plaque on which they had misspelled my name. I offered a few words about each student, congratulated them, and said finally, "This is what I wish for you: May you never be more active than when you are doing nothing . . ." I saw their smiles of recognition at the words of Cato, which I had written on the blackboard early in the course. They could also recall the moment when we had come to the denouement of Aristotle's brilliantly constructed thriller, the *Nicomachean Ethics*—the idea that in the contemplative life man was most like God. One or two, perhaps more of the students, closed their eyes. In the momentary stillness of the room it was possible to think.

A year after graduation, ten of the first sixteen Clemente Course graduates were attending four-year colleges or going to nursing school; four of them had received full scholarships to Bard College. The other graduates were attending community college or working full time.

The Aftermath

During the latter part of the first course, a psychiatrist waiting for his license in the United States, where he would become the chief of psychiatric services in a large facility for veterans, operated the videocamera that documented the classes. Near the end of the year he received his license and could no longer spare the time to do the videotaping. In summing up his observations, he said, "It is the best psychotherapy I have seen in a very long time."

Psychotherapy was never the intention of the course, unless the shift from reaction to reflective thinking can be described as psychotherapeutic. In some instances, however, there were distinct changes in the psychological orientation of the students. In others, there were none that I could recognize. The changes came largely in what I would describe as their political lives, using the definition of politics supposedly spoken by Pericles; that is, the students became more involved at the family, neighborhood, community, and state levels. Some who had not spoken a civil word to one or both parents for some years found themselves able to discuss philosophy or an especially touching poem. Others found new pleasures in reading to their children or just talking with them. The greatest changes, however, were intellectual: two went on to study for their doctorates, two became dentists, one became a nurse; others were attending college when last I spoke to them.

The dentists, one of whom had suffered from overwork (three jobs and the Clemente Course), had lunch with Sylvia and me long after the course was over. They were college students then. A few years later, the young woman phoned and offered to give us free dental care to repay our kindness to her and her brother. It was not an offer I could accept, and I regret it in a way, for I would like to see them again.

Sleepy went to Bard College, where his adviser, Donna Ford,

did all that she could to keep him enrolled there. He left Bard after two years and went to work in a furniture store in a nearby town, soon becoming the manager of the store. Two of the women in the class became the personal charges of Sylvia Shorris. Samantha Smoot lifted up her head and graduated from the Fashion Institute of Technology. She and I appeared together on a CNN program about the course. I joked that we were like Beauty and the Beast, but Samantha relied on more than her looks. On CNN television and on Public Radio International she spoke in carefully made sentences about the effect of the humanities on the lives of the poor.

Carmen, whom I had met while she was a client in a drug rehabilitation program, may have saved the course from disintegrating. Midway during the year the students began coming late to class, some of them complaining about the winter weather, others slightly out of the rhythm of attending after the Christmas break. Carmen, the oldest of them and the toughest, took a stand in front of the blackboard to address the class. That night she had come to class wearing a black leather motorcycle jacket; she was intimidating. She berated the other students for being late, for not completing their reading assignments, for losing their discipline. And then, without a change in the harsh character of her address, she said a simple truth: "This is my last chance."

I do not know how the students understood her oration. Carmen had spent ten years in prisons. She lived in a part of the Bronx so dangerous that when my wife sent her a dozen roses to celebrate the completion of a year without drugs, the deliveryman was afraid to go to the neighborhood. If the others were afraid of her, they could not have admitted their fear. If they pitied her, they were too kind to let on. However they understood her address to the class, they complied with her wishes: classes began on time.

Two years later, Carmen told me that she was enjoying college, except for her philosophy course. "My teacher is not too good," she said. And after a pause that I attributed to an unaccustomed moment of shyness, she said, "I had to help him."

When last I spoke with her, she had become the head of the counseling staff in the drug program where I had first met her almost a decade earlier.

The students who graduated that year all did well, with the exception of Pearl, the Asian woman. I had talked with her during the year after she had behaved badly in class, and she had told me a grim tale of death and the aged. I did not know if it was true. Several years later, I saw her at The Door. A magazine had asked for a photograph of Sylvia and me and some of the graduates of the first class. Carmen is there with her head leaning on Sylvia's shoulder, smiling and affectionate. David and Samantha and others are also in the photograph. But the Asian girl is not in the picture. She had thrown a tantrum, and the staff at The Door could not calm her. I don't know what happened to her after that.

The effect of the course on the other graduates has been almost universally good. Yet slightly less than half of the students did not graduate, which is about the same as the number of students who complete four-year colleges on time. What of the others? Did the weeks or months in the course have any effect? There was some evidence: a letter with a Texas postmark but no return address.

"The blonde from Texas" is how the writer described herself in the letter. She said that she did not have enough money to stay on at New York University; and "I didn't want to start back at the bottom, go back to the shelters, so I gave in and came back home. It has taken nine years, but I am finally back, pursuing what my heart wants . . . I will never forget the lessons I learned in that center on the Lower East Side."

CHAPTER 2

It's About Freedom

The church in North Lawndale where Martin Luther King, Jr., had preached was gone, only the stone steps remained. An American sadness hovered over the area, grief turned to disaffection. The places where buildings had been burned out during the riots after the assassination of King remained blank, the hulks had been razed, their remains hauled away, the cellars filled in; the lots had not become a place for gardens but for all things broken, discarded, unwanted, unloved, sickening, and dangerous. Police cars roared across the empty spaces in pursuit of someone, whoever it was that had fired the first gunshots of morning and ruined the peace cast over the city by the heavy summer mist.

"We'll start with the Alderman," I said to my companions, the man and woman who displayed their fitness through sleeveless summer shirts and a visitor from Wisconsin who came to study the course. "Michael Chandler. I know him." I did not tell them that I had been in the building across the street a day before a boy lay on the roof, peering over the edge at the street five stories below, a rifle at his side. It was late on a summer afternoon when it happened. Streams of cars, trucks, and occasional city buses flowed east from the factories on the far side of the city. The boy waited for a white Toyota sedan. He had been told that an enemy gangster was coming. His assignment was to kill him. He waited, watching for the white Toyota. A city bus passed, moving slowly. Then the white Toyota. The boy killed the driver with a single shot. The driver lost control of the car, and it crashed into a bus, and the bus ran up across the curbing and into the front of a building not far from the alderman's office.

The boy picked up the empty cartridge and fled down the long flights of gray wooden stairs at the back of the building. He did not know that he had made a terrible mistake: the shot had been on the mark, but the dead man in the white Toyota was not an enemy gangster, he was a weary factory worker coming home at the end of his shift.

After the killing, the tensions along the street increased, and the openness that had existed even after the rage and the fires after the assassination of Dr. King died away. The alderman whom we had counted on to help us recruit students was not available. The women who sat behind heavy wooden counters away from the front windows said that he was not in and they did not know when he would return.

When I protested that we had an appointment, they insisted that he was not in and not due back in the office any time soon.

I said we would wait.

They said it was no use.

I said that I knew the alderman, had included him in a program on National Public Radio and quoted him in a book. Just as the debate was becoming unpleasant, Chandler came out of his office and filled the room with aldermanic charm.

We explained the need to recruit students, and the alderman accepted the request as a test of his control over the district. Of course he could recruit students for the course: he would send his people out to recruit for us.

What kind of students did we want and how many did we need?

What age?

What size?

Male or female?

When and where did we want them?

The helpful strutting was old Chicago ward politics. I knew the sound of it. My father and Chandler's had both been low-level operatives in Chicago machine politics. Chandler and I had laughed at the similarities across generations, races, religions. The West Side of the city had changed and it had not changed at all. The alderman passed out business cards. I knew better than to go back to him.

Angel Ysaguirre of the Illinois Humanities Council and I went to Pilsen the next day, thinking that in the Latino section of the city, in a social service agency, we would find an interested audience. The agency had assembled a small group of students from its educational program. Angel and I went to the public library, checked out several books of Mesoamerican art and literature, and carried them to a small classroom in the agency. The students had heard the Náhuatl names of the gods of the Aztecs and even the names of some of the poets and Great Speakers who ruled their forbears, but they knew nothing more. Nezahualcoyotl, the poet and ruler, was to them the name of a vast slum on the outskirts of Mexico City, yet reading a Spanish text of one of his poems awakened them. These young people, mostly undocumented, with little hope for a decent life in America, embraced the work. And responding to the gentle questions of the Socratic method, they could talk about it. Dialogue was possible. Eventually, there would be a Clemente Course for Spanish speakers in Chicago.

Before that happened, there would have to be a course in English. Students would have to be recruited and a faculty assembled. Kristina Valaitis and her board of directors had made the decision to invest the Humanities Council's people, energy, and money in the Clemente Course, which would go under the name Odyssey in Illinois to distinguish it from the housing project called Clemente. She appointed Amy Thomas-Elder, a young instructor at the Graham School of General Education at the University of Chicago, to manage the course. Kristina had grown up in Cicero, not very far from the West Side, where I spent my early years. We laughed about our elegant origins: Capone came from her home territory and there had been terrible riots and killings on the sidewalks where I had played hit the penny so many years ago.

Kristina is a sweetly irresistible woman, one who goes to Italy every year to bask in the sun and the culture, but she drives what is generally known as a hard bargain when it came to financial matters. She came to the Humanities Council from her post as a professor of literature. She said that she took the job because she loved the idea of making the humanities available to many people. It entailed devotion and finesse, and as I soon saw, she had both. I made a thoughtless comment on politics to a meeting of her board of directors, and she exactly knew how to rescue the Clemente Course and me.

Amy is a runner, a young woman who likes to wear muscle shirts and compare chin-ups with Ysaguirre, her co-worker. It came as one surprise to find that the runner had been working toward a doctorate in divinity and another to learn of her love for the students and faculty she was to enlist in the course. The young woman I first met, who seemed all too competent, businesslike, raised a lively and charming daughter and wept when handing diplomas to graduates.

Amy introduced me to the first two candidates for the faculty, both from the University of Chicago. Robert von Halberg was perhaps forty-five years old, with graying hair cut short and brushed up straight in military style. He sat more like a boxer than a man who leaned over books to become a professor of Germanic Studies, American literature, and African-American poetry. He was the face and demeanor of Heidelberg in a Greek setting. The other professor, Danielle Allen, also sat up in an athletic way, but it was her hands, which rested on the table, that commanded the room, for her fingers were long and perfectly formed and she held them with natural grace. Her fields were classics and political philosophy and she held doctorates from Harvard and Cambridge.

I took some time to explain the idea of the course and to give a brief history, now and then pausing to allow von Halberg or Allen to ask a question. As I was talking, I watched Danielle Allen's hands. They lay perfectly still, which I came to understand as a gesture of contemplation. When I had finished, there was a silence, and then Danielle said, "Oh, I see: it's about freedom."

"You're hired," I said.

She laughed.

I asked von Halberg if he would also teach in the course, and he agreed. With Amy as site director, we had the core of another extraordinary faculty. I began to think it was possible to teach the humanities to hundreds, perhaps thousands of people, all of whom had been cheated, all of whom deserved the best teachers in America. The next time I visited Chicago, Amy was working on a second course in the city. Emily Auerbach and the Wisconsin Humanities Council were about to start a course in Madison. Yet another course was beginning just north of the Illinois/Wisconsin border at Racine; we were teaching in Mexico; and Danielle Allen had become a MacArthur fellow and dean of the Division of Humanities at the University of Chicago.

Of course, Mexico was very different from New York, but I and the small advisory board had made an assumption about the American courses that proved to be wrong. We expected something like a franchise, with methods, reading lists, and so on coming from the central organization. But the variables were so many and so great that the Clemente Course in Chicago would be much like starting over. And the North Side of Chicago would prove to be not at all like the South Side. And neither of those would be like Pilsen, where the course would have to be taught in Spanish. I thought that the humanities, at the very least, would have been the one constant, but even that proved not to be true. Amy Thomas-Elder and I argued about the need to have the same reading list everywhere. She said that no University of Chicago professor would be willing to teach someone else's reading list. I talked to several of the professors we were trying to recruit. Amy was right. Starting with Chicago, every course in every city and every country would begin with a struggle over the curriculum.

Chicago students were different, too. Many were older. Rita Falcon was still in her thirties when we started in Chicago, the mother of three children, in the midst of her struggle against the world. One of her children was "mentally disabled," she told me, with no sign of sadness or even resignation in her face. She said, "Not only that, he had a bone marrow transplant. So in regards to life—the path of education—I kind of like took a detour, because I had to take care of a pretty much terminally ill son. He's okay now. He had aplastic anemia, which is fairly new. Not too many people know about that. It's not a cancer. Aplastic anemia—you're not able to produce white cells, plus red cells and platelets are low. So he has disabilities, cognitively, but physically he's fine—but he needs a little bit of help. So yeah, I've been through some stuff."

She has a Chicago accent, and when she speaks of the worst of her life, she sounds tough; as if she was a girl again, in the projects, in Pilsen, or the only Latina in a white school. Today, at forty-four, she looks thirty-five. She does not shrink back from questions or hide from remembered wounds; a conversation with her is a struggle for control. Since we were talking about her life, I said almost nothing. She might be Italian, Spanish, Greek, a woman of Marseille; indigenous Mexico does not appear in her face or speech; she could have been someone else. Race is always an issue for her. She is Mexican—she does not ever say Mexican-American or Chicana or Latina—and she says the word as if it were a gauntlet thrown in the face of the world.

Her grandparents came from Mexico. Chicago was the end of the railroad line. The Spanish language was left behind somewhere along the way north. By the time Rita was old enough to remember, her mother was living in Cabrini Green, the most notorious of the so-called urban renewal projects built in the middle of the twentieth century. Cabrini Green is largely gone now, emptied of gangs and graffiti, torn down to make way for other kinds of housing in an effort to rid the ghettos of one aspect of the surround of force.

Rita Falcon remembers her childhood in the project: "Hispanics lived—Mexicans and Puerto Ricans—on the second and third floor. Black or African-Americans lived on top.

"The pressures . . ." she said. "I wanted to defy the odds and go against what everybody said would happen, meaning, your parents, her parents, aunts and uncles and sisters. We pretty much don't graduate, get on welfare. In regard to the household that I lived in, it was not to me a safe environment. There was drugs involved. There was violence involved, so I want to say that I beat the odds, but also fell into the vicious cycle of having children young, though I did graduate from high school, but I was three months pregnant when I graduated, repeated probably the same cycle as my mom, meaning married someone who did drugs and was violent, and infidelity was rampant."

It was then she said she met Amy and became part of the first class of the Clemente Course in Chicago. Rita was among the best students in the class. "You have to work, to strive to achieve. And that I do believe I have done."

"And would you have done it without the course?" I asked.

"Yes. It did catapult me to further education, obviously, but I was determined already. I was on that path, but the educational path, that's where the Clemente Course came in. The path of survival . . . I think I was on that route already.

"I've pretty much accomplished one of the goals that I set out to do: for my daughter to not grow up the way her aunts did, her grandmother. She is literally going for her master's at the University of Chicago. I have another daughter. She's fifteen and she's in a performing arts school."

Our conversation comes to an end, and then has a coda. Rita says that only people who have made the decision to get on the right path should come to the Clemente Course. Their decision must be like hers; it has to come before they enroll. She left no doubt that the hero was not me, not Amy, not Danielle Allen, not even the humanities; we were minor players. In this drama, Rita was the lead.

On the North Side of Chicago, near Evanston, within sight of the elevated trains, in a small community center, the Clemente students gathered in late autumn of 2010 to talk about the death of Socrates. Catherine Zurybida, an art historian, directed the site. Darrell Moore, a philosophy professor at DePaul University, conducted the class. Since there was no table of any size in the room, Moore stood at the head of the class, but it did not deter him from teaching the *Crito* using the method the ancient Athenian had practiced, but gently.

All the students were African-American or Latino. A few came late, making excuses as they arrived. Moore brushed the excuses away. He had read their papers, learned each student as if they were his family. He called on one of the students, a woman nearing thirty, dressed against the cold just coming to Chicago in late October. The question was about the jury that would judge Socrates: "Angela."

She spoke quickly. What were Socrates' strategies? "One of the strategies was defining the jury," she said. "He started off telling them, 'I don't speak your language.' He's not used to the mannerism of the court. This is his first time in court at seventy years old. So he brings the jury down to his level . . ."

"Or?"

"Or up to his level," she says, correcting herself, taught by the questioning word.

A few minutes later, after a student speaks about irony, he asks, "How does this relate to Leslie's point? She used this very example."

"Trying to use reverse psychology," the student answers. "Playing with their minds."

And then to Leslie: "What do you think about what Angela is saying about the point that you made earlier?"

Moore works the dialogue. He takes them back to the *Euthyphro*, which they read earlier, to the courthouse steps, where Socrates speaks. "And what is it he does?" asks Moore.

A student answers immediately. "It's what they say is corrupting the youth; he's making them think, questioning their knowledge and also making them search for the knowledge."

The language of the students comes out of the real city. It is not the perfect city Plato wished for, but the real streets of Chicago that produces the language; it is the Agora in 2010. Darrell Moore is corrupting the youth in the same way, with questions. But he is not a seventy-year-old Athenian, he is a slim young man, with dark skin. He is an aesthetician, handsome, himself the philosopher. He has earned his doctorate at Northwestern, been a fellow at the Frederick Douglass Institute, finds connection between aesthetics and political philosophy. He embraces the students with his glances and they respond and respond and respond. The students have already learned to laugh with him at the joy of learning. They talk about Socrates and his children as if they were family; philosophy has become that real to them.

The students say that the Athenian society thinks Socrates is dangerous, not merely a gadfly. Moore smiles, agreeing, encouraging. The students talk about the transmigration of the soul and the expectation that Socrates will not die but go to a place where he can talk with Homer.

One of the students, a young woman from Ethiopia, dressed and groomed to appear affluent, talks about the Athenians "waiting until his old age. They were acknowledging his work." She finds Plato telling the reader of this aspect of the dialogue, a kind of triumphant moment for philosophy, and Moore says very softly, "I didn't think about that."

He did not come to debate, but to teach. When the students raise the issue of what they see as Socrates' lack of concern for his sons, which they call "poor parenting," Moore takes them away to the heart of the dialogue. He asks what makes Socrates a good man, and the students respond with the argument of obedience to the law and they quote lines from the dialogues to defend their point.

It is finally the character of Socrates that they settle on, his refusal to be swayed, even by the threat of death, from his position of doing what he believes is the good. The idea of virtue emerges in the dialogue between the students, Moore, and the text. In what seems like minutes two hours have gone by. Moore gives the assignment for the next meeting of the class. They turn in papers. He promises to read them carefully for the next class.

It has not been an ideal dialogue, but it has been real. A group of men and women, new to the world of ideas in the autumn of their first year of attention to that world, are prompted by questions to learn to be questioners themselves. The class is over. The students gather around Moore. One by one, they leave. It is already cold in Chicago, the night wind is harsh, but the evening has been a success: citizens are being born.

On the South Side of the city, in the early afternoon, graduate of the Odyssey Course, a woman of great poise and eloquence who comes out of the tradition of black Protestant ministers who set out to remake the country one congregation at a time, talks about how she got her name. She had gone south from Chicago to one of the traditional black colleges. The heat there, she said, was terrible, a hundred and sixteen degrees. She laughed. For the first time, she said, the minister's daughter, who had dressed the part in Chicago, wore a strapless top. One of the other girls noticed a birthmark on her back, revealed by the tank top. She cried out that the birthmark was in the shape of the African continent. From that time on the daughter of the Reverend Porter, who had worked with Martin Luther King in Chicago, called herself Afrika.

Sis Afrika Porter speaks in a cultured voice, much like that of a trained actor, and she has an easy and very winning laugh, a diva's laugh, which she tempers with the deep-throated sound of agreement learned, I imagine, in responsive readings in her father's church. The effect is of overpowering charm. It comes as a surprise when she speaks in lovely voice of angers that go back for generations, all righteous angers, all more deeply, more passionately sounded, softly, with charm.

There is no anger in her younger son, Jahbril, who is eight years old and has already acted in a Chicago Lyric Opera production.

Jahbril, at his mother's request, stands tall, and proudly recites the work of Ralph Waldo Emerson. After the recitation, Jahbril turns his attention to a small recording device, deciphers its incomprehensible operating instructions, and begins recording the voices around him. Afrika is pleased, but in a stern way, for they are in public, and Jahbril is learning how to be both dignified and warm, but he is still more interested in the tiny recording device than in his mother's story. She begins:

"My dad's a retired Methodist minister and activist; he written a book—*The Autobiography of Black Male Violence*. My mom is an educator. She teaches at Literacy Chicago. The humanities have been around us for all of our lives. I grew up on the South Side, in Hyde Park, right here. We actually integrated our block in 1973. Right on Fifty-fourth and Greenwood. We were never invited to any events, anything. Our neighbors were white; they still are. We have three generations now. All my siblings have children and the children have children, and it's been the same thing. So I've grown up in a community—especially since the Obamas are from Hyde Park—if you look at it—they say Hyde Park is great. Not for Afrika.

"My friends came from where my church was—in Englewood, where most of the homicides happen in Chicago. Even up to a few months ago, my sister lived there with my parents. My parents are older, my father is legally blind. And my nephew was there. The neighbors were having a birthday party and my nephew didn't get invited. So because he knows them, he said, 'Well, I would like to come to the party.' [And they said] 'Well, we didn't know that you would be available.' Who lives like that? Who does that to a child? It's not humane.

"We went to the school that was an all-black school a block and a half from my home, but everyone else on my block went to the [University of] Chicago Lab School. Or they went to Academy. So I got to see it very early, and my father being who he was, very active

55

in civil rights, we got to learn about it to the point now where I found this flyer at the library and I thought, 'We've got to do this. This is great, this is what we do, this is who we are.' " She became a student and an organizer. "We did the first [Odyssey/Clemente] course, we did the second course, we did the third course. We did the first video course and the second video course, and now I'm calling, asking, 'What have you got now?' Whatever they have, we want to be in it. We thoroughly enjoyed it. And we [she and Artila Mims, who was sitting beside her] brought over twenty people to that course."

She has an analytical view of the racism of popular culture. Her grounding in the humanities comes to the fore as she looks at two television series: *Everybody Loves Raymond* and *Everybody Hates Chris.* The humor of the actor Chris Rock is not enough for her to overlook the message of the programs, especially as it is sent to children. Raymond is white; Chris is black. "The duality of the two programs is painful," she says, "when you are an inner-city young black male. Everybody loves Raymond and Raymond is lovable and the show is happy, the show is funny. But everybody hates Chris. You can't get past the visual when you see the billboards while you're driving or on the bus. You can grasp that without having seen the show.

"All the parents on the block where I grew up were professors right here at the university. So was my dad. Those were his colleagues, but it didn't mean anything because socially we weren't accepted. [They said] 'He worked with Marcus Garvey, he's a Garveyite, he wears that African clothing.'"

Artila Mims breaks in to ask, "Do you think that if you all had been assimilated, you would have been okay?"

"Oh, yes, definitely. We have friends that were, and everything was fine with them. They were invited to things that we weren't. We still have the relationship with them.

"From here, my goal for myself is I'm a full-time home educator. I have two sons, my fourteen-year-old is in high school, and he [Jahbril] is eight. My main focus is to parent positively."

She talks about the killings of young black men in Chicago, and turns to Plato for a solution: "Educating young black men will teach them about the Allegory of the Cave. They have to be able to think themselves out of going into the cave. They'll look at that [life] and think, this is a setup."

When she is angry, she talks at a rapid pace, in a much higher register. It is not hysteria, but a voice sharpened by anger, tinged with regret. Yet no anger shows in her face. Her face is a perfect palimpsest: the grown woman, the college girl, the adorable baby sister, all the pretty faces of a lifetime, and still young, a woman knowing the effect of her smile, enjoying it, enjoying her husband, sons, the pleasure of being, the blood of anger.

Father
I am not ready yet
my bones are still brittle
the dark still frightens me
I still hope
to find a man
who would steal my heart

Judy Razo writes in English now. She is one of the first graduates of the Spanish language Odyssey/Clemente Course in Chicago. Before I met her, she had sent me a sheaf of her poems and with it a letter about the pains of aspiration, the cruel advice given by friends who do not know when poetry that is lived cannot be said. Judy Razo is bursting with poetry, with words that are not always the words she wishes she could say. She came late to English, so that often she translates her thoughts from Spanish when she speaks, but if one listens closely, all that she feels, remembers, wishes, comes through her sentences and sighs. Nothing is lost but the poetry, testament to the betrayal of language inherent in translation. To sit in intense conversation with her is to hear the pained serenade of her sweet soprano voice and to be fixed by her eyes, to see in them the origin of the unexpressible poems, and to wish her the words to say them.

By the time we met she had moved on from the Spanish language course. She was a university student—in English—but she had never lost her connection to the Clemente/Odyssey Course. We spoke in English, with a Spanish word or phrase said now and then more for comfort than for clarity.

She said, "I was born in 1968 in Guanajuato and I moved to Guadalajara when I was eight years old, and from there I came here to Chicago. I was not doing anything with my life. I was just working to help my mom. I didn't go to school. So I didn't have anything for me. I stayed in Guadalajara until I was seventeen.

"I kept calling my aunt to see if I could come over here, and she said yes because they wanted to have Grandpa to come over here. I said, 'I'll take him over here.' So she paid for my ticket. My uncle, who is really rich, got me the visa. I traveled with my grandpa. We came by plane. I wouldn't come across the desert; I'm not that brave.

"That poem I just gave you . . . I just wrote it for Heritage Month, because they asked me if I wanted to write something. My mentor—she is a college teacher—she said, 'Write something, write something for the school. [In the poem] I talk about the things we leave behind when we come here.

"Where I lived [in Guanajuato] is really, really small. I always used to go to the big part of the small town. I always wanted to live where everything was really, really happening. You always have to go back to your reality, but I always thought, 'If I could get out of here, I could go somewhere else.' I was going like that, from side to side.

"Once I got to Guadalajara and I see everything that I wanted to see, then I was bored. I didn't want to just work; I wanted to go to school.

"My father was an alcoholic, so he wasn't reliable for us to survive. My brothers were little. I was the oldest, but there were three other ones after me . . . they died. The next one is eight years younger than me, so he couldn't help.

"When I was little my father trained me to be a butcher. I could take apart pigs. They were like two hundred pounds. So when I got to Guadalajara I was really skilled. I could work like an adult. Where Father worked, I was making twice as much, because I could kill the pig, cut it up, and cook it and sell it. And I was doing really good, like a salesperson. I was real young. I think I was like twelve.

"I used to go out and drink and everything, but I always wanted to go to school, and my mom said I couldn't because I had to take care of her and my brothers and my sisters and my father. I wanted to save money and come [to Chicago], but I didn't know how.

"I went to the cultural center, because there was like all kinds of people there—Brazilians and Africans and Arabic people, all kinds of people. I would go there just to talk to them, for them to tell me about their country and stuff. I wanted to be friends with them so they would send me stuff, photographs of places like San Francisco, Arizona, New York. I always kept friends; of course, the ones that were able to communicate with me in Spanish, because I didn't speak English.

"That was the highlight of my week. Every weekend, I would go there, and there was always somebody to talk to. Everybody would just hang out there at the cultural center. We would just sit and talk and smoke and tell jokes—all night, we would just hang out there all night. They were people of all ages, all walks of life. I think that is where I learned a lot about this country before coming here. It was in 1980. I came over here in 1985, November 25, 1985. I wasn't frightened, because I had waited so long. But I also knew that I wasn't going to come back. I told my mom that I wasn't coming back, because I didn't want to be half here, half there. It's so painful to separate. I just knew that I had to come here and start all over again. To me it was like a new beginning, a new life, and I was free. I just went for it. I didn't bring anything with me, nothing . . . oh, a book. I didn't bring any clothes, nothing, because I was gonna start all over again.

"My aunt, she grew up with nuns. I couldn't go anywhere, I couldn't have friends, nothing, just stay home and help her. She used to watch children, so I had to help her. Then I started working. This lady found me a job: I was gonna be a busboy. I was able to communicate enough. It was an Italian restaurant. It was good for me. The Italian family was really good to me. I practically moved in with them. But once again, the owner, the guy had a drinking problem, so I had to be like a babysitter. I would bring him home late at night. I worked there from 1986 to 1994.

"I got married the first time in 1992. I got married because he was an older person. He was sixty maybe and I was twenty-four, but he was adorable, a very nice person; but when I moved in, he became like psycho. I couldn't get phone calls, I couldn't go out with my friends. I waited and waited. I thought maybe he has to get used to me. I knew I was different and a little bit wild. I thought it wasn't worth going through all of that just to get legal status, so I applied for a divorce. He was Italian.

"The next one . . . I liked him, but not like love. I told him I was not a citizen, and I told him the whole process, and he said,

'I'll marry you.' He was African-American. We were the same age, twenty-six. I only stayed with him two years, and he died. He was a martial artist and he suffered epilepsy and he had a heart attack and died. It was really weird, because he was like the healthiest person, never smoke, drink.

"I always wanted to go to school. The old person [her first husband] said, 'First, you have to marry me, then go to school.' I didn't want to compromise my life like that. I didn't want to have any children. With the second one, I would just study at home. He would help me. He would tell me about the GED. He would help me read. I would go to the library with him.

"The third one, he told me that he had a drinking problem, and when he relapsed I tried to get away from him. I was just working, from nine in the morning until ten thirty at night. I used to manage a restaurant. I was seven months pregnant when I left him. And that's who I had a baby by.

"So now I find myself with a baby, and what am I gonna do? I have a baby, four weeks old, that I don't know anything about. I'm still responsible for my mom; my father had just passed away. And that's when I left the third one. I had him incarcerated, because he broke into the house and stole all the things I had purchased for the baby. I came home and the house was empty. So I confronted him and he beat me up again. That's when I knew I had to get away from him. I could have killed him that day. He was trying to kill the baby. He wanted to kill the baby. He was trying to get him away from me, and I wouldn't let him. He like broke a chair on my head. So you know what I did? I wrapped the baby in a towel and I took him under the bed to protect him. He dragged me out to the porch and he bent me over and he was trying to kill me, but I beat him to it. I threw him from the third floor. And nothing happened to him. That was twelve years ago. That was the end of a horrible thing.

"[Now,] I've been living with the same man for ten years. The person I'm with said, 'You're pregnant, you're too stressed out. Don't work.' That's when I volunteered for Americorps. I was doing ESL with adults, helping them with basic English, and then the director caught me that I didn't have any formal education. She said, 'Do you want to do the GED?' And from there, I met Tony Perrone [a professor from the University of Illinois at Chicago], who became my best friend ever. He told me about the Odyssey Project, so I started going to the Pilsen.[1] The students were mostly Mexican, all Mexican. No, there were some Colombians.

"It was scary. Really! I went only to the third grade and here I am in a whole classroom full of people. I don't know how to follow instructions. I don't know how to take notes. At the same time I got the bright idea of signing up at college. And my life was just crazy. I didn't know if I was coming or going. I was the oldest person in the classroom.

"It's a good thing that I had teachers like Aaron [Lambert]. He would sit with me and . . . 'No, not like this, like this.' You know, he would take a lot of time to teach me how to write. I didn't know punctuation. It was him and Professor [Mauricio] Tenorio, they took extra time with me.

"We read Socrates and Plato and Kant. But I really liked the history one, with Professor Tenorio. It's not only that he's a great teacher, but he's so funny, so animated, colorful. He would just sit there after school and try to explain to me how to write. I'm just as bad in English as I am in Spanish. I don't know. I've been teaching myself.

"I wanted to know more. I became curious about many things.

---

1 Pilsen is the mainly Mexican and Mexican-American section of Chicago. The Odyssey/Clemente Course there is taught in Spanish. The course was founded by Dra. Herlinda Suarez Zozaya de Valencia in conjunction with the National Autonomous University of Mexico and Amy Thomas-Elder of the Illinois Humanities Council.

I began asking the teachers, 'Let me know when there is a course so that I can take it. Like I'm always asking Mr. [Bart] Schultz. He doesn't know me, but I'm always sending e-mail.

"It really helped me to get the idea of going to school. I was lucky enough to have those teachers. They really helped me. If I did something bad or stupid [in a paper], he would switch it around; they would totally butcher my paper. *Just leave the title or something!* But they really helped me, because I had no idea, I didn't know anything. They really helped me to feel that I could make it.

"Most of my family, my in-laws and everything, they're constantly telling me that I'm a loser, that I'm never gonna finish school. They never gave me credit for anything that I've accomplished. Even when I went to China. For Christmas they gave me a little backpack. They play really cruel jokes. They just cut me off, in conversations, like that. If it wasn't for those professors, I think that I would quit.

"One of my professors—he was my mentor—he would go to my house and drag me out. He would come into my place, and he would drag me.

"Now, I'm going to Roosevelt [University] and to the Graham School [University of Chicago School of General Studies]. I'm studying psychology and gerontology."

As part of her studies Judy visits a nursing home to comfort the Spanish speakers there. A bit shyly, she said that she also observes them. She did not say that she reads poems to them or sings the love and sadness of her life.

CHAPTER 3

Appalachia in Wisconsin

Emily Auerbach contends that the Madison Odyssey Course is not a Clemente Course in the Humanities. And I suppose that by the strict definition of the course it is not. In Madison, the students come to class once a week instead of twice. They stay longer each time, but now and then they do exercises in the humanities that are less rigorous or dignified than I would like. If the Clemente Course were taught according to the original design, students and faculty would use only their last names preceded by the title of Mr. or Ms. as is common now in formal address. I think it adds to the dignity and order in the classroom. Emily uses hugs.

When the students are at their best in Madison, or so I think, it is often when they are reading and discussing and writing about Emily Dickinson. With Professor Auerbach's permission, I have taken a few paragraphs from their work.

James Horton wrote about Dickinson's #833, which is about poets lighting lamps. He said: "The poets illuminate the path. They are but sparks that create fire. Their ideas last longer than their physical minds. The flames or thoughts continue to allow us to peer through the darkness of the future. Each age is a lens, so as poets dissect the meaning of their lives [environment], it helps all humans understand their place in the world!

"I like writers who write about writing's purpose. One of the reasons I continue to write is to enlighten myself as well as others. I feel that all we have to contribute to other living beings is what we've learned in our own lives. More than technology, these lessons will allow our species to achieve its true potential."

Edwin Shumpert wrote of #254, which is about hope as a bird: "It expresses 'Hope' as a bird with feathers, to me meaning it has no boundaries, no limits, and can be found not in space but within—the real place to search. The image of the 'little bird' . . . says that regardless of the storms we may come across in life, with 'Hope' we can weather the storm and can be calm [warm] and steadfast . . . even in the midst of troubled waters.

"On a personal note, I was very moved emotionally because I've had to daily affirm within myself to never give up hope, and that hope is always a strength to lean on or call on. Both Gandhi and Dr. King, for example, always maintained hope at all cost or opposition."

Rhonda Johnson said of Dickinson's poem #576, which is about praying, "This poem reminds me of Blake's writings."

Wynetta Taylor said of #248 about being kept out of heaven: "She's asking why men treat women as second class. Why are women shut out of heaven, meaning the world? She felt that for women, being able to do what they wanted to do in life, being free, was heaven. For her, it was openly writing and being respected as a writer.

"For me, it's like racism when men think they're superior to women. I think any time anyone is shut out, fear is clearly at play. Anyone who is secure and sure of themselves would not feel threatened by anyone else. In fact, they would welcome everyone to join them—to spread their wings and fly."

Justin Wilson wrote his text after #1,587, which is about precious words: "This poem is about a man who begins to truly live once he starts to read. The words and concepts allow him to temporarily forget that he is but a man, living in poverty. Instead, these words allow him to soar, to experience other levels of reality.

"I chose this one because in many ways it is about me. My mother would read to me every night. It started when I was still in the womb and continued until I was four years old. At that point, when story time came she handed me the book and told me to read. See, the beautiful thing about reading is you can be anybody who ever lived, go places you've never been, and do the most amazing things. Ever since she handed me a book, I've been reading. I now read some two to three books a week for leisure in addition to my free research I do every day.

"There's a reason why I say that my mother was a saint, and it's because she released the shackles of my mind. My mother couldn't give me the material world, and she knew that; instead, she gave me the universe. She taught me how to fly and travel through dimensions.

"Dickinson has that role partly because of my love for her work."

The classes in Madison are as interesting and thoughtful about Socrates or Shakespeare or Sojourner Truth. It is an extraordinary place, as Kevin Riley, chancellor of the University of Wisconsin System, said at the 2010 graduation when he called the students "role models to others." And he is correct in his estimation of the effect of the students in the world, for their work reaches far beyond the classroom. The course reaches the community through the children of many of the students and through their families and friends, sometimes a significant part of a housing project or a densely populated neighborhood.

Dignity spreads outward from the classrooms. Although we have not quantified what happens to the children of people who attend the course, the anecdotal material tends to lead me to think that the day care we generally provide, linking the children to the educational experience of their parents, is a way to break the cycle of poverty. Sociologists looking at the children of our Maya students found them to be the best students in their rural primary school. In Chicago, Odyssey/Clemente graduate Afrika Porter's children are doing well in school and appearing in small parts in operas and plays alongside professional actors.

Sometimes I do not know how dignity grows, however. When I see the students in the Madison course wearing funny hats while reading Shakespeare, I am put off a bit, perhaps because I am a snob or not so brilliant a teacher as Emily. Fourteen of her students have now graduated from college; about two thirds of the graduates go on to some form of higher education. The statistics are good, but I think Emily and Amy Thomas-Elder in Chicago and Lela Hilton in Jefferson County, Washington, would agree college is only one indication of a successful life. College may contribute to happiness; but a healthy family, steady employment, a stable home, the enjoyment of music, art, literature, and participation in the community, that glorious political life Pericles talked about, may be equally good measures of happiness. Aristotle, as Odyssey/Clemente students learn, would say that the contemplative life is the one closest to God. Socrates would tell us that using the knowledge gained in the course to have a life of virtue would be the best road to happiness.

Nonetheless, college counts. And it is easier to measure than happiness. If some of the students in the Clemente Course are to get to college, they must generally complete the course. Madison has an astonishing record of retention. It happens partly because Emily is a very assiduous recruiter, which is where the retention rate begins. To do that she has become a first-rate publicist, consistently filling the local media with stories about the course, publishing a student newspaper, and keeping close contact with community organizations. She often has two or three times as many applicants as she has places. Even though she limits the number of students to thirty, she has more than once ended up with thirty-one graduates. It is not a subtle form of sleight-of-hand, but her willingness to admit a student who had to drop out because of illness or family problems and was able to return after acceptances were sent out or the year had begun.

All courses are not like hers. John Marsh, who was the director of a course at the University of Illinois for a while, said that he lost most of his students. And when it came time to get college credit for those who—more or less—remained, he said that he had to lie about their work. The difference between the results of Emily's work and John Marsh's is astonishing. I do not know John Marsh, but I think it is best that he no longer teaches a Clemente Course.

It is impossible to know quite why Emily's classes go so well. She says it was her connection and that of her parents to Berea College in Kentucky that is responsible for the creation of the Odyssey Course in Madison. It is not a Clemente Course, at least not in any official way. The Madison classes are much less formal than Clemente courses—hugging has a lot to do with pedagogy in the Madison course—yet Emily and her faculty achieve excellent results by teaching the humanities in their own fashion to people living in poverty, making Madison one of the best (un)-Clemente courses. It started either in Appalachia or when Jean Feraca brought it home to Wisconsin from a visit to Chicago to learn about the course and watch the founding of the first one there. Jean and Emily have made the changes, mainly by the insertion of their own personalities and the influence of the college in Appalachia—Berea—which is free to students who gain entrance and is, as generations of Auerbachs are fond of saying, "The only college where you have to be poor to go there."

Berea was founded before the Civil War, and was the first integrated college in the American South. After the war, laws were passed prohibiting integration and Berea obeyed the law, but set up another school nearby to educate blacks, and went to court. After many years, the law was overturned and Berea became integrated again. Two people who came out of the Berea experience are Emily's parents. I think that history has put the idea of free education for the poor, regardless of race or religion, in Emily's DNA. She directs a very successful course, whatever she wants to call it, but she told me that her dream is to start another Berea College. It would be difficult, but no more difficult than beginning the year with thirty students and finishing with thirty-one.

In the realm of magic, when I was last in Madison, Emily and Jean and I met with a group of people from several UW faculties and the head of the university's foundation. The University of Wisconsin, being a state institution, could not grant free credits to Emily's course, but when pressed, the head of the foundation said that it could replace the cost of the credits. From then on, it was a happy meeting.

There is always the question of what educational psychologists refer to as "outcomes." When Kegan Carter graduated from the University of Wisconsin (Madison) in 2009, it was in one sense the best of outcomes. Carter had come to the first class in Madison in 2003, having left Chicago for a less crowded, less dangerous place. She was pregnant and already had a four-year-old child when she arrived in Madison. For the first few months in her new hometown she slept in a small, crowded room at the YWCA. She found work, a place of her own, and managed to survive until she saw a flyer soliciting students for a free college course.

Once connected to Emily Auerbach and the Madison Odyssey Course, Kegan Carter had found a way out of poverty. She went to a technical college in Madison for two years, then moved up to the state university. To care for herself and her children while she went to college Carter worked either part time or full time when she could manage it, at minimum wage, and then as she became more educated, at higher paying jobs. And there was the Auerbach connection: Emily uses part of the money she raises to help sustain students while they attend the course and then afterward when they go on to college or build lives in other ways. Kegan Carter now works with the Madison Odyssey/Clemente Course while preparing to take GRE and LSAT exams.

Carter had the good luck to attend Odyssey/Clemente classes taught by Emily Auerbach, Jean Feraca, and the late Nellie Y. McKay, the author of books on Jean Toomer and Toni Morrison. From those three women Carter gained a sense of what she could be. They taught her to love freedom, which is the end of education and the hope of democracy.

CHAPTER 4

Black Leggings

O n the day when he spoke of the amaranth growing wild on the plains of Oklahoma, Howard touched his cheek and said with sadness that the color of his skin had grown lighter with age. I had known him for some years by then, and I had come to admire him and to value him as a good friend. He was a man of great dignity and many angers. He had been in South Dakota in the days when the American Indian Movement (AIM) was strong. He had seen whites spit on Indians on the street and I think he had been at Wounded Knee in 1973 when AIM and the Lakota had made a stand against the whites, but I am not certain of that. I had been there a few years earlier when there was still a sun dance on the Lakota Reservation. Howard had gone later, a representative of the Episcopal Church on a mission to make peace.

Howard and I talked about amaranth and Wounded Knee and many other things as we traveled long distances together across Oklahoma. I know his children, especially his daughter America, who is named for Will Rogers's mother, Mary America. And I have spent many hours talking with Howard and his wife, Mary Ellen, whom he describes as Cherokee royalty because of the family connection to Will Rogers and William Milam, who had been a principal chief of the Cherokee Nation. Mary Ellen was the acting director of the Cherokee Heritage Center then and Howard was a professor at the University of Arts and Sciences of Oklahoma. I was there because my wife had said to me one evening after we had started several Clemente courses, "What about the Indians?"

"What a fool I am!" was all that I could think to say in response. She made excuses for me, saying that I was sure to start courses for Indians even if she had not reminded me that I had written a book about Indians that had caught the attention of Senator Edward Kennedy. Or that I had gone to grade school with Indian children, descendants of the Tiguas, who fought a battle with the Kiowa Apaches at Hueco Tanks in 1837 so brutal that the story of it was told in pictographs painted on the walls of the tanks near Ysleta, Texas. The Tiguas threw live rattlesnakes into a cave where the Kiowas had taken refuge. And when the rattlesnakes didn't perform as intended, the Tiguas threw burning red chile peppers into the cave to smoke out their enemies. And I had sweeter memories as well: two Lakota children, Olivia Jumping Bull and Gary Tobacco, had taught my younger son to ride a horse, and since then he has not been entirely comfortable if he does not spend some part of a week on horseback.

And then came an invitation to go to Oklahoma.

When I first met Howard and Mary Ellen Meredith, they had walked into a bookstore together, two tall, lean people standing very straight, Howard in a suit and tie, looking like a Presbyterian minister, and Mary Ellen dressed as always in fine and slightly conservative clothes. I cannot remember why, but for some reason, I thought they were the governor and first lady of Oklahoma. They introduced themselves and we chatted for a while.

It happens sometimes that people meet and immediately become friends. It had not often happened to me, and I was surprised. Howard and I agreed about everything that came to mind as we talked. He could describe the rise of the land off in the distance and the way corn had come to Oklahoma and supplanted amaranth as the chief form of grain. I knew about the development of *teosintle*, a grass, that was coaxed into corn in Mexico more than three thousand years before it came north. He knew the history of treaties made and broken between Indians and the federal government, and so did I, having written a book about it. But his knowledge was far more detailed, and he spoke about it softly. I marveled at the way he could speak with great emotion and never change the pitch or volume of his words. Perhaps it was something he had learned in his work with the Episcopal Church. There were so many other things to talk about that I never got around to asking him.

In the course of our conversations we came to the decision that there ought to be a Cherokee Clemente Course, and he set about forming it. We had help from Anita May, who was then the executive director of the Oklahoma Humanities Council, and John Feaver, the president of the University of Science and Arts of Oklahoma (USAO). John was then in the process of bringing USAO to prominence. It had a long history as the first women's college west of the Mississippi and then as an ordinary liberal arts college, but John has made it into one of the best public liberal arts colleges in the nation. John Feaver was also dedicated to teaching Indian studies, although the number of students in the program had grown smaller as he demanded higher grades and test scores from entering students, including Indians, who suffered from inadequate primary and secondary education. He immediately agreed to be one of the sponsors of a Clemente Course and to give college credits to Clemente Course graduates, if they earned them.

Howard arranged a meeting with the Choctaws and Comanches as well. The Choctaws were represented by Dr. Lee Hester, a thickset man with a penchant for irony, which he directed at whites. When I said we would teach indigenous as well as Western philosophy, Hester claimed that there was no such thing as indigenous philosophy, and wouldn't be moved from that position. The Comanches were represented by Nita Pahdopony. When we were introduced, I thought it was another joke played on the white man, for the co-chairman of the Comanche Nation was a young woman of extremely delicate features and tiny white teeth. She said little, but stared at me intently. Howard said nothing. After Lee Hester was done with me, he sat back, obviously pleased by the wounds he had inflicted on the pretentious white man. I turned my attention to Nita Pahdopony, for I was certain that there was nothing to be gained by speaking to Hester. I began by telling her that we were teaching indigenous people in Mexico, and to open a dialogue with her I asked if she had been to Mexico. She said, "Comanches go there to kill them and steal their children."

Her teeth now looked very sharp. I was reminded by her answer that the Comanches were among the most ferocious of the original peoples of the Americas, and this delicate woman was the co-chair of the Comanche Nation. Rather than asking her anything else, I launched into a description of the Clemente Course, its history, and what we hoped would be the result of my visit to Oklahoma. She said nothing, her gaze so intent that I became uncomfortably conscious of my own face. She asked no questions, although I paused several times to give her an opening. And I was certainly not going to ask another question of her. After I finished my presentation, there was still nothing but silence in response. Finally, I asked, "Well, what do you think?"

She said, "Comanches are more succinct."

Years later, Nita and I became friends. She was an accomplished painter and an interesting, if not yet refined poet. She sometimes sent me her work, asking if I would help with a bit of editing. The Comanches have a college of their own, where Nita teaches now that she is no longer co-chair. She has some ailments, and she has not been shy about discussing them. I saw her again a year or so after our first meeting, and she was still very reserved, although ferocious might be a better description. When she sent me a Comanche/English dictionary, I understood more about her. It is a Uto-Aztecan language, related to Náhuatl, which is spoken by the Mexican Aztecs, but very different from that language, which is familiar to me. Náhuatl (*Nahua* means "clear speaker") is the language of a settled people. Comanche (*ntmt tekwapt*) is the language of hunter-gatherers of the plains.

After the meeting with Nita and Lee Hester, I had some doubts about the future of the Clemente Course in Oklahoma. Lee, too, has become a good friend, and a staunch supporter of Clemente courses as well as the head of the Indian Studies Department at USAO. Like Nita, however, he has suffered from illness over the last ten years or so, and as with Nita we have had long conversations in support of each other.

With the help of Lee and Nita and John Feaver and under the guiding hand of Howard Meredith, the process of starting courses went forward. By then, we were teaching Maya, Nahua (Aztec), and Cup'ik (Eskimo) students, and a gathering was held at USAO of indigenous scholars connected to the courses. They came to USAO at Chickasha, Oklahoma, to meet with the Cherokees, Kiowas, and Chickasaws to talk about how to start courses, and to form an organization, which they named the Pan-American Indigenous Humanities Center. The Mexicans were immediately comfortable with the Oklahomans. The centerpiece had been a poetic lecture about the indigenous world given by Alejandra García Quintanilla in English, which she had learned as a child and perfected while earning a doctorate at the University of North Carolina. She and Herlinda Suarez Zozaya of the Nahua Course and Jay Goombi (Kiowa) acted as translators for the others. The Pan-American Indian Humanities Center was founded. A board of directors was formed, and since I am not an Indian, I could only serve ex officio. Miguel Léon-

Portilla, the great Mexican scholar, published an article about the forming of the center in a quarterly magazine he edits. John Feaver and Howard Meredith became the leaders of the project since both men had the confidence of many Oklahoma tribes.

The work of establishing the courses moved ahead quickly. The Cherokee Course was to be largely under the influence of Eli No Fire, a fluent speaker of Tsalagi (possibly the correct name of the Cherokee language and people). Before dinner one evening at Tahlequah, the headquarters of the Cherokee Nation, we were entertained by a traditional Tsalagi storyteller and flutist before getting to work on the curriculum, which was to be bicultural and bilingual, in keeping with the conviction that the final stage of assimilation, the loss of the original language, had to be avoided, for it meant the end of the Tsalagi world. It was not a romantic view of indigenous peoples; everyone in the conversation knew that the loss of language and culture led to problems more damaging than mere unhappiness. The original peoples had been the victims of physical genocide followed by a continuing attempt to kill them as persons. They had suffered enforced removals, compulsory boarding schools, punishment for speaking their own language, race hatred, and killing poverty. These deprivations stole the sense of being complete persons. It was worse than physical torture, for it was painful to the soul, and the hurt was felt until the person died, leaving behind children who would fare no better than their parents, and perhaps not as well. I knew this and had written about it in *The Death of the Great Spirit*.[1] I thought I understood the nature of the victims of American genocide, but what I saw then and at many other times in Howard's face was more terrible. I saw rage in the mind of a gentle man.

---

1   *The Death of the Great Spirit: An Elegy for the American Indian* (New York: Simon & Schuster, 1971).

The Kiowa course began on the night of one of the worst rainstorms of the year. Roads flooded, bridges were washed out, leaving many of the students cut off from the small meeting place where tables had been set up in a semicircle to facilitate discussion. A group of students, about half the class, found a way through the storm to the small building where the class was to be held. In addition to the students, many of whom were women, there were several old storytellers in attendance, men who remembered or passed on stories of the Kiowa Apaches at war with their traditional enemies. Before the class began, an old man sat down beside me to tell a Kiowa story. Inspired by the weather, he began by describing a night worse than the one outside bearing down on the small building where we had gathered. Many years ago, he began, a Kiowa hunter found shelter from the storm in a cave. There was already a man inside, but he allowed the Kiowa to take shelter in the darkness alongside him. Neither man spoke for fear of giving himself away to the other. In the darkness, the two enemies passed the night together, saying nothing, sharing what little food they had. In the morning, after the storm had passed, the men crawled out of the cave, and the Kiowa saw that the man who had shared the cave with him was a Cheyenne. The old man laughed. "The Cheyenne were our enemies," he said. "So the Kiowa killed him." He looked at me then, his face set in a smile of pride. "It is a true story," he said. "That is how the Kiowas are."

The rain continued to fall. Tables set to the side of the small room overflowed with food for the large group of students and observers who had been expected. "Don't worry," one of the women said to me. "It will not be wasted."

Jay Goombi, son of J. T. Goombi, former chairman of the Kiowas and first vice president of the National Congress of American Indians, sat in one corner of the room, a big man, voluble, with a booming voice and powerful physical presence despite the fact that he had been injured in an automobile accident and had to get around in a wheelchair. As the first class was organized he became quiet and allowed his aunt, Alecia Keahbone Gonzales, to take her place in the center of the circle of tables that filled the small room of the informal church. Alecia, who had been a princess of the Kiowa Apache tribe in her youth, had become the most accomplished linguist and lexicographer in the Kiowa world. She wrote textbooks, compiled a dictionary, taught at both the high school and college level, and was, perhaps more than anyone except the writer N. Scott Momaday, the cultural center of the tribe.

She sat quietly while the students arranged themselves. Alecia's hair was gray, full and short. She wore pastel colors and spoke softly in a commanding voice. I knew her from earlier meetings. We greeted each other easily, but she was careful not to give the students the impression that I was in control of this first meeting of the class, which was to be a Kiowa meeting, not a European meeting. When the class was settled, with the help of Jay's strong voice, she welcomed the students, told them the Kiowa name of the course: *Yee P'ay Gyan Aim*, which means "Two Ways of Thinking," and asked how many of them spoke Kiowa. No one raised a hand or nodded. In the silence, looking straight ahead through her eyeglasses, undeterred by the lack of even one affirmation of a link to their culture through the magic of language, Alecia began humming very softly. After a minute, long enough for a melody to become clear, she asked them to hum with her, and a soft chorus arose. Then she began singing in Kiowa. One or two voices sang with her, softly, timidly, uncertain of the words. "Do you remember how your grandmothers sang to you?" she asked. And she sang again, the same simple melody. It was the cooing of the grandmothers. It was as if the students saw their grandmothers in Alecia's face and heard them in her voice. In another moment the students were in full throat, and Alecia said, "You see, you can speak Kiowa."

The course did not continue without incident. John Feaver had recruited J. Sanders Huguenin, a young professor with a brilliant academic record at an Eastern university, to teach at USAO. Sandy agreed to be Alecia's counterpart, teaching the European side of the bicultural course. He and the rest of his side of the faculty not only taught European (Western means something other than Western civilization in the American West) history, literature, and philosophy, they immersed themselves in Kiowa language and culture. The only problem came in Sandy's view of the course as a Kiowa response to European art and ideas. Howard Meredith and I thought the structure relegated Kiowa culture to second-class status. We did not think there was anything racist in Sandy's viewpoint, but it expressed the profound problem indigenous people suffered in a world dominated by Western culture. J. Sanders Huguenin, the highly educated young man who had come out west to launch his career in the classic American pattern, defended his position well. Howard and I explained what his idea meant to the Kiowas, and Huguenin himself became a defender of the position of equality. He attended the Kiowa language and culture section of the course, and over the years, until he left to become provost of the University of Virginia campus at Wise, Sandy became one of Alecia's best students and beloved of the Kiowas.

My connection with the Kiowa tribe grew stronger each year, mainly with Jay Goombi and his "Auntie Al." One evening, at Howard Meredith's house, I tried pulling Jay's wheelchair up the three stairs on the front porch. My error was in thinking that a man who quickly moved himself out of his automobile (Jay drove using hand levers for fuel and braking) was relatively light. I got him halfway up the stairs, then fell backwards, and sat down hard while Jay rolled down the steps and across several feet of the front walk. It was the kind of pratfall that cements friendships, and it would not be long before I understood how close I had come to the Kiowas.

At the close of the year 2000, I became very ill and could not meet certain obligations to the Kiowas. I told Julie Bohannon at USAO about it, and a week later, during the most unpleasant part of the illness, a small package arrived from Oklahoma. It contained an audiotape and a folded sheet of paper with a few lines written in Kiowa. Alecia had written a prayer song for me, and recorded it so that I could hear the song in New York City.

A week after that, a small white envelope arrived sent by the Kiowas via Julie. There were $18 inside. It was Kiowa prayer money, the modern equivalent of the arrowheads and gemstones and eagle feathers the Kiowas had offered up in prayer for the sick in some earlier time. And they had danced. They were not young men, and they were required to hold their staffs as they danced; the rule of the dance was that the staffs could not ever touch the earth.

I wrote a note of thanks to Alecia, using the few Kiowa words I knew. For reasons none of us understood, the words and the grammar were perfectly correct. The friendship grew deeper.

A few years after the beginning of the Kiowa Clemente Course, Howard had talked about the course with Lona Barrick, who was then starting to turn the Chickasaw Nation's arts and humanities programs into an important aspect of tribal life. Lona had recruited students and faculty for the first Chickasaw course, and she invited Howard and me to attend the first class to teach European literature for an hour before a Chickasaw speaker taught

Chickasaw vocabulary and grammar in the second half. It was, as always, an opportunity to travel across Oklahoma with Howard, talking about the grasslands and the shape of the hills and the history of the tribes now settled in Oklahoma after the long marches remembered as the Trail of Tears. Jacksonian democracy had not been kind to the Indians.

The time of the nations as Indians (Howard preferred that word to Native American) was in danger of coming to a close. There were only two fluent Wichita speakers left, and one of them was a white college professor far to the north. I did not know what to expect of the Chickasaws, and I was delighted to meet Lona Barrick, a stylish young woman then, and crisp. Over the years she has become even more businesslike, with a managerial style that pushes routine down to underlings. Nothing about her is harsh, she has no apparent sharp edges, but she does not hide from conflict. The Chickasaw Clemente Course has grown to three courses under her guidance, and she now heads the Pan-American Indian Humanities Center.

Howard and I waited with her outside the room that had been arranged for a Clemente Course class, talking about the course, telling her what we planned to do for the hour. When the class began, Howard sat at the head of the long table and I sat along one side. Lona did not sit at the table with us after she made introductions; she hovered, watching, the fierce aunt of the course. The other woman who caught my interest that evening sat directly across the table from me. She was thin and wrinkled and her skin was dark with many ages in the sun of Mississippi and Alabama, where the Chickasaws had lived before being forced to move to Oklahoma. Howard had told me on the way to the class that Mrs. Greenwood was one of the most culturally sophisticated members of the Chickasaw Nation. He was anxious to meet her, and so was I.

The class went along well enough for the first forty-five minutes. The students had been asked to read the *Allegory of the Cave* in preparation for the discussion, and most of them had done so. They struggled with contemporary analogues of Plato's work, but the questions brought them to an early stage of understanding—enough to let them feel the slight sting of thinking. Before the Chickasaw teacher took over the class, we read a poem from *In the Language of Kings: An Anthology of Mesoamerican Literature*[2] and talked about the Nahua poet/philosopher's questioning of reality and illusion. It was then that a woman sitting to my right, who said she was going to become a nurse, made a speech about the uselessness of all things Indian. She was glad to read European literature and philosophy, but she did not want to waste her time with Aztec or Chickasaw language or literature.

She said flatly that Chickasaw did not even have the words used in European ideas, so it was not possible to study philosophy in Chickasaw. The other students sitting around the table nodded agreement. Lona said nothing. I glanced over at Howard, and was not comforted. He looked worried, like a man watching a fire next door. It was not his house that was burning, but he could smell smoke. Since there was now nothing to lose, I said that we should choose some of the most difficult concepts in the works of Plato, and ask Mrs. Greenwood if the same concepts appeared in Chickasaw. Mrs. Greenwood agreed. I began with "illusion." Mrs. Greenwood immediately translated the word into Chickasaw. I picked out several other words, then chose a word that I thought might have no exact counterpart in a culture that looked more toward harmony than European ideas of good and evil. "Virtue," I said. And it was indeed a word that did not immediately call up a counterpart. In the moment that passed while Mrs. Greenwood searched through

---

2   Miguel León-Portilla and Earl Shorris, eds. (New York: W. W. Norton & Company, 2001).

her mind, my anxiety about the future of courses for Indians led to curious and disturbing fantasies. The history of the ahistorical world of Indian peoples, who considered life to be a great circle, was at grave risk. Was she too old for the task I had set for her? Or not old enough? Was the circle finally breaking there in a small room in a Chickasaw community center? I watched Mrs. Greenwood's face for a sign. The woman who sat next to me, plump and certain, casting away millennia, gave a sigh of satisfaction and farewell.

Mrs. Greenwood could hear the sound from across the table. She smiled, and spoke the Chickasaw words that together meant "virtue." I did not look at the plump woman, but at Howard, who smiled with a mixture of relief for what we understood as the survival of the original world yet again, and awe at the ability of the woman who contained the language, dreams, love, ideas, and the indomitable sense of rebellion (from which their name derives) of the Chickasaw culture, and could offer them to the world in which the plump woman chose to live. Not long afterward, Howard began driving from Tahlequah to the Chickasaw Reservation to record an oral history with Mrs. Greenwood.

He told me that he was worried about Mrs. Greenwood's health. He did not have long recording sessions with her, because she had a weak heart. After that, I did not hear from him for a long while. It was not Mrs. Greenwood but Howard who had become desperately ill. He was moved from the Meredith house at Tahlequah to the M. D. Anderson Cancer Hospital in Houston. I did not ever speak to him again, for he was too weak to accept a telephone call, but he did manage somehow to send a series of postal cards. They did not speak of his illness or of his hopes for heaven. He wrote as he had talked on our long drives across Oklahoma. He noted the coming of the seasons, the shadings of green in the trees, and the birds which he seemed to hear singing through the silence of glass windows.

Alecia Gonzales was nominated for the state Humanities Council's public humanities award in 2009. Julie Bohannon at USAO asked if I would write a letter in support of the nomination. In my letter, I told of the first night of the Kiowa Clemente Course. Alecia received the award, which pleased her very much. Soon afterward, however, Julie told me that Alecia was ill. I phoned her at home and then on her cell phone, where I found her sitting in a restaurant, waiting for her lunch to be served. We talked for a while, until I heard her say something to the waitress, and then to me, with the abruptness of a hungry woman, "Well, good-bye, Earl. My lunch is here."

The last time I talked to her, she was very ill. Jay Goombi said he would hold a telephone to her ear. "She won't last much longer," he said. "Talk to her."

I thought how she had sung for me. The next day, I wrote the eulogy to be spoken at her memorial service. I suppose it was my way of singing for her.

CHAPTER 5

Darfur

A tall, slim man stepped out from among the rows of cars parked in the dry, floodlit field in the heat of the equatorial night, and walked quickly toward us. He wore the tan cotton matching shirt and trousers common in North Africa. In the cold light of the high-intensity lamps I could see that he was not a black African. His skin was the creamy brown of the centuries-old Arab invasion of the continent.

"Shorris," he said.

"Mutasim."

"I have come from Addis this afternoon," he said. "I am waiting for you."

He smiled. I handed him fifteen hundred-dollar bills. "Now, it is your responsibility." He took the money and put it in his pocket without counting it. We embraced like old friends although we had never met before. The discomfort began immediately. The Ghanaians who had been standing there with me also smiled, but they did not embrace him or even shake his hand.

We climbed into a four-wheel-drive vehicle. The Ghanaians said they had reserved a room for me in the Hotel Mensvic, which was not far from the University of Ghana, where we would be working on our first Clemente Course in the Humanities on the African continent. Mutasim said that he had already found a room in a hotel close to the beach, and in that hotel he could cook his own meals. He said to me, speaking as if the Ghanaians were not there, "If you stay in my hotel, I will cook for you."

The Reverend Tony Bianchi, who had arranged my trip, said, speaking as if the Arab were not there, "The Mensvic is close to the university. His hotel is very distant."

"Then I will stay in the Mensvic," I said, and I told Mutasim that I would see him often while we were both in Accra, but I could not stay so far from the university because I had come to Ghana to do my work there.

I could not see Mutasim's face in the dark, but I sensed that something was going wrong. Bianchi and I had known each other since we first talked at a Clemente Course graduation in Chicago, and we had met at Schiphol in Amsterdam to make the last leg of the trip from the United States together. The work in Ghana was Bianchi's idea. Mutasim Yousif Mustapha had agreed to meet me there to talk about the possibility of another course in Africa, one for internally displaced persons (IDPs) from Darfur.

The meeting with Mutasim had begun at Kings College in Halifax, Nova Scotia. At the end of a public lecture there, a small brown woman, sitting in the front row at the far end of the large hall, had stood up to say, "My name is Huwaida Medani. I am here from Sudan. Would you also teach in Darfur?"

"Yes," I said. "Don't go away. Just wait right there." And turning back to the audience, I said, "Thank you for coming. I wish you a good evening."

The small woman remained in her place as the others filed out. I walked over to where she stood, keeping watch over her lest she change her mind out of shyness or some fear I sensed in her, but could not define. We shook hands and exchanged e-mail addresses. I said that I would write to her about Darfur. She turned and hurried off.

There was other work to do in Halifax: a course to strengthen, a faculty to debate about curriculum, a talk on the humanities to deliver to the class completing the Foundation Year[1] at Kings College, and the lively world of a fine liberal arts college to enjoy. I did not think much about Darfur and the small Arab woman whose Internet address I had scribbled somewhere in a notebook. Darfur seemed remote, impossible, and the behavior of the woman too mysterious for what had become the meat and potatoes work of teaching the humanities to the poor. For several weeks I put her address aside and attended to other work. When I came across it in the notebook, I sent her a brief note. She answered promptly, and we began a long correspondence, at first trying to coordinate the ideas of the Clemente Course, which were then still devoted mainly to teaching the same conception of the classics that Petrarch had defined as the humanities during the Renaissance.

She had no objection to the curriculum since she was then in Canada working on an advanced degree; the Western classics coincided with the thinking of her professors. To back up her words, she made an extraordinary offer, one that I could hardly refuse. She was so taken with the idea of the Clemente Course that she would fund a trip for her friend Mutasim Yousif (or Yousuf) Mustapha (or Mustafa depending on who is transliterating) to Ghana, where I would be establishing our first course in Africa. A three-way correspondence then ensued, with Mutasim expressing his agreement about the need for a Clemente Course for Darfuri IDPs. His English was serviceable, but imperfect. I have no Arabic. When there was a problem, Huwaida, who is fluent in both languages, solved it.

The first of many problems we would encounter with governments came when Mutasim explained that he could not travel from Sudan directly to Ghana. To get a visa to enter Ghana, Mustasim

---

1 A one-year required course in the liberal arts.

would have to travel to nearby Addis Ababa, Ethiopia, where he would make application at the Ghanaian consulate. He expected the visa to be processed in three days. Then he would catch a flight to Accra, which is 2,600 miles away, on the other side of the continent.

The complicated arrangements were going along well when Huwaida wrote to me that her niece, little Huwaida, a beautiful child whom she loved as if she were her own, had been diagnosed with cancer in one eye. She said that the money she was going to give to Mutasim had to be used instead to pay for the child's treatment. I said that she should devote herself to the child, and I would finance Mutasim's trip. Huwaida sent me a photograph of the little girl standing outside what appeared to be a small desert town or village. Although it was only a photograph, the brilliance of the sun, the baked ground, and the faded brown earthen buildings with their tiny windows transferred the heat of the North African desert to a screen 8,000 miles away. Huwaida had been born in this cruel land. Her father farmed whatever the scarce water would permit. Perhaps she had been like the little girl, sweet, alone, and somehow both happy and forlorn. Mutasim had grown up closer to the Nile, where the land is more fertile, yet I understood him, in his difficult life, as if he had been like the small boys off in the distance behind the girl kicking a soccer ball in the terrible sun of Sudan.

Almost every day Huwaida wrote about the little girl's suffering. The surgeons removed her eye, she endured chemotherapy, and nothing worked. The child died, the money was gone, the Darfuri filled the refugee camps, the killings went on, there was no opposition to Sudanese president al-Bashir. To attempt to teach the beauty and clarity of the humanities to the survivors of the nightmare had the allure of madness. The correspondence with Huwaida and Mutasim did not stop, although he had only a telephone line through which to send his letters, and at times he had to wait for hours just to get a place in the queue.

The Reverend Tony Bianchi and I continued moving ahead with the Clemente Course as part of his mission to Ghana. I told him about meeting Mutasim, which he thought was fine as long as Mutasim did not interfere with the work of the mission. Bianchi is a gentle man with an iron will that announces itself in his bearing and in the clean, geometric lines of his face. He speaks very softly, with the mildly lyrical accent of Twi, the version of Akan spoken in Accra, and the slightly British enunciation left in Ghana by its long years under English rule. The other Ghanaians standing at the first meeting with Mutasim were a driver and the Reverend Dr. Abraham Akrong, head of the largest dormitory complex at the University of Ghana in Legon and director of the Department of African Studies. Akrong is a large, thickly built man, who has a looming presence and a great, embracing laugh. He exhibits his administrative and personal force with relish. He and Bianchi are fast friends and have been since their days together in divinity school. The driver, who owned a fleet of sports utility vehicles, had been rescued from a life of addiction and misery by the Reverend Dr. Akrong, and he made no secret of his loyalty to his pastor.

It was a difficult situation for Mutasim, who managed to irritate the Ghanaians and me in a dozen different ways. Some of the problem came of his wish to stay in a hotel far from the university, necessitating long trips to pick him up and deliver him, something the Ghanaians had not bargained for, and which they did for Bianchi, who seemed to command such favors by the quiet certainty of his demeanor.

The work in Accra went forward in two distinct parts: Mutasim, who had taught Islamic literature in both Khartoum and Islamabad and who washed his feet five times a day as required by his faith, moved in one direction and the Christian pastors and their loyal coterie went in another. One was born in the arid villages of Sudan, the descendant of the ancient marriage of Arab and Nubian peoples, and spoke Arabic as his first language. The others were trilingual and quadrilingual West Africans, some of whom could speak and understand the language of the drums as well as spoken and written language. Their complex culture included the powerful influence of long British occupation as well as the pride of being the first African nation to throw off the yoke of colonialism. I had not brokered a good marriage.

Mutasim and the Ghanaians separated. There were no unpleasant words between them, but there was no communication other than a few words here and there. Mutasim was invited to meetings that he did not attend and not invited to others. At other times during the day and evening, he and I met to work on a curriculum for Darfur/Sudan that did not involve the Ghanaians. Darfur and Accra were soon farther apart in the city of Accra than on the map of Africa.

During our long months of correspondence, Mutasim had been looking at a sample curriculum I had sent to him, thinking he would work on the version that would be taught in Darfur/Sudan. When we met for dinner in the small restaurant at the Mensvic, he brought along a copy of *Riches for the Poor*, the book I had written about the theory of the course, and a few notes he had made, but nothing like a curriculum or reading list for the Darfur course. I had no choice but to greet the information with a shrug and the thought that we would eat promptly and begin work. He agreed, and we went about the business of eating the simple fare offered in the hotel dining room. Mutasim ordered a beer with his dinner, and being a man with little time for religion I was secretly pleased that a man who washed his feet and prayed five times a day was reasonable enough to enjoy cold beer in a warm clime.

We talked about his family, his wife and sons, all of whom he loved dearly. And then he told me about the heavy teaching load he had to carry at the university all the while studying for the exams to complete his final degree. He was a diligent and good-hearted man, I thought, and I began to like him. Among other winning aspects of his character, he made clear to me that he was husbanding his funds so that he could buy souvenirs for his children and a gift for his wife. I looked at his face carefully as he translated our agreements on the course and wrote his notes in neat Arabic script. The feat of speaking one language and making notes in another was one I mismanaged with great difficulty, and his talent for it, while not remarkable, was enough to increase my respect for him. Like many people who learn English more by reading than speaking, however, he was not at ease in conversation. We stumbled. I tried to be aware of the need to speak slowly and enunciate carefully all the while choosing simple words to form short, clear sentences. It made for Strunk & White sentences on my part as well as his, less the art of conversation than the imperfect laying of bricks.

Mutasim kept his diet as much as possible to fish and vegetables, and when he ate, it was but little. At first, I had imagined his emaciated body was a result of poverty or a lack of available food, but his endurance was remarkable, given his physical problems, which included malaria, tuberculosis, diabetes, and some unnamed ailments of the digestive tract. We sat close to each other, and I peered at his notes as if I could read them. I still held on to my original wrongheaded position about the reading list. We began with philosophy: Socrates, Plato, Aristotle, Kant, and Hume. Only original texts were to be considered. Art history was to begin with the caves at Lascaux. He carefully wrote down the names of periods and of specific paintings as I suggested them. He did not ask to include art from Arabic countries, although we did agree that the students should have a look at work from the Benin culture and compare it to Picasso. I said that the purpose of the art history section was to teach the students to see, a notion that puzzled him at first, but brought forth a smile after I apologized for speaking to him in less than common language. In the literature section we agreed on *Antigone*, one of Shakespeare's comedies, and a sheaf of British and American poems followed by some of the best work in Arabic, pre-Islamic to the present. I could not help him with the history of Sudan, especially Darfur, but I urged him to give the students documents to read, even if the documents were transcribed from the oral tradition.

We spent hours sitting at the table in the hotel restaurant. And although I had come to like Mutasim, I could not understand how he and his friend Huwaida, both Arabs, could be so concerned for the welfare of the Darfuri, who were being murdered, raped, driven from their villages, forced into crowded camps by government bombing and strafing and by the mainly Arab *janjaweed*, the militia who entered Darfuri villages mounted on camels or pickup trucks and murdered or displaced everyone. The killings that President George W. Bush had said amounted to genocide appeared from my great distance as a kind of race war: Arabs vs Africans. If that was the case, how different were Huwaida and Mutasim from the rest of the Sudanese? The Sudanese character was very much in the news then in Accra. The African Union (AU) was meeting in Ghana. A new head of the AU was to be chosen, and the office, which rotated among heads of state, had come around to Sudan. President Omar al-Bashir, the Sudanese chief executive behind the ongoing genocide in Darfur, was due to become the leader of the African nations. If that were to happen, the AU would not interfere with the genocide; the assassin would become a hero to the continent. Who would stop him? Certainly not the Sudanese. No Sudanese citizen would dare.

Weary after our hours of work, Mutasim and I spent a while at the kind of aimless chatter that often leads to friendship, and then he called a taxi to take him back to his hotel. We parted with many issues still unsettled. Where would we teach? How would we fund the project? How practical was it to teach the humanities in a form leading to thoughts of democracy in a country where members of the opposition could be imprisoned, tortured, raped, or murdered? What if Huwaida, Mutasim, and I were putting our prospective students and faculty into the hands of the Sudanese Secret Police? Neither Mutasim nor Huwaida nor I had spoken aloud of our trepidation as we moved toward establishing a course for Darfuri IDPs; I think we all knew that any expression of fear would lead to abandoning the work.

We were not to meet again for several days. I imagined that while I was working, Mutasim was lying on the beach near his hotel or cooking elegant vegetarian meals or washing his feet. My resentful thoughts turned out to be ill informed. Mutasim was not lying on the beach or cooking the vegetables he bought in the local markets, he was working very hard at starting a Clemente Course for the Darfuri. My frail friend had found himself in the company of the courageous.

It happened this way: Two men had come to Accra to engage al-Bashir and the African Union in debate. Mutasim had seen these men on television and read about them in the newspapers. One had traveled from Geneva, the other from Sudan, one was Fur and the other Masalit, and both were apparently willing to risk their lives for their people by speaking in public about Darfur and al-Bashir's responsibility for the killings. The previous night I had gained some appreciation for the power of al-Bashir. We had been forced to pull off to the side of the road while a convoy of SUVs went speeding by. It was al-Bashir himself, and there was something ominous about the bravado of the people beside me in the truck. If the next head of the AU could stop traffic and turn conversation into sudden laughter in Ghana, I could only imagine the extent of his power in Sudan. I could not grasp the meaning of the laughter of my companions.

Mutasim had apparently telephoned the two defiant men and arranged to meet them in the lobby of their hotel. He told them about the Clemente Course and invited them to meet us at the Mensvic. They agreed to meet for dinner the following night. Mutasim arrived on time. We took a table in the nearly empty restaurant, and waited. I asked about al-Bashir, Sudanese politics, the character of life under an oppressive government. Mutasim fended off the questions, which I put to him in blunt language, afraid that nuance would be lost or misunderstood. He was not cowardly— after all, he had come to Accra—and being Arab, educated, and Muslim he had little to fear in Sudan, yet he spoke very carefully about the political situation, almost as if he thought someone in the empty dining room might be listening. I did not press him. We went back to discussing children, the economics of a professor's life, our mutual friend, Huwaida, and little girl whom she had loved as if she were her own child.

After a time, we began to think that the defiant men were not coming. It could have been nothing more than a bit of posturing by Mutasim, or al-Bashir could have found a way to silence them, or they could have found a more promising meeting. I decided this last was the case, and said to Mutasim that I thought we should order dinner and discuss options for establishing a course that did not involve these men. He agreed. We had just begun dinner when his cell phone rang. He had a brief conversation in Arabic, and smiling, he said they were sorry to have cancelled our engagement and would like to meet us in two days at the same place. I agreed.

Once again, Mutasim and I met in the hotel dining room, and waited for the two men. In the intervening days, the AU had met, an election had been held, and the results were not as had long been expected. The African Union had passed over Omar al-Bashir in favor of John Kufuor of Ghana. The Darfuris had humiliated the man who was destroying them by the hundreds of thousands and displacing them by the millions. I knew al-Bashir's reputation, I had seen the entourage speed past us. I did not expect his daring antagonists to keep their appointment.

When two burly, dark-skinned African men dressed in very British pinstripe suits entered the hotel dining room, I glanced at them and turned back to my conversation with Mutasim. The two were either British businessmen or government officials. One carried himself in the slightly accusatory manner of a litigator, shoulders set against the onslaught of the opposition, ready to pounce. The other had a small mustache and wore glasses. The men were not smiling. Something seemed to be wrong. Perhaps they knew that Mutasim and I had exchanged our dollars for Ghanaian cedis on the black market. Mutasim leapt to his feet and greeted them both with delight and relief—the men in business suits returned his greeting with what seemed to me too much formality, arranging the relationship. These were the two he had told me about: Abdelbagi Jibril and Mohamed Abdalla El Doma. "Jibril" was the Arabic version of Gabriel, according to Mutasim. Mohamed was a familiar enough name. It was clear to them who was the American. They spoke to me in English. I invited them to be my guests for dinner.

The two men and Mutasim ordered beer and I ordered a glass of the hotel's execrable wine. The men in business suits had impeccable European manners nicely mixed with the gracious style of the Fur and Masalit and sure sense of right and wrong that comes with long practice at being courageous. They conveyed the confidence I had seen before in some old soldiers and a few successful bullfighters. Abdelbagi Jibril introduced himself as the executive director of the Darfur Relief and Documentation Center and Mohamed Abdalla El Doma said he was the head of the Darfur Bar Association. Before dinner they gave me copies of the work they had been doing in Accra, speaking on radio and television, circulating written materials to the newspapers, visiting the delegations from other African nations, all to keep al-Bashir from his moment of transcontinental glory. And they had succeeded. They were pleased, but not content. They understood this victory as only a small thing. The suffering in Darfur went on.

Since both men were fluent in English, I was able to explain the idea of the Clemente Course to them. They grasped it quickly, leaping ahead of my description with their questions. Several years later, El Doma wrote to me about his thoughts during that first meeting: "I heard him carefully, but frankly speaking there were questions which spring into my mind: Is Mr. Shorris, who is speaking, dreaming or is he not serious about the course, which seemed to be impossible at that time? Funny [sic] enough, he was confident about the course in Darfur."

The two men ate with appetite while I continued my overly long and detailed description of the curriculum, the Socratic method, and my insistence that there be women as well as men in the course and that we have at least one woman on the Darfur/Sudan board of directors that we would establish in Khartoum. They agreed to everything I suggested, but for one aspect of the course. I said that we should teach the poor, defining "poor" as those people most economically, politically, and educationally disadvantaged. They did not think it would be useful to teach the very poor in the camps. According to Abdelbagi and El Doma, both of whom knew the IDP camps very well, what was needed was to teach the Clemente Course to the leaders, both men and women.

We discussed the issue of who would attend the course, but it was really no discussion at all: they had come to a decision. Soon enough, I realized that we would be teaching the leaders or we would not be teaching anyone. Curiously, the conversation never turned to the conditions in the IDP camps where we planned to teach. The horrors of the ongoing work of genocide lay on the table as if some sickening repast had been carried out of the dry fields by the dead of Darfur and spread before us. The work I proposed seemed both urgent and superfluous. We agreed that we would do this work, because I had proposed it and because we did not know what else to do. I asked if it was dangerous, and they did not make a joke about me, but said in response to my question that they would help to set up the course.

We had met with handshakes; we parted with embraces. Mutasim stayed behind, and for the first time we talked about the realities of the course: where would we find a classroom? Where would we find faculty? Who would recruit the students? Who would be the course director? How much would each professor be paid? And then there was the question of the government. Would the students be tortured, sent to prison, or murdered? "We must get a license from the government," Mutasim said. "Otherwise it will have to be done in secret, and that would be dangerous."

He did not ask about the money to pay the cost of the course and I did not bring up the subject, for I had no idea about where to find the funds or even where to look. I did not know how to raise funds, and I had never applied for a grant. El Doma and Abdelbagi had intuited this lack in me. Mutasim, I would soon learn, thought all Americans are rich.

The next day I spoke to the Reverend Dr. Abraham Akrong about the course we were planning to set up in Sudan. We were drinking beer, I was eating chicken, and he was eating a fish in the Ghanaian manner, expertly picking the meat off the bones with his fingers. "We are going to have an all-African board of directors," I told him. "Would you be willing to be a member of the board? I think that having the Master of Legon House on the board would protect the students and faculty."

Abraham's expertise with the fish was such that he did not pause in picking the bones while he thought about my request. Instead of answering the question, however, he tried to help me understand what I was proposing for the Darfuri. "In Africa, there will always be one person who is reporting everything to the government. You cannot have a secret from the government in Sudan."

"Will they harm the students or the faculty?"

"Not necessarily," he said. "But they will know." And then he laughed and drank down his beer and told me he would gladly serve on the board. He did not like Mutasim very much, although he was too polite to say so. He said that he would like to meet Abdelbagi Jibril and Mohamed Abdalla El Doma. I said that I would try to arrange the meeting, although both men had completed their work in Accra and would be leaving soon.

Two days later, when Mutasim and I were having a final dinner in the hotel before he was to return to Khartoum, the hotel desk clerk came into the restaurant and announced that Mohamed had come to the front desk asking for Shorris in Room 305. "That's me," I said, and stood up to greet Mohamed Abdallah El Doma, for I knew no one else named Mohamed in Accra. "Please tell him to come in."

Mutasim touched my arm and whispered, "He is a thief."

"El Doma?"

"You will see. Mohamed is coming." And he directed me by a nod in the direction of the restaurant entrance to look at an African man in a shabby business suit coming our way. "Shorris?" the man said, taking what appeared to be a business card from his pocket and holding it out to me. I nodded. Mutasim said nothing. The man approached our table, talking as he came, "I am Mohamed. . . . ," and then said the rest of his name, which I did not quite understand. "I have a business here of making items for export. You are here for business. You have money to invest. We can make profits with these items."

"He is not here for business," Mutasim said.

"I have no money to invest," I said. "You are mistaken."

The man apologized and left. I thought I saw the hurt in his face when I said I had no money. He withdrew the business card in what I took to be a sign of parsimony. When the man was out of earshot, Mutasim said, "He was sitting in the lobby when you came with your Ghanaian friends. He listens to your room number. He knows the name of El Doma from the newspaper. You must now change your room. He is going to rob you in your room."

"I have nothing of value. Papers. A little clothing. Some medicine."

"He knows your room."

On the way out that evening I asked the desk clerk, with whom I had become familiar enough to make a joke here and there, if he knew the man named Mohamed who had been asking for me.

"*Daabi*," he said, continuing my fruitless lessons in Twi.

"*Meda ase*," I replied, but I did not feel very thankful, considering the fact that a robbery or at best a burglary was now imminent.

Mutasim and I continued to talk about the course. We had to get a license from the government, secure a place in which to hold classes, find a way to bring people from several camps into that location, get the money, the faculty, the students, agreement on the curriculum, and I had to teach the teachers how to teach. By the next night, as I lay in my room wondering when I was going to be robbed by Mohamed the Stranger, I began to think of the project as the other Mohamed, El Doma, told me it looked to him: *Mr. Shorris is dreaming . . . he is not serious.* I thought that I could not do it. A trip to Khartoum was impossible. I had no visa, no airline ticket, I would run out of the Malarone antimalarial tablets and some other medicine, and I had not one word of Arabic. It would all have to be done by the sweet, slightly timid, slightly unpleasant Mutasim and the two fearless men in barrister's garb. The last thing

I could do for Darfur while Mutasim and I were still in Ghana was to invite him to attend the class I was going to teach to demonstrate the Socratic method. The Ghanaians would make a videotape of it, convert the tape to a DVD, send the DVD to me in New York. I would have it copied (if I could find a machine that was compatible with the one used in Accra), then send it to Khartoum, hoping they had a machine compatible with the one we used in New York. Without the DVD, I was afraid that the teaching method would be very different from what we use in the Clemente Course.

The last time I saw Mutasim was during the demonstration of the Socratic method. At the break between the philosophy and literature classes, we stood outside the classroom in the open air eating fruit that had been covered with cloths to keep the flies away. We stood together, planning the next steps. I began to worry about him: if he did not get a license, if the government thought the course was subversive, if there was an uprising, or if someone he worked with knew about the American and the government thought that was, in itself, subversive . . .

Mutasim and I were both going home that afternoon. He looked so thin! He had so many diseases, so many burdens, such long hours; what had I thrust upon him? We had a long, brotherly embrace. A taxi came for him, Akrong's driver came for me. Mutasim carried everything he owned, including the souvenirs for his children and the gift for his wife, in a small cloth bag. He wore a tan matching shirt and trousers as he had every time I saw him. I waved to him, and he waved back through the window of the taxi as it sped off across a muddy field. The work in Darfur would depend on him.

CHAPTER 6

Hawakeer

Mutasim had a talent for meeting people who could help the Clemente Course. By the time he arrived back in Khartoum, he had managed to meet the UNESCO ambassador to the African Union, and convince him to join our Darfur/Sudan board of directors. Dr. Idris Yousif Ahmed also joined the board. Dr. Idris held important posts in three worlds: he had received a doctorate from the University of Newcastle for his work in electrical engineering. He holds one of the key positions in the traditional structure of his *hawakeer* (section of Darfur); he was a member of the Pan-African Parliament of the African Union; and he was responsible for the design of Sudan's modern telecommunications system. Idris, Abdelbagi, and El Doma are key members of the rational opposition to the al-Bashir government. Abdelbagi cannot return to Sudan, but the other two have, so far, been able to live in opposition both to the genocidal government and to the Sudanese liberation groups striving to bring down the government through civil war. El Doma spent much of his time in South Sudan, trying to stave off another war when South Sudan gained its independence.

Since the board was an all-African organization (I was only ex officio), primarily Sudanese, the organization could not be expelled from the country as al-Bashir continued his effort to drive out all

NGOs. Similarly, the faculty and students would all be Sudanese: they could be killed or imprisoned, but like the board of directors, they could not be expelled. There was no reason to harm them, however. We had organized with Akrong's prediction in mind. He was undoubtedly correct that working in secret would produce a spy within our midst. The Darfur/Sudan Clemente Course in the Humanities was entirely open and all-African. Mutasim would have to suffer through a ferocious bureaucracy, but he would be able to get a license from the government social services department. Once he had the license, he and I and everyone connected with the course would feel safe.

The next step was to gather the faculty, and Mutasim was somehow able to assemble an extraordinary group of professors, only one of whom was Darfuri. The rest were Arabs. I do not know why they agreed to teach IDPs in a course invented by an American. It may have been the money, but that was only a small part of the motivation. At least three members of the faculty were comfortably fixed. Two were rich. In a country where the government threw dissenting students out of fourth-story windows, it is not an easy thing to commit to teaching the victims. I would see later that it is easier to punish the victims than to embrace them. The courage and steadfastness of the faculty would become clear. I would come to love the man who had irritated the Ghanaians and me.

Mutasim, who has a PhD in Arabic literature, went first to his friend Ismat Mahmoud Ahmed, head of the Philosophy Department at the University of Khartoum, and then to Rashid Diab, who had earned a PhD in art history and painting in Spain and come home to found the Dara Art Centre. As a painter Rashid had exhibited widely in Europe as well as North Africa, and as an entrepreneur he had built a gleaming white museum space, which one entered by mounting wide, accommodating steps to sit in green gardens or assemble in spotless halls. Ismat was a brilliant young philosopher working in Islamic philosophy who was also deeply interested in modern moral philosophers like John Rawls.

To teach Fur language and culture, Mutasim turned to Dr. Idris Yousif Ahmed, author of the only book on the Fur language (published in Canada). Idris had been a member of both the African Union Parliament and the Sudanese Parliament. He was the father of twelve children, a former Eisenhower fellow, and a man known and respected not only in his own country but across much of Africa. Idris, who quickly became the center of the work, let it be known that this was a good thing for the people of the hakura.[1] Based on his many strands of influence, recruiting the men and women who held leadership positions in the camps went quickly. As the time for starting classes drew near, Idris invited the professors to meet in his house to watch the video of the demonstration class.

The meetings were open, familial, with Idris's children playing free in the house while the conversations went on. Huwaida sat with them one day, and on another, Valerie Laforce, a humanitarian aid worker who had been expelled from her work in the huge Kalma Camp near Nyala, the capital of South Darfur, visited the meeting. During that period I spoke with Valerie almost every evening via Skype. She was in a safe house next door to the Danish Embassy, waiting to find out if there was some way to convince the al-Bashir government to rescind the order for her to leave Sudan. Al-Bashir had found another, more sinister way to carry on the genocide. By cutting off humanitarian aid and fomenting intertribal rivalries in the camps, he was allowing disease, hunger, and banditry to carry on the work that had been done by the *janjaweed* and the Sudanese military.

While Valerie waited in the safe house, when we talked, which

---

1   *Hawakeer* refers to a single area of Darfur; *hakura* is the inclusive name of all *hawakeer*.

was almost every night (morning in Sudan), I could hear the mix of feelings in her voice. She never said that she was frightened, but she did speak of the Sudanese government reading e-mail that came to aid workers, and because we were speaking via Skype and she did not think the police intercepted the conversation, she talked about the police taking female aid workers to their headquarters to interrogate them. Valerie described the police as huge, menacing men, who terrified the aid workers. Some of the women found the interrogations so terrifying that years later they still bore the psychological scars of the terror.

I wanted to protect her, but I had no influence with either the Sudanese or the U.S. government. The best I could do was to say, "If you have a problem, call this number . . . It is Dr. Idris. Tell him we are friends, and say that I told you he could help." Which is how Valerie Laforce of Medicine Hat, Canada, came to be visiting the faculty of the Clemente Course in the home of Dr. Idris Yousif Ahmed.

As she and I talked and the faculty worked on the curricula and reading lists, it became clear that the aid workers and the faculty were of similar character. The humanitarian workers wanted to remain in Darfur despite their fear of the police and the increasing violence in the camps. The Darfur/Sudan Clemente Course faculty were willing to risk teaching J. S. Mill's *On Liberty* in a country run by a dictator who would soon be indicted by the International Criminal Court. The distinction between moral acts and moral courage is not subtle. I think it is a moral act to teach the humanities to the poor, but it is an act of moral courage to fight for human rights in the midst of genocide or to teach Mill to the Darfuri in Khartoum.[2]

Before we could recruit students, two issues remained to be solved. First, we had to settle on the curriculum. Would the fac-

---

2 Going to Darfur was impossible for me. Humanitarian workers were being expelled, and I would fall into that category. And I was still recovering from a bug picked up in another refugee camp. Moral courage would have to belong to others.

ulty in an Arabic-speaking country of mixed indigenous and Arabic cultures, where the influence of Islam was very strong in every aspect of life, teach art and ideas from the West? The answer could be found in the history of philosophy and in the famous verse of the Light in the Qur'an (24, 35–40):[3] "Allah is the Light of the heavens and the earth. The parable of His Light is as if there were a niche, and within it a lamp; the lamp enclosed in glass; the glass a brilliant star lit from a blessed tree, an olive neither of the East nor of the West whose oil is well-nigh luminous though fire scarce touched it. Light upon Light! Allah doth guide whom He will to His Light." There was this wisdom from the Prophet and, in the great Arabic philosopher al Kindi, the agreement with Aristotle that we should incorporate what went before in our thinking now. It was perfectly fine to teach both Plato and Aristotle to our students. And the verse of the Light extended the scope of the course. Islam and the West would be parallel, not antagonistic.

Ismat Mahmoud and I went over the philosophy section. Bart Schultz, the professor of philosophy at the University of Chicago, suggested that we add J. S. Mill to the readings, and Ismat not only agreed but said that he wanted Bart to teach him John Rawls. At the same time, Ismat was teaching me Arabic philosophy. The interchange among Bart, Ismat, Mutasim, Idris, the painter Rashid, and me was, in the deepest sense, thrilling, for this exchange went on while the U.S. government declared Sudan a terrorist country and the Sudanese government engaged in murder so extensive that it merited the term "genocide." There were cultural problems, however. It was impossible to find enough copies of Shakespeare's plays in Arabic translation. Although Mutasim and I had settled on a comedy, no comedy was available in sufficient numbers. The only work he could find in quantity was *Julius Caesar*.

---

3   Assembled here from several translations.

Idris sent a brief curriculum for the Fur section and then expanded it into a model approach to an indigenous culture. Rashid opened his Dara Art Centre to the course. In my search for funding, I wrote to Aryeh Neier, president of George Soros's Open Society Institute (OSI). It would prove to be the best and worst of the American side of the Darfur/Sudan Clemente Course. Neier, whom I knew slightly but had not seen for years, answered my letter immediately. OSI would support the course. But getting the money to Khartoum was a problem. To get around the U.S. embargo on funds to Sudan OSI sent money to Abdelbagi Jibril in Geneva. Abdelbagi deposited the funds in a Swiss bank, where they were converted into Sudanese currency, which was then hand-carried in small tranches into Sudan or wired to bank accounts, again in small tranches to avoid attracting notice. The conversion of the money in Switzerland ate up 10 percent of the grant, which was made up through a gift from the mother of Lela Hilton, site director of a Clemente Course in Jefferson County, Washington.

Once the money was in the bank, the course could go forward with recruiting students from camps within busing distance of Khartoum. The name of Dr. Idris Yousif Ahmed was all that was needed to assure the leaders of the displaced people, both male and female, that the Clemente Course in the Humanities was a worth-while endeavor. Idris was irresistible. Thirty-one students, nine of whom were women, signed on. I do not know what he said to them, but he and I have never talked without laughing. I call him "younger brother," and he laughs. When we spoke of the forthcoming marriage of his daughter, we laughed over my good luck in having sons, who do not need a dowry. He has two wives; I have but one. I did not pry into the life of a man with two wives and twelve children, but we did chuckle over the number of dowries he would have to pay. When it came to serious matters, however, Idris was always quick and clear on what could or could not be done. Mutasim was the director of the course, but Idris was the dean, guiding it as he did virtually all the many efforts in which he was involved. The horrors in Darfur had diverted him from his business career; the search for peace and an end to suffering had taken his time and mind. Yet it did not keep him from laughing, even at the bad jokes made by his older brother, whom he addressed always as "Shorris."

Halfway through the course, Bart Schultz, director of the Civic Knowledge Project at the University of Chicago, invited the Darfur/Sudan faculty to speak at the university. Matthew Santirocco, dean of the College of Arts and Sciences at New York University, invited them to NYU. Schultz arranged for the airfare; Santirocco arranged for lodging in New York and a dinner in celebration of them after they spoke at NYU. Tickets were purchased, posters were made, invitations were sent, and the faculty left Khartoum for Cairo, which was the nearest place to apply for a visa to enter the United States. The success of the course had been astonishing. In photographs made on the first day of the course the students sat with their heads lowered, except for the four traditional chiefs, the *omdas*, who sat staff in hand, white caftans and turbans gleaming, staring stonily ahead. Valerie Laforce ascribed their demeanor to the Fur discomfort with confrontation, which is how they may have understood the idea of teaching by the Socratic method; that is, they understood questions as confrontation. Ismat had feared the worst when teaching by the Socratic method.

In Cairo, the U.S. Embassy visa officer took the passports of the professors and arranged for interviews. Dr. Ismat Mahmoud Ahmed, chairman of the Department of Philosophy at the University of Khartoum, the man with whom I had negotiated—in English—a curriculum for the philosophy section of the course, was told that his application was denied because his command of English was not sufficient for him to lecture at the universities that had invited him. Ismat's wife had warned him about dealing with Americans. The visa officer confirmed her view. But the State Department had only just begun its work of creating enemies of the United States. No fifth column could have operated more effectively.

The visa officer took the passports of the others and sent them to Washington, telling the Sudanese that they would receive their visas in three days. On the fourth day, Mutasim told me that he and the others were running short of money to pay for their hotel rooms and meals. On the sixth day, it was clear that the Sudanese were in trouble. Ismat had gone home; Dr. Idris had sent his passport via courier instead of going to Cairo; Rashid the painter had a Spanish passport and so quickly received a visa. Mutasim waited. Every morning he went to stand outside the gate of the embassy to ask when he was going to receive his visa. Every evening, he sent me an e-mail describing his troubles. No longer able to pay for his hotel room, he moved in with an acquaintance. He could not go home, for he had no identification—the U.S. government had his passport. Every evening, I phoned the embassy in Cairo to plead for Mutasim's passport to be returned to him. Mutasim waited. Penniless, without identification, he was stranded. In order to send him money to enable him to buy food and telephone his family in Sudan, we arranged a complicated transfer system. He sent me the name and passport number of a friend who would go to the Western Union office with him. I wired the money to his friend, who picked it up at the Western Union office and gave it to Mutasim.

The time for the Sudanese to leave from Khartoum to fly to Jordan, where they would change to a flight to Chicago, was fast approaching. Mutasim was panicked. The U.S. Embassy would tell him nothing, not even permit him to speak to anyone to plead his case.

In the end, only Abdelbagi, traveling on a Swiss passport, and Huwaida, with her Canadian passport, were able to come to Chicago. They had already arrived when Mutasim sent us an e-mail from Cairo: although his trip to the United States had been cancelled, the U.S. Embassy would not return his passport. He had spent the money I had sent to him, and he was again penniless. He did not have enough money to use the computer at an Internet café for more than a few minutes, he was staying in the home of an acquaintance, and every day when he went to the U.S. Embassy he was turned away at the gate. Mutasim's passport was in Washington, according to the press officer at the embassy in Cairo. Once again, we wired funds to the Western Union office in Cairo. This time, it was Bart Schultz and the University of Chicago's turn, and Bart and the university were good about it.

Two days later, without apology or explanation, the visa office at the U.S. Embassy returned Mutasim's passport, permitting him to leave Cairo. The Clemente Course went forward, but other projects did not. He and I had once talked about starting a Clemente Course in Islamabad. Mutasim had friends there, had taught Islamic studies at the university, and thought that teaching the humanities would contribute to the well-being and self-esteem of the poor of Pakistan. After the incident in Cairo, we did not talk about democracy in Islamabad anymore.

The University of Chicago and New York University soldiered on with the talks by the Darfuri despite the State Department. Abdelbagi and Huwaida spoke well about the situation in Darfur and the effect of teaching the Clemente Course. Near the end of the presentation in Chicago, people in the audience were invited up onto the stage. One of "the Lost Boys," children who had been rescued from the civil war in Sudan and brought to the United States, now in his early twenties, dressed in a perfectly pressed blue suit, slim, handsome, took his place on the stage and spoke with grace and without apparent rancor of his ordeal. He had been orphaned in South Sudan in 1985, when he was seven years old.

Alone, bereft of family, friends, and the tools of living, frightened by the air attacks of the Sudanese government, he had begun walking through the jungle and across stretches of the sub-Saharan desert. Somehow surviving the dangers of thirst, hunger, carnivorous animals, poisonous snakes, and stinging insects, he had crossed out of Sudan into Ethiopia, then walked east and south into Kenya, where an American rescue group picked him up and brought him to Michigan.

After describing his ordeal, he turned on Abdelbagi Jibril, accusing the Fur, in particular one Fur member of the Sudanese Air Force, of strafing and bombing the defenseless people of southern Sudan. Abdelbagi denied the accusation. The Lost Boy insisted. Their voices rose in pitch as the intensity of the accusations grew. Then a man in the audience, Olivier Kamanzi, a Rwandan living and working in the United States, stood up to speak. He is a big man, and in his yellow and brown spotted Rwandan pants suit he looked even bigger and more muscular, a man shivering with physical and intellectual intensity. I knew Olivier and his fiancée, who sat beside him, wearing a white ruffled dress. Olivier was then an executive in the international division of Citibank. He said, "My parents were both murdered in the Rwandan genocide. I was away in school in Switzerland when it happened. Only forgiveness has enabled me to survive."

The room fell into quiet; the spokesman for the Lost Boys returned to his place in the audience.

After the State Department denied Ismat's visa application on the grounds that he could not speak English, I asked him to write, in English, the remarks he would have made at the universities in Chicago and New York. The e-mail he sent, edited mainly for length, was read at both gatherings. I apologize for my immodesty in including the second paragraph, which tells more about his character than mine.

Dear esteemed Ladies and gentlemen,

Please let me express my immense gratitude and appreciation to you for all the real feeling you show in sympathy and the continuous support that you give to the people of Darfur, who face one of the worst catastrophes that were ever faced by any people in the modern world.

Also my thanks and appreciation is extended to the Clemente Course in the Humanities and New York University and the University of Chicago's Civic Knowledge Project. I would like to especially express my thanks and gratitude to my teacher and old brother Earl Shorris for the invitation to join the staff of the Clemente Course in Humanities / Darfur program as a teacher of the subject of philosophy and for giving me the chance to participate in offering a little help and support that the people of Darfur deserve. I also thank him for his patience and generosity that is manifested within a number of discussions that continued until I was able to grasp the dimensions, nature, method, curricula and objectives of the idea, hence it was possible to rush into this experiment with hope and trust to achieve success.

The Clemente Course in the Humanities / Darfur is similar to the other courses, inside or outside the United States, with regard to efforts to achieve social change through the Humanities. In conformity with this vision the course offers studies in literature, philosophy, history, history of art and critical thinking. The course is distinct from other courses by the introduction of the Fur Language and culture.

The Philosophy curriculum is comprised of three major parts. The first part is Greek Philosophy thorugh the study of a group of Plato's texts like *Apology*, *Crito* and some chapters of *The Republic*, especially those chapters that deal with issues of justice, the nature of the state and the allegory of the cave.

The second part comprises a number of philosophical issues in the area of moral and political philosophy through the study of different selected texts of some philosophers like Hobbes, John Locke, David Hume, Immanuel Kant and John Stuart Mill.

The third part comprises the introduction of some texts of a number of Muslim philosophers, like Al Kindi and Averroes. All such texts stress the importance of the philosophical thinking and refute the contradiction between religion and philosophy. These texts, although very important, are not known to many in our country. The importance of these texts lies in the fact that they establish and urge dialogue, tolerance for others, and call for openness towards the theoretical production of the humanities. Also they accept [right reason] from wherever it comes.

The course started with 31 students, among them nine ladies, with different age groups ranging from the fifties down to the twenties. All the students have regular education below the secondary level, with a minority having studied in the Khalwa (a traditional school mainly for knowing the Koran by heart). All the students were affected by the war situation in Darfur. Four of them are traditional leaders at their areas.

At first I was much afraid to depend on the Socratic Method as the only method of introducing philosophy, and I remember that at the first lecture I described my role just like that of the traffic man, to orgranize the traffic, not to drive the cars. The students themselves shall drive and determine the direction of the knowledge generated through purposeful dialogue in the class. My function shall not go beyond the organization of the dialogue. Really, I was concerned that there may be no cars in the streets, but what took place was in contrast to my fears. My problem was the existence of overcrowding and jams of intensive intelligent ideas and constructive points of view. There was always a feeling among all that the time of the class went quickly and we need more.

I think there are many factors that make the Socratic Method successful and effective in dealing with the philosophical issues; among them might be the richness of the traditional culture of the Fur people, for they inherited a stable political system continued for centuries. The Fur Sultanate is considered among the oldest kingdoms of the area. This stability through time has created a rich cultural environment. The folk memory of the Fur is filled with many traditions, stories, sayings, poetry and oddities. Taking this heritage into consideration the Socratic Method tends to urge the minds of the students to look within this heritage to bring out the essence through an intelligent, thrilling dialogue. So when a philosophical concept is introduced for the first time, then we find close correlations with the culture of the Fur people. This is what gave these philosophical classes vigor and pleasure.

In this context, the students felt that the philosophical issues are not merely formal cold issues that have nothing to do with the reality of their life. Philosophy now is not a tinkling talk as they thought before; they are now able to tackle the philosophical issues as they find them in their stories, sayings and poetry. I felt deeply that their new approach gave them trust in philosophy and its ability to provide real tools that assist them to understand reality and the mode of relationships between different parties in addition to being able to discover the virtues and shortcomings of that reality.

Thus the students got a suitable ability to grasp the points of strength and weakness in the issues facing them; they are also able to point out a number of alternatives to better deal with this reality.

This deep understanding consolidated the desire of the students towards positive change and to overcome the disappointment and fear of the future which continues to roam around them. There is now a real intention to change the painful and dark situation of injustice and coercion that has prevailed for many years. This intention is now supported by deep understanding of the moral and political dimensions of the problems of Darfur.

There is a psychological aspect which I consider one of the deepest effects. It moved me to the extent of crying, because of the pride I have in the wide window of hope open to overcome this crisis. At the beginning of the class there was a prevailing feeling of despair, but as the study progressed that feeling was replaced by hope, this might be one of the reasons that strengthened my trust in philosophy much more than before. Philosophy would be rendered of no use if it did not soothe and comfort us in our grief and concerns, or did not help to find a window of hope And that opens more windows for us.

I am so pleased by this positive change and the development of awareness in this circle of students. I think it is a must for all those who consider this positive effect to work to widen this circle and call for the continuation of such programs to include all Darfur areas, especially because the direct target is the simple people who were overwhelmed by the war and stripped of their security, stability and hope of peaceful life.

Thanks to you all. Thanks to my teacher who honored me by reading this paper.

Ismat

The work in Sudan went on without interference from the al-Bashir government through the end of the academic year. Graduation was a grand occasion featuring many speeches and a curious shift from the Darfuri wish to avoid confrontation to a Socratic daring in its criticism of authority. Omda Zakaria Mohamed Nour said that he spoke for the students. He began with Muslim homage to Allah, and he spoke always with embellishments, repetitions, prayers, and flowers. "In the Name of God the Beneficent and the Merciful, Our respected Staff Member, Our dear Guests and our Fellow Students, Peace be upon you and God's Mercy."

He went on: "This Course was really very important and has added a lot to our knowledge as students; however, perfection is for God alone, so that for any work there must be some positive aspects and some drawbacks. The positive aspects are more; however, let us speak of one or two drawbacks that accompanied the Course to avoid them in the next ones through early resolution and good preparation here in Sudan and maybe outside for the welfare of human beings living similar conditions.

"The first drawback is . . ." He went on to lay out with perfect accuracy the early failings of the course and the marvel of order and seriousness that Dr. Idris brought to it. Although he did not refer to the Socratic method, as Ismat and I have, he said two astonishingly perceptive things about the course. First, "Students and Lecturers form one family," which is one of the precepts of the teaching method, and he noted the cultural change: "We have learned to be aggressive, daring, clear, should not give in easily, and discuss logically."

In great good humor, filled with hope for our work in Darfur, we all began work on the second year of the course. The situation in

Darfur had not improved significantly. The number of deaths was down, but the camps had become increasingly dangerous. Roving bandits hijacked vehicles, women who went out to gather wood were attacked and raped, disease spread. I maintained contact with the New York headquarters of OSI, although a bureaucratic shift had moved George Soros's African headquarters from New York to locations in Africa. Darfur was moved to OSI's East Africa operation under Binaifer Nowrojee and Anne Gathumbi. I put together a full presentation, describing everything that had gone on during the first year, and the newfound willingness of the University of Khartoum to give us classroom space and college credits for our graduates.

Given George Soros's public expressions of concern about Darfur, I thought that his foundation, OSI, would continue to want to help the victims of the genocide. After all, our work had been successful, and the cost was low, about $45,000 for the entire academic year, including transportation and a small food allowance, as well as books. It came to $1,451 per student, including 10 percent taken by the Swiss banks to change dollars into Sudanese currency.[4] The Sudanese began recruiting students for the second year of the course. Then an e-mail response to our proposal to Ms. Nowrojee and Ms. Gathumbi came from a program assistant (a largely clerical post) at the Soros East Africa operation. It was a form letter: three canned paragraphs that did not even mention the name of the proposal. The foundation had turned its attention to South Sudan. Darfur was no longer in the press. We would have to begin again.

---

4   The Sudanese pound is worth about 40 cents in U.S. currency, but prices in Sudan are inflated by the country's oil wealth.

CHAPTER 7

A Crack in the Foundation

We were a curious quartet: Leon Botstein, president of Bard College, trustee of the Open Society Institute, conductor of the American Symphony Orchestra, brilliant, expansive, mercurial, as men who wish to affect many worlds must be; Robert Martin, outwardly cool, a handsome fellow vetted at Yale in philosophy, trained at the Curtis School of Music, who contained within him a giggle at the absurd that he could not always repress, which made of the vice president and co-director of the music festival a charming fellow; Martin Kempner, a heavy-boned man who had dreamed of playing baseball in the major leagues, had chosen instead to study philosophy, but after a series of academic jobs, a fine teacher had been left to earn his living as a salesman, a man reaching, a self-appointed sufferer/king; and me.

Sitting with the other three in the near darkness of Susan Soros's office at the Bard Center for the Decorative Arts, Leon agreed that Bard College would support the Clemente Course in the Humanities. Bard would offer course credits to students who merited them and employ a full-time director. After he had made that offer, Botstein said that we would need a board of directors. Moving at his usual pace, he said to me, "You will be the chairman. And who will be your board members?" I was unused to making decisions at his speed, but I managed to name Starling Lawrence, author and editor-in-chief of W. W. Norton; Hon. David Dinkins, former mayor of New York City; Grace Glueck; Stuart Stritzler-Levine, dean of Bard College; Peter Sourian, author, professor at Bard; and Dr. Jaime Inclán. Robert Martin, vice president for Academic Affairs at Bard, would be responsible for Bard's expenditures. His longtime friend Martin Kempner would take my position as director of the course, and I would return to writing books. Leon, who had arrived at Bard in 1975, when the small liberal arts college was in its economic and pedagogical death throes, had turned it into one of the most interesting and innovative educational institutions in the country. Botstein had always been in a hurry, becoming president of Franconia College when he was twenty-three years old, and moving on to Bard less than seven years later. This evening was no exception. The details were left to Martin, Kempner, and me to work out. Botstein had declared himself and the college the institutional spirit of the endeavor.

In that brief meeting, while a car waited outside to take Leon back up to Bard at Annandale-on-Hudson, there were many handshakes, but such things as reporting relationships and oversight of expenses, curriculum, and so on, were not discussed. We all left the building feeling happy. In time, all the problems of a growing organization befell us. Not every university or college wanted to submit to oversight by another, which I should have expected, and Leon thought it best if Bard confined its work to courses in the United States. Bard, like other educational institutions, was becoming an international organization and the Clemente Course would have been an unnecessary complication in an already difficult operation.

The first meetings of the little board with no teeth produced the idea that the courses would follow the curriculum set out in the beginning. There would be no deviation from the plan. We would be a sort of franchise; the name McDonald's actually came up in the discussions, and no one laughed. As the course developed and expanded, it became clear that there would be variations based on the preferences of the professor. If a professor loved Keats more than Shelley, there would be skylarks rather than nightingales in the spoken world of the classroom. If a professor loved Aristotle far more than Plato, there would be a less mystical, more orderly approach to ethics. One history professor might wish to discover the soul of the nation through the Declaration while another would step gingerly from Hutcheson to Locke to Paine and then to Jefferson. Art history could be taught looking backward from the abstract impressionists to the Chauvet cave or forward from Chauvet to Picasso. How the site directors taught the course seemed to be influenced by place, not only continent and country, but state by state, city by city. The McDonald's menu expanded with every new course and professor. As Amy Thomas-Elder said to me early in our expansion to Chicago, "No professor worth her salt is going to agree to teach the course exactly the way you want it."

Sometimes the differences were so great that a course did not fit at all within the general sense of the Clemente Course. The English faculty at the University of Victoria, British Columbia, a fine university, of great reputation, told me that the faculty was so immersed in the ideas of deconstruction[1] that they refused to teach the important works generally thought to be the foundation

---

1   A means for understanding literature, grown out of the writings of Jacques Derrida, who owed his ideas to Martin Heidegger. In the United States, Paul de Man developed the Yale School of deconstructionists. After his death, de Man was discovered to have written explicitly anti-Semitic texts. His relation to Heidegger, a Nazi sympathizer, via Derrida, has tainted all three men and the deconstructionist school. Nonetheless, the deconstructionist view of literature practiced at Victoria University at the turn of the century continues to interest people more concerned with the views of the audience than the intentions of the author. Richard Rorty, a product in part of Derrida's ideas, was the most admired of that general school, especially in his later years.

of literature in the world. They were going to deconstruct "comic books." Victoria taught an admirable course for the poor for some years. It was an outgrowth of the Clemente Course, but the reading list was very different: many of the works read by the students are secondary source political works. The course at the University of British Columbia (UBC) has migrated from the original curriculum over the years, but it remains one of the most venerable and successful courses in the world. I think that my dear friend, the late Michael Ames, who had founded the course along with Am Johal, would be enormously pleased to see the results of his work. He is best known for his stewardship of the famed anthropological museum at UBC, but in his later years he had become very involved in the UBC version of the Clemente Course. Near the end of his days, when he was suffering terribly from the ravages of lymphoma and the side effects of the chemotherapy, he was invited to speak at a conference held in the Far East. It was about museums, and he was expected to speak about the museum he had headed up for many years. Instead, he wrote a presentation about the UBC version of the Clemente Course. I was flattered when he sent it to me, asking if I would read through it and make whatever comments I thought necessary. It was lovely, cleanly written, not personal, but from the very heart of his person. I told him that I could not suggest any changes in the text and asked if I might crib a few thoughts from it.

We had similar health problems, but his were far worse. It was painful for him to walk or stand, because the chemicals had destroyed the sheathing of his peripheral nerves. He was getting weaker as the days went by. Nothing could be done. In the end of life this great, tall man with whom I had walked the streets of the downtown East Side of Vancouver could not make the trip to Southeast Asia. I wrote something about him that was read at his memorial, but it was insufficient to the man.

At the two extremes of Canada, Vancouver Island University in the west and King's College in the east, different versions of the course appeared. The course at Vancouver Island University followed the original curriculum and recruited students who were able, with some effort, to do the work. The Halifax consortium, which included St. Mary's College, was put together by a management consultant and Mary Lu Redden, the wife of a Protestant minister. It is not as rigorous as the original model, but a softer version, designed to accommodate students wounded by nature as well as by society.

King's, the oldest chartered university in Canada, founded by tories who left New York during the Revolution (the original King's is now Columbia University), retains its British traditions. Students and faculty wear academic gowns and say Latin grace at formal meals. King's is generally considered the best undergraduate college in Canada largely because of its Foundation Year, a core course in the humanities. On the day before giving the annual Foundation Year lecture, I taught a class in the Halifax version of the Clemente Course. I had been in Halifax for several days by then, had given a public lecture and had discussed the program on local radio and television stations all in the routine of being some support to a course, but Halifax had not been quite what I expected. Recruiting black students was an insurmountable problem in the community, which was more divided along racial lines than any I had encountered in the American South. To break down the pattern I asked that the town librarian, a black woman, be added to the little board of directors that had been assembled to manage and fund the course. She was invited, gladly joined, but no black students came.

The founder of the course, an Anglican priest, won me over immediately. He was a wise man, I believed, with the best intentions. And I was not mistaken in that judgment. He was the sort of priest they make movies about, highly educated, the chaplain of King's College, a marvelously articulate man, devoted to the institution, the individual students, and the larger community. Yet there was nothing soft about him. He had a kind of hard-edged goodness that seemed at times more fit for war than academia. The more time I spent with him, the more I liked him. I thought that he and God had chosen each other well. I did not yet know what a disturbance he and Halifax would cause in my settled understanding of the humanities.

I had been spending much of my time in Halifax with the Reverend Gary Thorne when I met up with him one afternoon with his son, who is intellectually disabled. There was nothing strange about the young man; it was just a shadow across a gentle life. We were introduced. The father and son then had a brief conversation. There were not many words, no demonstrative gestures, but there on a pathway alongside a green near the college I saw that the man and the boy loved each other in very much the way I loved my own sons. There was no apparent breach because of the intellectual difference. *Agape*, I thought, a concept that does not often come in the course of daily life. And now it was there in the forefront of my mind on the green in Halifax. In the afternoon, while I prepare to teach the Halifax version of the Clemente Course, the love between father and son caused me to make a kind of inventory of love in Halifax. A grand scholar, who would drown my Foundation Year lecture in the voluble charm of his introduction, cared for his wife who lived in a wheelchair, and snapped at the world with icy wit.

Sophos had been my plan from the moment Niecie and I had spoken in the prison; *agape* was a different process. I associated it with the churchmen and the gentlewomen and was neither and had never intended to be. On an earlier afternoon in Halfiax, Mary Lu Redden, the wife of a minister and the imaginative, interesting director of the Halifax course, had spoken of our college days, the troubles of children in our time, and she had answered my reticence with an honesty that left me no response but silence. We were driving through the town as she spoke. We passed the church her husband pastored. She spoke of memories, but I heard her speaking of other people as if she were a metaphor.

Nothing in Halifax was as it first appeared. Mary Lu Redden was an attractive young matron, the minister's wife, seemingly the product of a sweet but shallow life. Susan Barthos, who was with us in the car as we drove through the town, was a businesswoman, so crisp in her communication I thought she might shatter if we were to disagree. She had a son in Africa and she did not live in Halifax but in a place north of the city along the empty ocean coast among fishermen and what I imagined were the long, white silences of Nova Scotia. She divided her life among businesses and charities, and there was in her conversation some referent passion stated in the absence, a puzzle, some part of her life that brought her to the Clemente Course and, as I was to learn, to the particular assemblage of students who awaited me in the classroom that evening.

It was a literature section, although the Halifax course, I learned, was not ordered into the five aspects of the humanities that Petrarch had given us for a structure. I had asked that the students read several chapters of *Don Quixote*, thinking we would have a good time with a windmill and a copper basin and perhaps a little detective work about the true author of the novel.

The students were assembled, seated in a circle when I arrived. When I looked around at them, I was surprised. There was only one person of color, the result, I assumed, of the racial divide in Halifax. She was by far the most carefully dressed and seemed the most alert of the group, an impression that would be borne out later as I came to know her. The others seemed different from the usual Clemente Course students, most of whom had the determination of strivers in their faces when I first looked at them. After a while they would sort themselves into individuals, wearing instinctive histories on their faces—sitting, leaning, slumping, fidgeting, rocking, according to the lives they brought to the classroom.

These students were more difficult to read. Since I did not know them, I began the class with a sort of chat, trying to gauge the kind of questions they would respond to. One spoke of having been institutionalized, another mentioned the medications he took for psychosis, a raw-boned woman dressed in something that might be called a pinafore said she was worried about her children who were outside in the hall. The students were all polite, attentive, but some of them, I knew, would never be able to grasp ideas in the required depth. They read Dante and Homer and for that evening Cervantes, but I did not think that some of them could ever grasp the idea of the Homeric Age coming to a close as Achilles surrendered the body of brave Hector to his father, Priam. Nor would they ever understand the meaning of the barber's basin on *Don Quixote*.

To begin, I asked them who wrote *Don Quixote*. After some probing, one of them said, "Cervantes." I asked if they were sure Miguel Cervantes was of that opinion. Question after question did not produce the story of the found manuscript, the translation from the Arabic, the excuse for the madness and fantasy in the character of Arabic writing, although that was contained in the chapter I had asked them to read. Perhaps I was at fault. It would have made it a less complicated evening to blame it all upon my head. I would have left Halifax more sure of what I knew about the humanities.

After the class, we gathered in the hall for a light supper of cold cuts and dessert. The conversation continued at the same level. The students were not stupid. It would have been a mistake even to consider that as a possibility; they were troubled, more deeply wounded than the students who came to the course in other cities, other countries. *Sophos* was not the only aim of this course, that was not why Mary Lu had recruited these students. Halifax was different. These students would read great literature, they would have first-rate teachers, but the love between the father and the son on the pathway beside the green was the driving idea here. *Agape.* I had not even considered it. Had anyone? What about the psychiatrist awaiting his license who had told Dr. Inclán it was the best psychotherapy he ever had seen? Why had I dismissed his comment as interesting, but peripheral?

That night, as I lay in a comfortable bed in a Halifax hotel, I suffered the introspection I should have practiced at the beginning of the course. And there is always the most difficult question to struggle with in the twisted sheets of sleepless uncertainty: If I was wrong then, how was I to know that I am not wrong now? Waking and sleeping, my thoughts went to the discussion of opposites in the *Phaedo.* Opposites are always about matters of life and death. Fire and ice. Were *sophos* and *agape* opposites or components of the good?

When morning came, blue and cold, beside the northern sea, I was no longer the smug student of the humanities who had come to Halifax. The chaplain, the minister's wife, the crisp woman who lived among silent fishermen, the students who would never grasp the meaning of the forms had been my midwives. I knew what I had to tell the Foundation Year graduates, but I did not know how to tell them.

That morning, for the love of the humanities, I attacked. To avoid the conflict between faith and reason, I did not choose the errors of times long past, but looked to the students of the humanities in Germany as it went mad in the years leading up to World War II. Rather than argue a theory, I told them of a historian who had run a concentration camp, of pianists in the SS, of the great architect Albert Speer, and of Martin Heidegger, the greatest philosopher of the period, the man who gave the idea of existentialism to the world. The evidence is irrefutable, I told them: Heidegger was a Nazi.

The genius of the humanities lies in its imperfection. Unlike religion, it is not the work of God, but of man. Criticism of the humanities inheres in the very idea of a selection of great works to be read slowly and contemplated for the duration of one's life. The humanities are self-correcting, not in each individual work, not even in each era. Heidegger slept with Hannah Arendt, who must have known. The Yale University deconstructionist scholar Paul de Man wrote a vicious anti-Semitic article or two in a Belgian newspaper run by Nazi sympathizers. But they are gone now, Heidegger and de Man, and even Arendt, who must have known. The humanities are self-critical because they are in the world. They are "heard melodies." To love them is to know when we are wrong, to allow the self-critical character of the humanities to guide us in the long journey of the world. That is why when we study the humanities we are hopeful.

I do not think the students were pleased by the lecture, but I glanced up now and then toward the balcony where I saw the chaplain's face, and I knew that for once I was not wrong.

Only a few years later, my hopes for Halifax were rewarded when my friend, the philsopher Anne Leavitt, was named president of King's College. The Halifax course would go on, and King's, the grand Canadian liberal arts college, would be an even more embracing and thoughtful home to the Foundation Year.

CHAPTER 8

On Revolutionary Ground

Like most Americans, I connect the Revolution to Lexington and Concord when I think of Massachusetts, as if those towns were bound to history and not to life, and even though I have been to the museum in New Bedford, Captain Ahab seems to me to have sailed out of Boston Harbor rather than New Bedford. After a long time, history and life become bound up in the larger subject of what a person can do in his or her time. For example, the work of David Tebaldi at the Massachusetts Humanities Foundation (known now as MassHumanities) seems to me to have to do with a revolution in thinking that David brought to Massachusetts. MassHumanities, where he has been executive director since 1985, does not have its offices on what we think of as revolutionary ground, but in Northampton. MassHumanities works with the University of Massachusetts Dartmouth and Bard College and teaches in social service agencies in Boston and New Bedford. It struggles every year to raise money to pay professors and sometimes has to allow a course to suffer a hiatus.

Tebaldi, a scholar who has taught philosophy at Amherst College and the University of Wyoming, came home to become the lively mind of MassHumanities. He is soft-spoken, with a short, neatly trimmed beard that does not hide his expressions but enhances them so that his smile is a happy conflagration. Tebaldi had read a section of *New American Blues* in *Harper's* magazine. It interested him enough to start a course. To learn more about it, he sent Kristin O'Connell to Washington to listen to talks Martin Kempner and I gave at a meeting of state humanities councils. When the board of directors of MassHumanities was presented with the idea of teaching the humanities to poor people, several members balked. They told him that helping poor people was a fine social service, but not something that fit the idea of a state humanities council. Tebaldi and his allies maintained their view, and the board agreed to an experiment. For one year.

At the end of that year, a student went before the board to talk about her experience in the course. It was the student who won over the board. They agreed to make the Clemente Course a key program for the state council. It had long been their goal to make the humanities available to the less privileged people of the state, and they saw the course as a way to do it. They quickly realized, as if John Donne had been there to advise them, that no student was an island. The course spread the ideas and appreciations of the humanities to the student's children and other family members and on to people in the student's church group—even to neighbors and neighborhoods.

Tebaldi and Kristin O'Connell, the assistant director of MassHumanities, went forward. While Tebaldi, as executive director, took the risk, O'Connell was both stern supervisor and dear friend to the course, the faculty, and students. Tebaldi said that she was "the soul of the course."

Almost from the outset, class observations and student interviews showed that the idea worked, although not perfectly. It never works perfectly. But it can succeed, if the faculty is excellent and the students are devoted and there is enough money to pay the teachers. While Tebaldi brought the council to a place of increasing influence in Massachusetts, Kristin devoted much of her time to the course. Every year, she worked with social service agencies to provide day care for the students' children during class, helped with the recruiting of faculty and site directors, and sat in on many classes. A longitudinal study of the courses was begun, class notes were collected, graduation ceremonies were arranged, and students were guided onto the next stage in their education, often at a nearby college. Some sites worked better than others, but ten years on, working with Bard College and the University of Massachusetts Dartmouth (at Pace Head Start) in New Bedford and in Dorchester at Codman Square, MassHumanities had seen hundreds of students through the course. The faculty in the Massachusetts courses come from UMass Dartmouth, Harvard, Tufts, Brown, and other fine colleges and universities in the area.

Given the quality of the faculty and their institutional affiliations, one might expect attendance to be perfect, with assignments completed on time. That is rarely the case. Many of the students cannot overcome family problems, poor health, the lack of a quiet place to study, or old habits. Every student makes a courageous decision to come to the course, but the transition from a life in what I think of as a "surround of force"—where one has little time to do anything other than react to circumstances—to a life of reflection is difficult. The humanities make the transition possible, but not instantaneously and not always. The class reports collected by Tebaldi and O'Connell show the struggle of this metamorphosis. In them, the frustrations and glories of the women and men who teach the courses, whom I think of as heaven-sent, are evident.

I have changed all the names in a selection of these teachers' reports, which follows (with the exception of the series of reports on a philosophy class), lest anyone find it uncomfortable to read them. None has been otherwise edited. They were written at breakneck speed with no intention other than to indicate what happened in the classroom.

Dante, selections from *The Inferno*

This class went as many of my classes on *The Inferno* go. As we slowly made our way through the assigned cantos, I'd pause at particular images (Virgil's calling a demon a "carnival of bloat" is my favorite) to get them to really think about what the metaphors meant, or what it means when Virgil says he & the other pre-Christian dead suffer desire without hope. It seemed to me, as it has seemed before, that they did the reading but were intimidated & perhaps a bit overwhelmed by it. Every year the majority of mid-term essays are on *The Inferno*, so it seems they like it, but aren't able to articulate their ideas in class. This group was less talkative than other Clemente classes with the notable exceptions of T & M.

Some issues that came up that have come up in other years: M asked if this was fiction or nonfiction; A protested that some of what Dante said "wasn't true." We got into the ways Dante's religiosity is different from both 21st century & Biblical theories, but I'm not sure that satisfied the people for whom A spoke.

The high point of the discussion was G saying, in regard to the sinners being segregated into different rings w/Virgil & his cohorts in the most bearable, "How you gonna be having cliques in hell?" This sort of statement is one of the things I love about teaching in this program. It allowed us to talk a bit about the stratification of the Medieval world view, so from a teaching standpoint it was great. But it was great, too, in that I can't imagine my Tufts students ever having the temerity to ask such a question, to question Dante's basic architecture of *The Inferno*. I think a lot of the students we teach elsewhere have, despite their very many advantages, had that fresh kind of attitude towards knowledge trained out of them.

We made our annual pilgrimage to the MFA on Wednesday and it was, as usual, a great time and too short. Despite the coldest weather of the winter so far, most of the students made it to Codman early where we loaded up our convoy and headed over to the Museum of Fine Arts. The subject of the class was Impressionism, and we spent most of our time in one room, looking at Monets, Renoirs, and a smattering of Cézanne, Gauguin, Caillebotte and Cassatt. The class has reached that wonderful point where it's teaching itself. The hard part with this group is still just trying to contain all the comments. They immediately picked up on the color, the brush-strokes, the resolution of the images from stepping back. They also asked a number of questions about the galleries that allowed me to talk about some of the different museum departments: conservation, lighting, registrar, and curatorial.

After our short class (our regular two hours was eaten up by the traveling time), I took them into an adjacent room to see Turner's "Slave Ship." We had discussed the story in class but the actual painting has so much more detail and texture that they quickly picked up on how much they are missing by just looking at slides and books. "We're going to come back here next week, right?" asked R. I wish. Many people said they wished we could stay longer. Shane, who has been quiet in class, was easier for me to spot last night, holding up her hand, patiently waiting for a chance to make another of her good comments. On the way home she mentioned that she had popped her head in another room and saw a Botticelli. Did you recognize it from the style? I asked. Well, she knew she was familiar with the artist but she had to read the label to remember his name.

After I mentioned that Renoir used contrast rather than black paint to suggest shadow on the faces of the dancers of Bougival, they stared at my face and saw green and blue and purple all over me. (R saw J staring at her face looking for color and exclaimed,

"It's not fair, I can't see your face! [under her Islamic veil]" and they cracked each other up.)

Ezra and Andrea enthusiastically went off exploring. Q asked about taking photographs of paintings to enlarge and put on her wall at home and I suggested that buying a reproduction in the shop would probably be more cost effective and likely better quality. And H, who missed a few classes last year, seemed to really bond with I, who set off an alarm and teasingly blamed her friend for it.

The individuals have become a group and refer to themselves as such. In the van on the way home they talked about who had dropped out and wondered about them. "Jack," E asked. "Are we the best class you ever had?" They are shaping up to be.

Because we spent almost the entire previous session in discussion about Douglass, I began our fourth class with a mini-lecture on "Slavery and Freedom" and the "Coming of the Civil War." I explained the crucial historical difference (à la Ira Berlin) between "societies with slaves" and "slave societies" (the difference being the extent to which slavery provided the social and economic foundation of society). I also gave a brief "long" history of slavery, dating back to antiquity, to make the point that "racialized slavery" (the kind of slavery wherein "race" is used as the principal justification for human bondage) is a relatively recent historical phenomenon, "perfected," as it were, in the United States from the "Age of Revolution" to the Civil War. I talked about Edmund Morgan's formulation of the "slavery-freedom paradox" (the simultaneous rise of slavery and freedom in America) and Barbara Jeanne Fields's provocative thesis that "race," as an ideological category, emerges in the U.S. during the last quarter of the 18th century. I was intentionally historiographic here, trying to get them to understand how fundamentally the "story of slavery and freedom" has changed in the last generation or so. Some of them—B, P, S, and others—were pretty floored by this (for instance, they were shocked to learn that black people had not always, or necessarily, been slaves) and so I had to explain, against some resistance, that slavery was not a static institution: that it varied quite widely across time and space (hence the growing divisions between the North and the South). This required a bit of insistence on my part—the first time I've relied on the "Trust me, I'm a historian, I know this" line of defense—but it seemed to have worked (for the most part).

Then, I explained to them that American history during the period of the Revolution to the Civil War can be characterized— in one sense—as the story of bitter conflict over the existence and extension of slavery as America grew in size and scope. I went through a brief chronology: Louisiana Purchase (1803), Missouri Compromise (1820), Mexican War (1845–48), Compromise of 1850, Kansas-Nebraska Act (1854), "Bleeding" Kansas (1855), *Dred Scott* (1857), and Harper's Ferry (1859). I also provided a map of the country in 1860, pointing out the major territorial acquisitions and state admissions throughout the first half of the 19th century, and gave them statistics about the growth in various "populations" (slave, free black, and overall).

Then we launched into a discussion divided pretty equally among three sets of primary texts: John Brown's last speech to the jury; selections from Mary Boykin Chesnut's diary; and Lincoln's speeches (First Inaugural, Gettysburg Address, and Second Inaugural).

People were floored by Brown, especially after I described the courthouse scene from his trial (Brown chained to a board on the floor, threats of his kidnapping and murder by abolitionists and proslavery advocates, respectively, throughout his trial, etc.). Bridget and Ruby picked up on his overt religious language; Ethel and Linda related his last speech to the courageous stance of Socrates before his death. J, S, and M wanted to know more about Harper's Ferry—and "what he was really guilty of"—and L wanted to know if he "really was crazy." I turned that question around, asking, "Is it crazy for a man to be willing to die for one's beliefs?" They got the point, and immediately began making connections between Socrates and Brown—something that Brown himself encouraged in his prison letters. I shocked most of them, though, when I casually divulged (late in the discussion) that Brown was white. You could hear the gasps in the room. I asked them, "How many of you thought Brown was black?" Most every hand went up. I laughed, and asked why it was so hard to imagine that a white man would be willing to die for black people. P responded, "Because so few have been willing to do it." This inspired a long, productive tangent about interracial sympathy and solidarity—evidence of it, prospects for it, obstacles to it—wherein the consensus was that it is very rare but crucially important.

We moved, then, to the Civil War. I talked about the prophetic quality of Brown's life and death: how the violence and bloodshed of those years foreshadowed the brutality that would come. Truth be told, I laid it on a bit thick here—I find myself struggling with Iraq more and more each day—and so I was talking about war in ways that were both historical and contemporary. I was trying to get them to understand how high the stakes were during the Civil War, and in our own time. There was a palpable silence in the class as I talked about the 620,000 people who died, the 4 million slaves who were liberated, the President (in my opinion, our best President) who gave his life for this cause.

They were really feeling it now, as was I. My voice nearly cracked. M, L, L, and A were moved almost to tears; M actually had to excuse herself from the room to take a breath in the lobby. As she was leaving, P said, "This makes me so sad that they had to go through this." Then B added, "But thank God they did." Silent nodding throughout the room.

It was one of those moments—unique, in some respects, to the

Clemente Course—where students feel a connection with the past in a way that stirs them and gives them pause.

After something of a moment of silence, we launched into a discussion of Chesnut's diary. I was stunned by their reaction: they loved it! Linda said it "floored" her (and then took my copy of the whole diary home with her to read). B said it was "amazing." E said it was "like nothing I've ever read." Ditto for M. In some respects, I think Chesnut's diary satisfied some of the curiosity they had about the "other" perspective on slavery, but still, they were struck by the sympathy she had for the slaves she witnessed at auction—and the connection, as Claude and L noted, that she was making between her struggle as an "unhappy" woman and the struggle of female slaves. P and K likened her—in a positive way—to Stowe, in terms of how she narrated the scenes of the slave auction. L was also preoccupied with the "misery of her false life," stuck in a marriage that seemed troubled, childless (P speculated that she wanted children, but that her husband could/would not provide her with them), and forced to socialize with all these elites "against her will" (B's reading).

I was struck, over and over, about how active and imaginative their readings were: seizing on suggestive moments in the text—was she unhappy, depressed, longing for liaisons with other men, antislavery, fully on board with secession?—to offer informed (and sometimes quite provocative) readings of Chesnut's "inner life." I was also struck by how much sympathy the women in the class—especially the black women—had for Chesnut. B pointed out how her life was full of "tensions"—between her real sympathies and desires and the obligations of elite life—and suggested that the war had placed these into sharper relief. S said that reading her diary was like watching "someone who is ADD but off their medication." We all laughed (and then B made a joke about Chesnut's references to morphine and alcohol). All in all, this was the best discussion of

Chesnut's diary I've ever had with students, at any level. A real high point of the course so far.

Lastly, we came to Lincoln. I had them talk about how the three speeches (and the Emancipation Proclamation) allow us to trace Lincoln's evolution in terms of thinking about race, slavery, abolition, and Union during the Civil War. They were largely sympathetic to Lincoln—"I keep thinking about his awful and unnecessary death," Ethel said—but they still took issue with how slow he was to embrace the abolitionist cause. We talked at length about the perception of Lincoln (how he was viewed by the Confederacy, by the slaves and other black leaders, by Northerners) versus the reality of Lincoln (what he really believed, his convictions and doubts, etc.). Again, they seemed to be quite preoccupied with Lincoln's "psychology," and I told them that this placed them squarely within the larger historical debates about the Sixteenth President.

At the end of the day, I think the consensus was that Lincoln was antislavery but not fully evolved in terms of his thinking about race. They gave good textual evidence to support this interpretation, and made note of the beauty and simplicity of his prose/speaking style. More than one student contrasted this with the current Republican President.

We concluded class with a brief discussion of Lincoln's more frequent use of religious imagery as the war goes on, especially the tension he posits (in the Second Inaugural) between a wrathful Old Testament God and the redemptive spirit (of Jesus) that animates the final paragraph. I suggested that we can read this speech as an allegory for the nation: as a call to us to either own up to our past sins in order to beckon a new era of peace, or as a question—which I offered to them not only as a historical dilemma, but as a philosophical one as well. Several of the students left the room talking about Lincoln in relation to Socrates!

Well, Augustine is no Sophocles. Despite the fact that quite a few people said this was the easiest reading to understand so far, the discussion was a bit slow. That being said, a couple of people (notably M & D) participated who haven't before, so that was a good sign.

I started class by going over a list of suggested essay topics. A good percentage of this group don't have very good listening skills, or at least didn't the other night, so the idea that only ONE question needed to be answered had to be gone over a few times, as did details on other assignments. Several students reacted to the assignments as if they had never seen them before & Judith even said, "what syllabus?" in a way that didn't mean which syllabus but rather, you never gave us a syllabus. Sigh. For at least the next few classes I'm going to start by asking for questions about assignments, the syllabus, etc. Maybe that'll help.

I started the discussion by talking about epiphanies, telling them that the choice of religion in Augustine's time had political consequences & that Augustine believed in conversion not thru miracles but thru reason. I forget what questions I posed at the discussion's start (I was beating back a migraine, so my memory of class is vaguer than it should be), but none seemed to be generating anything. We went thru plot summary (this is the chapter on Augustine's conversion) very slowly. Despite some saying this was the easiest reading yet, few seemed to have any memory of the text. The possible humiliation & risk involved in publicly refuting that w/which you had previously been identified seemed interesting to them as did Augustine's hope that god would make him "chaste but not yet." I suggested that we all have feelings like this when we know we should change but receive pleasure from old habits. H compared this to trying to quit smoking & R compared it to trying to get back to the gym. Generally, interest was mild, tho, and there was a fair amount of restlessness in the class; I had to call for quiet a couple of times. Bless her heart, tho, E made a comment that began "Building on what she said"—a great sign of listening to each other & considering each other's ideas.

Nicole had an impressive understanding of the text but kept moving away from Augustine to her own experiences with religion so I, painfully aware of the veiled and now-sound-asleep Judith sitting 2 feet away from me, tried to keep heading her off into more secular channels. Augustine tells four conversion stories in these pages, all of them thru books. I tried to get them to think about that, & about the possible fact that his experience mirrors theirs right now, of changing your life thru books. Thud went that idea. Thud also went my attempt to allow them to vent: should this be a classic? I asked, hoping that even if they didn't have much to say about the reading specifically, maybe we could at least get a discussion going of what they're looking for in literature. Nods all around. Yes, this should be a classic. Why? No comment—except for N's that it's important to know that god always forgives you & is there for you, etc.

I finished class by talking about Dante & his belief that literature should be written in the language everyday people speak (next week I'll introduce the word "vernacular"). I told them that Augustine's & Dante's favorite author was Virgil & asked them to consider the distance in time between Augustine & Dante & between us & Dante (900ish year gaps each). Did they think that was weird, interesting, anything? Do they think their favorite music is the same as Dante's? Yes, said A. Or at least not right now, but people probably listened to that stuff in the 50s, 60s, & 70s. There were a few mumbles of dissent so I picked up on them to say, right, we have very different tastes than Dante probably had and that after Dante we're going to see culture moving a lot faster, thus preparing the ground for next week's brief talk on Gutenberg & the Reformation. The class wasn't quite as turgid as I'm making it out. There were times that several people had their hands up at once & times when people were just speaking out. Compared to *Antigone*, tho, this class was slow. My migraine didn't help either—things always seem worse when my head hurts.

Looking forward to a headache-free Dante class,

Signature

Reports of Two Classes with the Same Students Follow: Class A

Tonight's class was exhausting, challenging, and took a few years out of me! The whole class had read very enthusiastically Plato's *Crito*. The atmosphere was extremely relaxed and students started out concerned that some of the familiar faces—Ed, Al—had not resurfaced since the end of last semester.

I was immediately struck by how closely the students had read the work. Almost all of them launched immediately into a critique of Crito (the man). "Socrates probably expected more of him," J said. Many felt that he was not a free and independent spirit and had not grasped Socrates' contempt for the "lazy follower" mentality. "He cared more about public opinion than the examined life," said L (who made great comments throughout the session). We tried to figure out Socrates' startling pronouncement: "I only wish that ordinary people had an unlimited capacity for doing harm; then they might have an unlimited power for doing good. . . . Actually they have neither . . . they simply act at random." We all agreed that this was a shocking statement, but S summed it up in an extraordinary way. She compared Socrates' human being to a glass that could change shape and size according to its content. If the glass was absolutely full, then it would swell and become potentially as large as the earth; if the glass was near empty, then it would be as

139

small as a raisin. The glass, she concluded, is the human potential according to Socrates. It can be everything and it can be nothing. Then referring to the comment about evil, F explained that what Socrates loathed above all else was the smug and complacent person. At least an evil person has energy and determination. He or she has made something out of life, even if the results are disastrous. In some ways, this person is closer to somebody with high aspirations because, in F's inimitable words, he or she is more than a "living dead."

This was a great discussion. Everybody participated. Nobody took Socrates' statement to mean anything other than "the unexamined life is even worse than the evil life because it has squandered human potential."

Things became a little less dispassionate when I asked a few hypothetical questions. Since they had all felt very close to Socrates' unwavering principles, I asked them to imagine the following scenario: There is a job opening. It is the job of your dreams. It involves saving children and really making a difference in the world. To get this job you need certain qualifications plus a higher degree which you don't yet have. The person you are competing against for the position is a horrible individual, who, besides his academic degree, would be terrible for the job. He hates children and could even possibly harm them.

When I asked who would lie to get that job (I raised my hand first), only C half-raised his. An amazing "fight" ensued: B looked at me with horror and said that she could never respect somebody who lies about such important matters. C, usually very jolly, became very serious and told me that if we all lied about our degrees to get what we wanted, the whole world would turn into chaos. O noted that it was outrageous that I was "playing God" by believing that I, and not the other fellow, would make the difference. In other words, I was playing God instead of playing by the rules. C meekly asserted that he would definitely lie if he knew that his competitor was a child molester. But he was immediately attacked. Even F, who usually has a constant smile on her face, became quite agitated and gloomy. It was as though my confession—I would lie for alleged good reasons—had put my "knowledge/wisdom" as a professor, as a guide to Plato, in jeopardy. It was a powerful moment.

What impressed and surprised me about the discussion was that they took my proclamation ("I would lie about this") as seriously as Socrates took his pledge to his idea of justice and lawfulness. What was odd was that (except for C, P, and L1) those who spoke refused categorically to see the other side—the all-too-human desire to break the law for a good cause. When flames started shooting out of B's eyes, T reminded her that it was just a hypothesis and that I had never actually taken this job. I must admit that I had expected the "humanitarian" argument to have more candidates. Many of the students felt that lying was just not an option, no matter what. When C asked how we might have reacted if asked to hide Jews in our home during the Nazi era, remarkably few said they would lie. They would have told the truth no matter what. This was becoming so heated that I tried to introduce something more abstract. The famous discussion about the Chinaman in Rousseau and in *Crime and Punishment* (it is also in Balzac's *Père Goriot*): if you could simply press a button and kill (unbeknownst of all, never to be found out) this evil character (the old Chinaman), and save thousands of lives, would you do it? I was stunned that it did not even seem to tempt them! Again, P, H, and L were tempted, but nobody else. Perhaps what I found most striking was that a good 80 percent of the class hung onto the idea of consistency and virtue with great passion. They mentioned the fear of chaos and it was obvious that, after relating so well to Socrates, they did not want to open up an unsettling (and unsocratic) possibility.

I could not help finding that religion, while providing such a reassuring framework, was blocking their critical powers. As a teacher, I must say that it was a difficult moment. Whether to push on or to go on to something else. What is going to happen when we do Kant! I'm not sure they need him as so many seem to embody the categorical imperative already! I'll have to bring them some John Stuart Mill to give a bit more tension to the Kant week.

I escaped from this discussion by asking them to rethink the problem through Antigone. What did Creon stand for? What did Antigone's rebellion represent, etc. That worked very well and M, S, and L were very animated, making the distinction between Creon's self-serving lawmaking and Socrates' "pure" and selfless relationship to justice. It was a great class, but I must confess that it made me realize I would have to find a way to broach topics that would not necessarily be able to be resolved after a Christian manner.

Class B

Yesterday's class was very inspiring. I felt a bit guilty having my class read literature rather than philosophy, so started out explaining why Dostoevsky's *Notes from the Underground* was not one of Nietzsche's favorite books (he rewrote his preface to *Daybreak*, opening the book with these "underground" lines: "In this book we find a 'subterrestrial' at work, digging, mining, undermining"), but a book that was conceived out of the philosophies of Plato, Augustine, and Kant.

I had each of them read a sentence from the book. O, who was in top form yesterday, could not stop laughing. "I know just the type. He's just like my mother. A complainer who wants attention and goes in and out of hospitals just to be noticed." I picked up on her point and asked the class how they would feel if they were a publisher and received a manuscript that seems to be written by a raving madman, reveling in his toothache, and telling us that he's a nobody. What are we doing reading books about nobodies—and, to boot, in a philosophy class? How would Plato have responded to this novel? Everybody agreed that he would have hated it and that the publisher would have probably tossed it in the garbage. Why? Because it was about weakness, not strength, and instead of giving you a model for good living, it is self-indulgent and formless. I was really thrilled at the way the students were linking Dostoevsky to our other works. Suddenly, what had seemed at times rather abstract (Kant in particular) was coming to life. C kept alluding to the nameless narrator's "being a punk and a coward." It was great to see that she could talk about him like someone she knew. "I can't help liking him even though he's a loser." I asked them whether they found it strange that a "loser" could be the main character of a great book. What would it teach us to be reading about somebody who can not only not get his act together, but who seems to contradict himself every other word? Janice, who was never a great fan of our utopian philosophers, defended this as an expression of real life.

Besides, added S, when he goes on and on about his toothache, he is trying to make things "more alive." The class picked up on that notion; people do all kinds of irrational things because they want to feel themselves living. Doing what is expected of you just makes you one of the group; we all want to have a special voice.

One of the great things this particular class accomplished was to allow abstractions (Plato's Allegory of the Cave, Kant's categorical imperative) to take a far more concrete shape. Because of the looseness of Dostoevsky's prose, the students felt that they could let go and be much more candid about ethics. While most had been very pious about never lying or acting for ulterior motives, today things were different. They were puzzled and relieved by the fact that a fictional character dared to write so negatively about himself. Many of them had written diaries and admitted that they edited some of the less attractive things about themselves for fear that somebody found the diary. This made the discussion turn on issues of transparency, honesty, and mostly self-knowledge. Can we ever present ourselves to others in a negative light? Or will there always be an element of deceit—don't we always find excuses for ourselves, no matter how awful we have been? I asked them to think about Dostoevsky's character, not as somebody writing down his notes (although that is what he is doing), but somebody who has a "bug" attached to his brain that records for us his entire train of thoughts. Many students thought this was a fascinating notion: if somebody could record all our thoughts, the end result would be a big soup full of the most clashing ingredients. Dostoevsky was the brilliant archeologist who dared to make us look deep into our dark sides. Mildred nodded enthusiastically throughout. And even Francine, who can become quite upset when we talk about the "evil" side of human nature, seemed very receptive.

Another thing that clicked was the fact that modern literature was both taking issue with, and yet deeply marked by, the very notion of human perfectibility. Even though Dostoevsky's underground man overtly spat on such a notion, his thoughts were always hovering around platonic and kantian ideals. This took us back to Mill's attack on Kant: how can we really know whose motives are good, who acts virtuously for the sake of virtue alone? Dostoevsky, despite the fact that he was a great debunker of Mill, points to the near impossibility to know ourselves. Paul read us a wonderful passage: "who was it who first declared that a man does evil only because he does not know his real interest?" and developed the notion of freedom. This made us think about Augustine and his stolen pears. We don't only act out of self-interest. Something pushes us to do the unexplainable.

I asked J whether she believed that if she got everything she wished for, if the world became an entirely rational place, as "figure-outable" as a mathematical equation, would she be happy.

She barely had the time to answer. Most everybody clamored that it would be boring, that we would all be the same, etc. From there we spoke about boredom. Why is boredom so important in this novel? Did Adam and Eve eat from the forbidden fruit because they were bored in the Garden of Eden? O remarked that everything we do comes from the desire to conquer someone or something. That means that we can't ever be content, it's against our nature. C pointed out that if we go on group holidays, what we are really doing is duplicating our work environment. "We come home completely exhausted." We work, not only because we have to, but because the alternative (absolute free time) would be thoroughly destabilizing.

I read them a great quote from Nietzsche about our horror of leisure. Leisure frightens us because it gives us all the time in the world to think about our human condition. Which brought us back to the underground man spending so much time thinking. One student pointed out, perhaps Janice, that the underground man was both the one to point out that "to think too much is a disease," while being the prime victim of that disease. We spoke about polyphony and how Dostoevsky managed to present at least two points of view for every question. Like Socrates, M added. It was like having Socrates and Thrasymachus in one body and it was good for us to be confused and not to be given one single truth.

In 2007, MassHumanities began a longitudinal study of the results of their courses. Students were interviewed at graduation and then year after year to gauge the longer-term effects of the course. A total of 129 students made their own judgments of their lives and hopes and woes on paper—48 of them in face-to-face interviews as well.

The results of this longitudinal study confirmed the work done in the 1995–96 academic years at the Clemente Center. In the earlier study a different method was used: the students were pre- and post-tested with a battery of standard psychological tests. The question for the research then, as it is now, was how far the students had progressed from a life of reaction to one of reflection, and what part the course had played in this progress—if indeed there was progress.

The MassHumanities research found that the graduates wanted to continue their education. Half of them hoped to go to a community college and the other half wanted to earn a bachelor's degree at a four-year college. However, financing further education was a problem. Most of them had to work at a job, or even two. They would have to attend college part time, but they were willing to do so. They did not speak of their hopes with blind optimism; they understood that the high cost of post-secondary education was a barrier they might not be able to overcome. They had the unhappy example of one of their classmates who was accepted by a four-year college, but could not afford to attend.

On a personal level, the Massachusetts students, like those at the Clemente Center, had a strong sense of accomplishment. Most of them believed that attending the course had improved the quality of their lives, and the lives of their families, their friends, and their communities. The students admired their teachers ("for their passion and commitment," the researchers said), praised the curriculum, agreed that their lives had been changed, felt more self-esteem. They said that they had learned how to think; they were wed to the humanities forever. The extent of their embrace of community showed in the choice of careers that attracted them: teaching and the helping professions.

All was not perfect, however. Like graduates of the course everywhere, from Khartoum to Korea to Chicago, they had gained sufficient confidence in themselves and their ideas to take a critical view of the world. It was the next step in their lives that worried them. The students did not know where to go next. They asked for classes in how to fill out application forms for college admission and especially for financial aid. They needed counseling, they said.

The dropout problem bothered students, causing a curious mix of self-interest and sadness. They said that trying to hold on to students took up too much of the professors' time. Yet the loss of classmates saddened them. Better screening, they said, would go a long way toward solving the problem.

The quality of the criticism was a good indicator of the ability of the MassHumanities courses to meet their goals. The students were no longer timid about their views, their criticism showed the use of analytical skills in the real world, and rather than merely complaining they offered good ideas about improving the course. There had been a change in their lives: they were now active participants in a democratic society.

CHAPTER 9

Yaaveskaniryaraq

The beginning of my friendship with the Yup'ik and Cup'ik people of the Yukon-Kuskokwim Delta came at the expense of the governor of Alaska. I hadn't intended to insult the governor in front of the entire state Democratic Convention, but he had made a terrible blunder, one that required a response from the next speaker on the program.

I had been invited to the convention by Steve Lindbeck, who was then executive director of the Alaska Humanities Forum. This was the first state Democratic Convention to be held in the bush. To some people, a trip to the Yukon-Kuskokwim Delta from New York might have seemed more like a punishment than an honor. The only way to get to Bethel from Anchorage was to cross the Kuskokwim Mountains by air. And there are no direct flights to Anchorage from Manhattan. It is a very long trip.

The ground in Bethel in spring, during the thaw, is deep and ubiquitous mud. Liquor and beer cannot be sold in the Y-K Delta, but it was not illegal to have a bottle. The area is designated officially as neither wet nor dry, but "damp." In winter, the Kuskokwim River freezes solidly enough to become a road that can hold an automobile or a light truck. In spring, travel upriver beyond Bethel to Akiak, Akiachak, or Tuluksak requires a Hovercraft, because the river can no longer support an automobile and the great chunks of ice floating toward the sea would destroy the hull of a boat. In summer, the river is open to motorboats or kayaks, if a person is willing to brave swarms of the largest mosquitos in North America.

It was still an honor to have been invited to speak to the first convention held in the bush. If it had been scheduled for the winter darkness, I would have made the trip. Lindbeck and I had not talked about starting a Clemente Course in the bush, but by that time I was confident enough to start a course anywhere.

The community center in Bethel had a large meeting room filled with pipeline workers, union organizers, politicians, publicists, teachers, business owners, professors, Alaska Natives, civil servants, and a few grizzled and bearded old men who looked like they belonged on a movie set about the gold rush. Steve Lindbeck sat across the room. The son of a Navy man, born in Alaska, tall, with straight yellow hair and a full frame, he is at ease behind a desk or telling stories about a moose that strolled into the neighborhood kicking hell out of anyone or anything that interrupted its wanderings. Steve may know everyone in the state, and if there is a person, Democrat or Republican, rich or poor, Native or Gussaq,[1] who doesn't trust him, I have yet to hear about him or her.

No one could have made a better introduction to Alaska Native people than Steve, unless it was his Yup'ik counterpart, Mike Williams. Born in Akiak, just up the river from Bethel, Mike was still in the early days of middle age. He still mushed along behind a dogsled every March in the Iditarod, crossing over 1,100 miles of frozen tundra, enduring weeks of snowstorms and cold that reached 100 degrees below zero. He and I talked about politics, the race and racism. Mike had been a drunk, like so many people in the Delta, and now he mushed across Alaska to raise money for programs to

---

1   From Cossack, used by the C/Yupiit for Caucasian. The first white settlers in Alaska were Russians, establishing a settlement in 1784.

discourage drinking by young people. He was a revered figure by the time we met, a man as thick and strong as a tree stump, bored by much of the routine of the meeting, politely waiting for Governor Tony Knowles to address the convention.

I saw him wince when the governor spoke of Alaska's pride in the men who had settled the territory, the pioneers, men who came up north from California and Oregon, Oklahoma and Texas. After the applause for the governor, it was my turn. I said that I wanted to correct the governor's error: "The people who settled the state, the pioneers, were the Yupiit, Cupiit, Inupiat, Inuit, Tsimshian, Tlingit . . ."[2] I tried not to look at the governor, but it was impossible. He and his wife were sitting directly in front of me, only a few feet away. Two expressionless and wintry stones. It crossed my mind that they were the frozen north, and I felt like laughing, beset by silliness over the trouble I had brought on myself. If there was to be a Clemente Course in the bush, there would be no help from the governor.

As if to corroborate my anxiety about the prospective course, the governor and his wife shook many hands after the meeting, but not mine. When I approached him to say I hadn't meant the correction as an insult to him, only to set the record straight or some other cowardly cliché, he refused to speak to me. I needn't have been so worried, for only a moment later, when I shook hands with Mike Williams, I knew from the way he smiled that there was going to be a Clemente Course in the Yukon-Kuskokwim Delta.

It did not come about easily. The next day, the delegates were invited to travel up the river on the Hovercraft that delivered the U.S. mail. There were no seats aboard the freighter, and it made

---

2   Cup'ik and Yup'ik are generally adjectives, although they may also be nouns, as in "I speak Cup'ik." Cupiit and Yupiit are plural nouns. Cup'ik is a dialect of Yup'ik, the language used in most of the twenty-six villages. The two are often written as C/Yup'ik.

a horrendous noise as it traveled through the air a few feet over the massive chunks of ice floating in the river below us. On the way upriver I spoke with Elsie Mather, whom I had met at lunch the previous day, about teaching the C/Yup'ik humanities. She was widely known as an authority in Yup'ik storytelling and language. We got on so well, shouting to each other through the noise of the engine all the way to Akiak, that I was sure she would be our course director. The next day, she did not show up for a meeting about the course, and I never saw or heard from her again. I learned later that the leaders of her church told her to spend her efforts converting people to the Moravian Church rather than teaching the Yup'ik humanities. Elsie Mather is a fine scholar; and I was sorry that her church disagreed with our work.

When the Hovercraft anchored at Akiak, there was no dock, and as I looked over the side I saw only what looked like grass growing up out of the river between the Hovercraft and the shore, which was twenty feet away. As the passengers clambered over the side, I expected them to sink into the icy river. I was astonished to see them walking across the grass toward the shore. I waited until most of them had made their way to shore, and seeing that no one sank, I too climbed off the Hovercraft and onto the grass. It was even more astonishing to find myself held up out of the water by thick tubular grasses. Once I stepped off the grass onto the shore, however, I did sink. My shoes, made for walking on city streets, were sucked down into the oozing mud almost to the ankle.

In the evening, back in Bethel there was a supper in the basement of the community center. Everyone interested in the course sat at one long picnic table. Steve Lindbeck had gathered the group, which included Utuan (Lucy) Sparck and Tacuk (Cecelia) Ulroan. As the state Democratic Party and members of the Bethel community lined up for a dinner that was being served in small paper bowls through a half-open Dutch door at one end of the room, Steve and

Utuan urged me to have dinner. I joined the line. When it came my turn, the person serving the food ladled what looked like stew into a paper bowl. Then he asked if I would like some seal oil for flavor. A woman two places back in the line shouted for him not to put too much in the bowl. "He's a Gussaq," she said. The server smiled, added a spoonful of what looked like cooking oil to the stew, and handed me the bowl, a plastic spoon, and a piece of hardtack.

I joined Steve and Uut (Utuan's nickname) at the table. Uut is a charming woman, with a soft, husky voice, and a very gentle manner. Unlike most traditional C/Yup'ik people, Uut does not follow the native rule of good manners in conversation by remaining silent for ten seconds or more after the other person finished speaking. The custom is to wait long enough to give the other person time to continue speaking if he or she chose to do so. It is unnerving, at first, to engage in conversation with a traditional Native person. Tacuk (another nickname) follows the traditional form; Uut is polite, but converses at a more Occidental pace. She is the widow of Harold Sparck, a man who came to Alaska in 1968, married a pretty young Cup'ik girl, and settled in to become the most effective political and social activist in the Y-K Delta during his lifetime.

The Cupiit and Steve watched as I tasted the moose meat stew seasoned with seal oil. I have never tasted food, medicine, or the worst of my own sickness as foul-tasting as that stew. I could not wash the taste away with water or soft drinks, and I could not chew it away with hardtack, mints, or candy. While I gagged, Uut explained that the Yupiit, who live far from the sea, developed a taste for the oil that was hauled overland from the ocean to Bethel. In the course of the journey, the seal oil, which cannot be preserved like fish or berries, turns rancid. The flavor of rancid seal oil became the delight of the people who lived far from the sea. And that is what I ate.

Someone removed my nauseating meal and replaced it with a bowl of unseasoned moose meat stew, saying: "It will clear your palate." The stew had a mild, not rancid flavor, but the meat was the toughest thing I had ever eaten. "Old moose," said Uut. And everyone seated at the long table laughed.

I thought I had done with my suffering for the day when the drumming started. The C/Yupiit play rhythms, using reeds to beat on skins stretched over large hoops. The sound is sharp, but variable, depending upon the area of the hoop, the direction and vehemence of the blow. And there are dynamics, because the reed smack can be sounded more or less sharply. It is more complex than Lakota or Apache drumming, but not nearly as complex as the sounds made by the "talking drums" of Africa. Traditional C/Yupiit dancing includes masks, headdresses, dance fans, and singing. It is elaborate and can be very beautiful. When Uut insisted that I join the dancing, it was not beautiful. The dance form developed during the many hundreds, perhaps thousands of years when the C/Yupiit spent the long Alaskan winters in communal housing, with little space and low ceilings. The dancing was performed by kneeling men, with women standing behind them, and everyone moving their hands in keeping with the rhythm of the music and the telling of the story of the song. I did not kneel properly, and I did not seem to fly like a bird or hunt like a wolf while the singers told the story of the dance. Uut, having raised five children, including a set of triplets, was patient with my clumsiness and ignorance, but before long even she capitulated, and we returned to the table to the ironic applause of our companions.

That evening, I had a chat with the clerk who occasionally appeared at the hotel. He was a Mexican from the town of Alamos, where the owner of the hotel spent her winters. I had an idea. Since there was someone in Bethel who could translate from Spanish, it would be possible to bring an indigenous Clemente Course professor from Merida to Bethel to explain how the course worked for indigenous people. Steve Lindbeck and Uut and the other person who was most likely to direct the course in the Y-K Delta, Tacuk Ulroan, agreed. It would not be an aging Gussaq but a handsome young Maya teacher who would tell the story of the course to groups of C/Yup'ik teachers and elders. I sent an e-mail to Miguel May in Merida, and he agreed to make the journey from the Caribbean to within a few hundred miles of the Bering Sea.

Miguel was a far better promoter of the course than I could have been. By the time he left the Y-K Delta, it was agreed that there should be a Clemente Course in Chevak, a village of about six hundred people situated along a river that emptied into the Bering Sea.

I went back to Anchorage, over the mountains to Bethel, up the river to Akiak, where an extraordinary meeting was held. I had been reading everything I could find about C/Yup'ik culture, preparing to work with Utuan and Tacuk and Ariss (Joe Slats, head of the Yupiit School District) on the curriculum. We met in the Yupiit School District library. A most extraordinary man attended that meeting and many others that we had on the way to starting the course: Uyaquq (Joe Lomack).[3] Joe, who had helped to build the Bethel airport, and worked for many years as a health aide, had retired by then and taken up his position as an elder in the C/Yup'ik world. In the Akiak meeting the C/Yup'ik course gained its name, *Yaaveskaniryaraq* ("Moving forward to gain wisdom"). As we discussed the curriculum, the gorgeous complexity of C/Yup'ik culture emerged. There was a discussion of the difference between the Christian and C/Yup'ik conceptions of God and *Ellam Yua*. Much of the time in the meeting was spent trying to help me

---

3   I have described some of the conversation in that meeting in an article in *Harper's* magazine, "The Last Word" (August 2000), which was reprinted in Robert Atwan, ed., *Best American Essays* (Boston: Houghton Mifflin, 2001).

understand this basic concept, which is the unifying concept at the center of C/Yup'ik thinking.

I have heard it described by various anthropologists, both amateur and professional, as everything from "fish" to "wind" to some sort of great person, a bit too much like the Great Spirit (*Wakan Tanka*) of the Siouan people, to plain old animism. One of the men at the meeting held up a paper cup that had been filled with coffee, and said that the cup was like the Gussaq (white man) conception of God above the world (*Agayun*, the Christian notion). The C/Yup'ik idea is *Ellam Yua*, the phrase sometimes translated as "God," though it has no such meaning. *Ella* means "consciousness" and "world" or "universe"; in other contexts it means "outdoors," "weather," and "air." *Yua* is the more complex notion, for it is the possessive form of *yuk*, which means "person," and what can a person own in the natural world other than his or her personhood?

The Yupiit have a word for consciousness, another for mind, yet another for the physical brain itself, and there is this business of *yua*. According to Tacuk, if a person sees a piece of driftwood on the frozen tundra, he or she must turn it over to expose the other side to the air. It is a gift to the *yua* of the wood. If one behaves that way toward the wood, perhaps one day the wood will return the favor. Hunting-and-gathering follows the same rules: the seal, salmon, herring, duck, moose, caribou, cloudberry, all things living and inanimate—all have this *yua*, and all are deserving of kindness. Was this pantheism, foolishness, a system of morals? What would Kant say? Was this a version of the categorical imperative, "Act only on that maxim through which you can at the same time will that it should become a universal law"?

Ellam Yua—in two words ethics is born of metaphysics. Or is it the other way round? The concept was as close to the *logos* of the pre-Socratics as anything I could imagine. I tried to understand the idea by comparing it to other notions that I knew better, the

Mesoamerican Ometeotl, God of Duality, the Mother/Father, Tloque Nahuaque (the Close and the Near), meaning omnipresent.

"Seen and not seen," Uut said, as complete a description as the spoken and unspoken of a writer's world. I thought I understood what Uyaquq was saying, but each time I asked a question or tried to rephrase what had been indicated to me with sweeping gestures or smiles or eyes that became an entrance to some kind of intensity I did not recognize, I was both puzzled and excited, unable to relate the thinking to the life of the people.

Until several people arrived late to the meeting, having attended a funeral service in Tuluksuk further upriver, I would have subscribed to any of the simple definitions just to get out of what seemed to me like an incomprehensible version of an Eastern philosophy. Uut asked the latecomers to describe where they had been. They made no excuses. Instead, they told me about the C/Yup'ik idea of the afterlife as a journey in a kayak down a great underground stream. The kayak was steered away from eddy pools and undertows by the thoughts of those who remained on earth. Social immortality? Of course. By then I realized that a Clemente Course for the people of Chevak would be as complex as the course for the Maya.

I had spent much of my life reading and thinking about the Maya. I could work on that course and the one for the Nahuas. The problem in Alaska was very different. I had not grown up with the language or written books about the culture. The great Mexican historian Miguel León-Portilla had consented to work on a book about Mesoamerican literature with me. I could not even speak to Uyaquq in his own language. I knew far too little about the C/Yupiit even to participate in developing the curriculum. Who would do it?

What had begun as a kind of lark had become a serious intellectual problem. I met with Michael Krauss, director of the Alaska

Native Language Center at the University of Alaska at Fairbanks, to talk about language and culture, and with Uut Sparck as translator I sat on the floor in her house in Bethel for many hours listening to Joe Lomack talk about C/Yup'ik ideas. Because the language is agglutinative, one can add almost innumerable suffixes to a word, and the more eloquent a speaker, the more suffixes. Joe seemed to enjoy adding more than a dozen, now and again closer to two dozen suffixes. Uut, whose fluency put her at ease in most conversations, had to work hard to translate his ideas. We all knew that much was being lost. I thought I heard a view of the world going silent as I sat there. If the language was to be saved in all or even part of its brilliant complexity, it would be necessary to save the method and the curriculum of the course they named *Yaaveskaniryaraq* (which means teaching in the Yup'ik Way, i.e., "Moving forward to gain wisdom").

To stir up interest in the course among the C/Yupiit Uut, Joe, Tacuk, Steve, and I flew up to Akiachak in a bush plane. I sat next to the pilot the first time out, and it did not make me the least bit happy to see him biting his fingernails as we taxied out to the runway. He managed to keep the wings parallel to the ground on the takeoff, and to follow the river north to Akiak, navigating by landmarks. When we arrived, Joe and the two women spoke on the local radio station in Yup'ik, and I said a few words about the Clemente Course in English.

It was the beginning of the establishment of the course, which was unlike any educational endeavor that had ever happened in the villages. Fortunately, the explanation of the work by Uyaquq (Joe) and Uut and Tacuk was more than satisfactory. We had done the same show in Bethel, and had become more proficient at explaining what we intended to do. Joe was revered as an elder, although his round, bald head and sweet face did not bespeak wisdom. He was the most modest person of great learning I had ever met. On the way out to Chevak, going toward the sea, Joe and I sat together in the back of a small two-engine plane held together with duct tape. Streams of frigid air came in through gaps in the aluminum skin of the old Beechcraft. Joe and I talked partly to keep warm. When speaking English, he had a way of going straight to the point. As we neared Chevak, I asked him how cold it got in winter out there at the edge of the Bering Sea.

"Hundred below," he said.

"What happens if you go outside when it's a hundred below?"

"Getting dead."

Joe looked askance at the lace-up boots I had taken to wearing in the mud. He wore rubber boots over many pairs of socks, ate Akutaq[4] with two fingers for a spoon, was opposed to drinking water in large quantities, and didn't mind pissing in a bucket. In return for his advice about waterproof boots and drinking water, I peppered him with questions about ethics and metaphysics. When we had trouble with a concept, Tacuk or Uut often helped. Joe was a Christian, a member of the Moravian Church, but it was in the C/ Yup'ik world that he was happy.

Joe and I sat together at a dance performance in Chevak that afternoon, two chubby, balding fellows who didn't dance. People from the village came to talk to Uyaquq. They spoke in Cup'ik and made gestures of reverence and gave him gifts of food and fresh seal oil. After he left on the afternoon flight, I spent the rest of the afternoon talking about Cup'ik ethics. What seems like animism to the

---

4   A dessert eaten as many as four times a day, made now of Crisco, fish, berries, and vegetable oil as a modern substitute for a food originally made of moose, caribou, whale, seal oil and other kinds of fat mixed with berries and fish.

uninitiated was told this way: If you are out on the tundra in winter and you see a piece of wood, turn it over so that it will dry in the sun, then the *yua* of the wood will return the favor to you. When I inquired further about the meaning of it, Tacuk explained that the dry wood might then be used by the next traveler to make a fire.

I slept in Chevak that night on the floor of the Kashunamiut School District building lying on one gym mat and covered over with two others. A local family fed me and drove me to the school seated on the metal bars on the back of a four-wheeler. It was very cold.

The next day, we met to discuss the course with potential students and teachers in Chevak. I rode again on the back of the four-wheeler, which was badly in need of some sort of cushion, but it was warmer in the sun, and I was glad for that and the sharpness of the air off the sea. I missed Joe. When he left, it was as if the world had been diminished. I looked out toward the sea, remembering that he had told me there were only two directions: toward the sea and away from the sea. Later, in a conversation about the *ircinrrraq* world, which is a C/Yup'ik idea of a miniature world, a kind of alternate reality, there was a question raised about the directions in that world. Were they the same as in the world in which the conversation was taking place or were they opposite? The *ircinrrraq* world is sometimes described now as meaning a place of little people, like Leprechauns, but the elders who came to teach in the Yaaveskaniryaraq version of the Clemente Course had an older, more sophisticated understanding of the ideas that had come to the people who lived and danced and told stories and worked magic in the low houses of the Cupiit.

As much as I listened and read, I could only understand a little of what went on around me. In the first meeting with the people who would teach and attend the course, a young man sitting next to me said of a much older woman sitting across the table, "I am her mother." I nodded wisely, knowing that it was a joke on the Gussaq. But it was not a joke. Cup'ik kinship structures are so complex and so utterly unrelated to anything in the European culture that a young man could be the mother of an old woman. I was in a dreamworld, one in which *ircinrrraq* meant as much to me as the alternate reality physical world postulated by the most sophisticated contemporary scientists.

Clearly, I could not help to produce a curriculum for Yaaveskaniryaraq. It would have to be done by Tacuk and Uut, working with Joe Lomack and perhaps with Paul John, another of the great elders of the Y-K Delta. To earn college credits for the course seemed impossible. It was developed by two Cup'ik women, both of whom were educated in two cultures. But they were high school teachers, not college professors. My one hope was that Ted Kassier, then one of the deans at the University of Alaska at Anchorage, would help me to solve the problem. Before I went back to Bethel, and from Bethel to Anchorage, I told the people in Chevak that I would speak to Ted.

It was a bit of a long shot. In Alaska, the rule was that institutions of higher education imposed courses on the Native people. This would have to be just the opposite, a kind of *ircinrrraq* world of education. I spoke to Ted about it. His field is Spanish literature, not linguistics or anthropology, but he was willing to look at what Tacuk Ulroan would put together. I told him that it would be Cup'ik culture and language, but that it would use the same five sections that we used in the other Clemente courses. Somehow we would sort the whole into its parts. When Tacuk delivered the curriculum to him, Ted asked her to make some changes so that it would fit with state guidelines. She made the changes, and he arranged for college credit for the students of Yaaveskaniryaraq.

Six years after the start of Yaaveskaniryaraq, Ray Barnhart, professor of cross-cultural studies at the University of Alaska at

Fairbanks, told me that the Yaaveskaniryaraq model had been adopted by many of the indigenous tribes in Alaska. Yet maintaining the C/Yup'ik course was difficult. Utuan Sparck had moved to Anchorage; Tacuk Ulroan suffered from arthritis; and Joe Lomack, Uyaquq, was seriously ill. Uut and I spoke regularly, trying to settle a dispute among two traditional groups in Chevak. I had phone calls to make to the Kashunamiut School District and Uut had set up a meeting with the new executive director of the Alaska Humanities Forum. Airfare from Anchorage to Chevak via Bethel had become outrageously expensive, the elders were dying out, the stories had begun to be lost or confused in the retelling; but the Yaaveskaniryaraq graduates had learned something about the world of *Ellam Yua*. And they now spoke fluent Cup'ik. It was not yet done. There would be one more generation, and perhaps even one more after that, and. . . .

CHAPTER 10

Cervantes in Buenos Aires

T heir concert hall was an unfinished concrete block building reached by crossing over an open sewer. It had been
raining that morning, and the water running through
the sewer had washed away most of the odor. The water ran fast,
brown over the green-streaked bottom. On the far side of the sewer
a path through the mud had been made of flat stones. The stones
floated on the saturated ground, making it more difficult to walk
the length of the building to the entrance on the far side.

Inside the building there was no heat, and it was still early in
the day, before the warming. The players made no mention of the
cold. The oldest was still in his teens and the youngest was only
eight years old. They had gathered to rehearse with their conductor, Adrian Crocce, a thin, intense young man who employed the
system of music education developed by the Venezuelan José Antonio Abreu. They played *Caminito*, the infinitely sad song of Buenos Aires, about the little road that shall go on, and like the lover,
never to return. Of all the tangos, *Caminito* is the most tragic.
The orchestra was made up of violins, violas, and cellos; and they
played together in many times, and now and then as if they read
disparate signatures, but withal the melody came through in a rec-
ognizable way, sweet and sad, commentary on their lives. Later,
they played an almost lilting *Humoresque* and a serious *Pomp and*

Circumstance; the seventeen players had been together for eighteen months.

A violist wore a baseball cap turned back to front, a violinist had his stocking cap pulled down to his ears. The tiniest one sat among the violins and the prettiest girl held a cello between her knees and allowed the personal sound to transport her. Five of the players, including the oldest of them, were the children of graduates of the Clemente Course in the Humanities. In the barrio of Las Tunas, on unpaved streets, where the water flows from pumps in the middle of the street and there is no sewerage system but the ditch and the rain, the children played Dvořák and tended to the strings of their polished wood instruments. The parents of the players had read Hobbes and knew a little of Ortega y Gasset and Cortázar and Cervantes and Lorca and García Márquez. They had learned to see the work of Michaelangelo and Goya and Picasso. And now their children played Dvořák and Beethoven, and although it was not certain that they knew the lyric or held out such hope, they played *"Somewhere Over the Rainbow."*

Caminito was the unforgettable song. It had stayed with me since my first visit to Buenos Aires, when the students sat in chairs and cross-legged on the floor of Claudia Paladino's apartment high in a building overlooking much of the city. Claudia, who had been one of the founders of the organization that hosted the Clemente Course, had invited the students to drink wine and eat empanadas and talk, and mostly to sing. A friend of Claudia's, a woman with thick blond hair, the daughter of *tangueros,* drank wine and permitted herself to be persuaded to sing. She sang many songs, and they were all good songs, but it was when she sang *Caminito* that the room changed. I sat between the singer and Claudia's son, Ezekiel, a boy in his late teens, dark-haired and already a handsome man full of music and gentleness. The daughter of the *tangueros* sang in full throat in a dark register in the half-light of the apartment. The students were silhouettes against the background of the lights of the great port city. Patricio Grehan, who still carried the Irish passport of his father's nationality, sat among the students, a man as tall as a tree, a heavy-limbed, serious man, who won over whomever he met. He had left the priesthood by then but had not abandoned his vocation. Claudia, the widow of an officer of the state, herself a success, an orderly and lovely woman. Like Grehan, she had taken good acts for her vocation, and like him, she was serious. She spoke in the voice of Buenos Aires—*porteño*, they say—and the students, too, spoke in that voice, with many Spanish sounds changed into the sound of rushing water.

When the woman beside me sang *Caminito,* there was at first only her strong voice, ". . . since you left / Never to return . . ." and ". . . you shall soon become a shadow / A shadow like me." She sang, and soon there were other voices, a low humming, a choir of sadness, so deep the room fairly sang along with them. One heard all the sadness of the history of the tango, the music of the poor people of the port of Buenos Aires in the time before Perón and his Evita. The students and I had talked together a few days earlier in the tiny library of the Centro para Desarrollo Local (Center for Local Development) in the barrio of Las Tunas, in the town of Tigre, on the northern edge of the city of Buenos Aires. I had asked Claudia and Patricio if they could provide the students with a few selected pages of the Borges story about *Pierre Menard, Author of the Quixote,* and several chapters from the beginning of the Cervantes novel, as well as chapter XXXVII. We would then be able to talk about Don Quixote losing his mind because of reading too many books. They would also know how Cervantes claimed the novel was based on a found manuscript and be able to connect that to the Borges story about Pierre Menard writing the novel. The argument in chapter XXXII would make them laugh, because they were in a humanities course and Don Quixote was claiming that the military was a better profession than the humanities (the name the old Spaniards gave to the study of law). The Borges story would teach them about fiction in its time and the ability of great novels to transcend changes in culture, even language.

To begin the class I asked, "What are the most famous words in the Spanish language?" There was a quiet moment while the class considered the question and the questioner, then one student raised her hand, and said, "*En un lugar de la Mancha, de cuyo nombre no quiero acordarme....*"[1] These were the opening lines of the *Quijote*.[2] I asked if someone would explain what Borges had told us about this novel, and the dialogue began. It took no more than a few questions before they grasped the importance of the Borges story. In it, Pierre Menard has written the *Quijote* letter for letter like the original, but the perfect duplicate is utterly unlike the original.

"What is Borges telling us about reading great literature?" I asked. "Can a classic text be the same now as it was four hundred years ago? How should we approach it? What should we expect of it?" I showed them my copy of the beautiful Royal Spanish Academy edition of the *Quijote* published to celebrate the four hundredth anniversary of the work. "Now, do you think this is the book Cervantes wrote?"

There was still some consternation.

"Then it must be the book Pierre Menard wrote."

"No," said one student.

"Of course not. It is the book I wrote."

And they laughed, and it was the beginning of understanding what Borges had meant about the same words being a different book in different times. "And for different readers?" one student asked.

---

1   "In a place in La Mancha, the name of which I do not choose to recall...."

2   In Spanish conversation the book is known as "the *Quijote*" rather than *Don Quixote*. It is very much like an Italian speaking of "the Poet" rather than Dante Alighieri.

"What do you think?"

We turned then to the early chapters in which Cervantes had laid out the structure of the novel. They began to gather the idea of the many levels of invention of the work, although it was told in simple language. As the second hour of the class was beginning to ebb, I asked if they would turn to chapter XXXVII. "What is the name of this course?" I asked.

"The Clemente Course in the Humanities."

"And what is chapter XXXVII about?"

"Arms and the law."

The version they had read did not have a footnote explaining that law and the humanities were synonymous at the time of the writing of the *Quijote*. I provided the footnote, and then we began to discuss the dialogue in which Quijote proves that the study of arms, which has as its aim the establishment of peace, is far better than the humanities (law), which aims to bring about justice. Peace, according to the Knight of the Sad Figure, is closest to the aim of Jesus.

"Is this what Cervantes truly believed?"

"He was a soldier," said one.

"He was a writer," said another.

"Is this book about Cervantes or the Knight of the Sad Figure? Does Cervantes want us to think this is the truth? Or is it irony?"

And then the dialogue danced through questions of irony and structure. We stayed a long time on the structure of the novel, for it is so often read as if the structure were no more than the tale of a dreamer. What could not be discerned from reading so little of the novel was the question of irony and whether a comic novel is ironic or that the only comedy is irony. They had not yet read Plato so they did not know much about irony, but there were their own lives set out upon the table surrounded by students, and it may have been that they all thought the entrance of a person from a distant place and another language to teach them in his lumpy Spanish was as ironic as the adventures of the man from the unremembered town in Spain.

Two days later, in the auditorium of the Banco Frances, Viviana Barreto, Dr. Eduardo Zimmerman—rector of the Universidad de San Andrés, an Oxford-educated historian who taught the history section of the course—and I were on a panel that discussed the humanities and the education of the poor. Zimmerman and another professor were interesting and well-spoken, but Viviana Barreto, who had been one of the students engaged in the dialogue about Cervantes, was the most eloquent of the speakers. When a man in the audience identified himself as the leader of the wealthy community separated from Las Tunas by a high wall, I suggested that we tear a hole in the wall. Then it was Viviana's turn. The audience had watched her carefully, for they must have thought she would be afraid or clumsy or even vulgar, but she surprised them, surprised us all, for all through the afternoon she soared, and when she responded to the man who lived on the other side of the wall, she was graceful: she did not mention the proposal for the breach, she said nothing about the wall, she spoke of true wealth— she said it belonged to people who knew the humanities.

Despite her eloquence and my pleadings, the directors of the Universidad de San Andrés did not accept Viviana Barreto as a student. They were like many universities in the United States, which insist upon the conventional academic credentials for admission. Martin Bohmer, dean of the Law School, Eduardo Zimmerman, the rector, and José Luis Galimidi in the Philosophy Department, all taught in the Las Tunas Clemente Course, but the university would not permit any of the graduates of their classes to matriculate. Viviana managed to enroll in another university, not so famous or so geared to teaching the children of the rich. Her work was good, and while she was there, she became a member of the staff of the Center for Local Development.

Viviana was among the graduates of the course who came one night to sit in a great circle and talk about what they had learned. It was the beginning of August, the end of winter in Buenos Aires, and the weather was still capricious: cold nights and an angry rain interrupted what should have been spring. The evening of the conversation, the open sewer between the road and the concrete building ran at flood. The slip of a foot on the muddy passage over the sewer invited an ugly catastrophe. The stones of the walkway floated on the mud, and as we negotiated the path we wondered how much worse it would be when the meeting was over. It was raining hard and would soon be dark. Inside the concrete house, the end of sunlight brought the stone cold into the air. There was no heat inside the building. Claudia and Patricio each said a few words to introduce Sylvia, my wife, and me to the students who had graduated in the classes after the night of Borges and the structure of a tale told by a voice within a voice within the voice of the author. It was a time for the graduates to reflect upon what had happened since they made the decision to leave the lives they had expected and enter a world that would forever separate them from the barrio of Las Tunas.

Not all the graduates had come that evening, but more than twenty-five had walked or driven through the rain. A woman who sat next to me in the circle defined the world as she had come to understand it. She said, *Hay gente pobre y pobre gente*—"The poor and the pitiful." It was the distinction she drew between those who had studied the humanities and those who had not. She was the oldest of all the students who had come to the course, still young, but already a grandmother, proud of the grandson who played in the youth orchestra. She wore a puffy jacket and had severely defined features. "When you get old, you should keep on growing," the grandmother of Las Tunas said. She spoke in precise sentences. Listening to her, one had the sense of an orderly existence, clear and loving. She took off her coat and offered it to my wife to cover her knees. They spoke to each other with glances, two women with shared ancestry in the Spanish sun, grandmothers. The graduates watched them, listened to their conversation in their much traveled language, and were put at ease.

A handsome young man who sat beside a plain woman who was his wife said that he had learned a lot in the class. And then, as if he were retelling the tale of the prisoner who emerges from the cave in Plato's allegory and returns, filled with the knowledge he found in the sunlight, wishing to bring it back to the prisoners below, the handsome young man said, "But you can't go into a tavern and change the lives of a bunch of drunks. They wouldn't know what you were talking about. I do this [continue to study the humanities] for my children and for myself, to be a better person, to give them better lives." And then they talked about how difficult it was to recruit people to come to the class, how fear was a greater barrier than the weariness one feels at the end of a long day in a factory or a store. We were asking people to step off a cliff, into another world.

It was at that moment, after fifteen years with the Clemente Course, that my wife and I understood that the students were not merely interesting or capable, but heroic. She said of the first day in the classroom, the breaking out of the surround of force into the light of the humanities, "It is an act of courage."

One graduate spoke of opening her life, and then others took up the theme. They spoke of the humanities as if they were a set of keys to the world, the narrow world of Las Tunas where the humanities helped them to solve the problems that surrounded them, crushing their lives, and the wider world of poems and museums and the history of the world. "After the first forty years," said one man, "do not waste the next forty years."

On the very first day of my first visit to the Centro, Claudia had introduced me to a man who stood in a large patch of turned earth outside the first of several buildings. I did not know what he was doing there. He was a slim man, balding, perhaps fifty years old, or a few more or less. He had very soft features and a blurry voice. In the turned earth he had been planting vegetables. All his life he had been a gardener, he said. Now, he had become a teacher as well; he taught the people of the barrio how to grow vegetables. It was his aim to turn the wasted land into many tiny farms. The nutritionist at the Centro, Sandra Szikla, supported his work. He attended many classes in the Clemente Course. He was not like the pretty young woman whose jealous husband phoned her three or four times during a single class. He gave his attention to the dialogue as he did to the earth. He seemed lonely, and when he spoke, his ideas were like his voice, blurred and gentle. On the evening when all the graduates sat in a circle, he took me aside to tell me that of all the things he had learned he liked philosophy best.

After the conversation with the graduates, my wife and I talked for a while with Silvia Wagener. We sat in a small house reached by walking along a wet and gritty path. There had never been anyone quite like Silvia in any of the classes. On the evening of Borges and Cervantes, she had been the most eager to speak. She sat far from me, near the vegetable gardener, at the other end of the long table that served for a circle in the narrow space of the library; at the greatest distance from the woman whose husband phoned. Although I did not know it then, it was Silvia's husband who had urged her to come to the course. He sent her to study as if she were his ward as well as his wife. They had been married for several years; he knew her well by then, the ferocity of her dreams.

She had been born in Pacheco, a barrio larger than Las Tunas and just as poor. At the age of thirteen, she dropped out high school, her parents' marriage began falling apart, and she left the barrio where she was born and came to Las Tunas. She did not say whether the move was to seek a new place to begin or an escape from failure. People said of her then that she was in full rebellion against the rules of that world, a girl with eyes that looked like fire and a great head of reddish-brown hair. As she speaks about her life, there is no hint of regret; that was her life. She speaks directly, almost in outline. What seems like wildness, what has become a fierce grip on life, prevents the melancholy of poverty; she will not be caged, she cannot accept limits.

It did not take long before the wild life settled into the gritty existence of a woman with two sons by a man who spoke of them as his "mistakes." Then came the struggle. The father of her children would not contribute to their support. He lived nearby, but would not even visit his mistakes; he gave them nothing. She went to the authorities to ask for help, to force him to support his children. There was no help, there had been no marriage, there were only the children. They lived on beans, and when they could afford it, meat. They survived because of a godmother. Four times a week, they were invited to her dinner table. On the other days there were the beans. The father of her children married, and had children with his new wife.

Silvia worked. She cleaned houses. For a time she sold clothing in a store. She cleaned houses again, and then found a job in a factory, but it was the worst kind of work, the least skilled and lowest paying: she cleaned the floors. She earned 450 pesos a month, less than half of what was needed to rise above the poverty line.[3] For

---

3   The Foundation for Latin American Research estimated the minimum cost for food per person—the poverty line—in Argentina in 2010 at 330 pesos a month.

ten years she lived as a single mother. The ferocity of her youth was turned to the defense of her children.

Then, as if a prison sentence had been completed or commuted, the ten years of living as a single mother ended. She does not speak of romance, of the rebellious girl, that other life. Suddenly it was over. She married a man who embraced her and her children. He urged her to go back and complete high school. They had a son together. Now she had three children and the beginning of a settled life, but she could not be settled: she volunteered to work in a library. The work appealed to something in her as strong as rebellion. She was pleased to be working among the books and the people who read them. And it was enough. She asked for no more. She was comfortable in her life, perhaps for the first time, when Claudia Paladino came to talk with her about a course taught by professors from the Universidad de San Andrés. At first, Silvia declined the offer.

In retrospect, however, she said, "There are some memories that a woman treasures all her life. When the Clemente Course started I was in a very difficult time of my life, and it was my husband who insisted that I had to find out if it was too late to begin, and I went there, and I will be eternally grateful that he insisted, because after that everything else happened: work in the office, the desire to study, which had been sleeping but not forgotten, and the ability to do the work."

She spoke about the professors who had taught her: "They never said that a person made an error. They insisted on people speaking about the text. Using the Socratic method, they made me think so hard that smoke came out of my head." She laughed. We talked easily. She had become one of the people who loved the humanities. She led others to the work. In 2007, she became the course coordinator and began her studies in social psychology at the Escuela Privada de Psicologia de Pichon Rivera. She had completed three years, and in one more year she would be able to work with groups, but not individuals. "If I go for two more years . . . ," she said, and laughed at her own ambition. She was forty years old. Her oldest son was twenty and the youngest only seven. She had the same ferocity I had seen when I taught the first class many years earlier. I am sure she is still of the opinion that humanities are more wonderful than war, no matter what Cervantes had written.

Silvia and my wife and I left the tiny house where we had been talking and walked back toward the car. A heavy, cold rain continued to fall. The stones of the path floated on the mud. It was difficult to see in the moonless night. Silvia walked beside my wife, holding her arm, steadying her on the shifting stones. We embraced, old friends now, no longer teacher and student. One act of courage leads to another. The humanities do not inhibit the fire; they enrich it. Even in the rain-drenched darkness I thought I saw the fire in her eyes, and it was certain that the rain had not drowned the wildness in her hair.

CHAPTER 11

A Hole in the Wall

They say there is a "wall" in Charleston. I first heard about it from a local historian. In response, I told her that part of the reason I had agreed to go to Charleston was to knock a hole in the wall. The historian looked at me and laughed, and looked again, and said, "Well, I believe you will."

I did not knock a hole in the wall that separates blacks and whites in Charleston, but Dr. Mary Ann Kohli and the president of Trident Technical College, Dr. Mary Thornley, and a person from the Charleston Heritage Foundation, who invited our students, black or white, to visit the historic houses in the city, did open a space for some dark-skinned people to travel through. Mary Ann Kohli did most of the work; her students say that she is their angel.

We met at the Charleston airport. I walked slowly toward her, trying to gauge the day ahead by the look of the woman who was waiting for me. I had expected an older woman, a plain woman, and serious, and she was young and stylish, a surprise. I looked at her very carefully, for I had just come from a bad experience at a venerable old college in Lexington, Kentucky, and I did not want to misread this visit too.

What was there to see? A face full of wonder, not at all child-like, yet with the innocence of a child. She was consumed by love, it was plain to see. But for whom? I laughed at myself and all the judgments I had made based on evidence caught in a glance. She took it for a smile of recognition and smiled in return. She held up my name on a book I had written. It was an assurance: "Yes, you've come to the right place. Welcome to the American South." When I drew closer, I realized it had been her hair that sent the complex signal I had been reading. Her hair was very thick and cut short; in the style of young boys, but she was not a boy, nor was there any-thing masculine in her face or stance.

Cancer.

Would she tell me? Should I ask? What is the protocol for inquiring about the chemotherapy regimen of a young woman who had neglected to mention it in the brief and very formal correspon-dence that led to our meeting at the airport? It made me queasy when I should have been happy to see her. The flight from Lexing-ton to Charleston on a small, wobbly plane had been enriched by conversation with the curator of the historic Charleston mansions. I was glad to have arrived on the ground, but the thought of the forthcoming cancer conversation unnerved me. I had only recently completed a few months of chemotherapy and radiation, and there were few things I liked less than the whine of the survivor class. I had decided that people either recover from the disease or they do not, and that the only unassailable medical advice comes from those who have not recovered.

The woman and I chatted easily, saying nothing of importance other than about the schedule for the day. She had planned a day without respite, one that left no time for conversation about the woes of the cancer patient or those who pretended their cancers had been cured. She was not averse to woes, as I would learn, only to defeat. I liked her. But I thought she might be too soft in the

way she dealt with the world to attend to all the problems of starting a Clemente Course. Perhaps it was the grace in her speech or
the accent of a highly educated Southern woman that I mistook for
weakness. Within a few minutes the conversation moved on to the
work, and I saw that she had made up her mind to have a success.
The gentle professor was rich in compassion, literate, and I thought
she possessed the will to overcome obstacles. If anyone could start
a Clemente Course in the American South, she could.

We did not see each other again for several years, until Mary
Ann and Carrie Thompson, the fund-raiser for Trident Technical
College, came to New York for an award ceremony. Mary Ann had
become a well-known figure in Charleston by then, a teacher with
national recognition; she was also a talented recruiter, fund-raiser,
and publicist for the Clemente Course. Our communication came
mainly via the Internet and occasional videotapes that Mary Ann
sent of graduations, classes, and the variety of things she had to organize to raise the money to buy books, pay the faculty (never including herself), put food on the table for students who could not afford
it, provide transportation, locate and pay for the repair of comput-
ers, and so on and on. She was a born autobiographer, a graceful
writer who liked to write. I learned the names of her pets and her
friends, the foibles of her marriage and the end of it. She sent poems.
Her favorite was the fourteeth-century Persian lyric poet Hafez. His
work gave her comfort in difficult moments and revealed the route
to thinking about her work. Trident Technical College, the Clemente Course, and other activities took up more than a day every day.
I marveled at her energy and goodwill and her determination to
break through the walls of ignorance or unfairness.

Among the first things she did in what would become the Sisy-
phean task of fund-raising was to offer a café and talent show for all
those willing to bake cakes or buy tickets. She sent me a videotape
of the show. Students in the Charleston Clemente Course were the

performers. Most of the money they raised would be theirs. It would not be very much, and the amount was Mary Ann's first lesson in the need to apply her waking hours to finances. Mary Thornley, the president of the college, was a staunch supporter of the idea of the Clemente Course and of Mary Ann's work, but Thornley was running an institution with almost 60,000 students on its various campuses, and she had to rely on a bureaucracy to manage it.

Like all bureaucracies, this one was less than perfect. Some of the people between Mary Thornley and Mary Ann Kohli were not supporters of Mary Ann Kohli or Mary Thornley or the Clemente Course or what they considered the violation of the rules of the draconian universe they imagined to give themselves comfort. Thornley could not intervene to shield Kohli and the Clemente Course from the bureaucrats without tearing apart the organizational structure of the college. The administration of the college of 60,000 students demanded that Mary Ann turn over part of the tiny proceeds from the café to the institution. She had not only the problems of the uneducated poor to deal with, she was at the mercy of several Dickensian characters who stood between her and the president of the college. If the situation became intolerable, Mary Ann could ask me to speak to President Thornley, but we did not know the limits of Thornley's support, and there was no appeal beyond Mary Thornley; we were hesitant.

The café did not bring in as much money as the planners dreamed, but it allowed the students to demonstrate their ability to stand up and sing or play the saxophone or recite a poem. A black woman named Fouche, a woman as thick as a mountain, took the stage to sing "Amazing Grace." Her voice was strong, and she did not say the words as professional singers do, she prayed in tune with the melody and sometimes not in tune, and when she lost the melody in the words, the song still reached the listeners. It was in the café that was not a café that Fouche sang: she made the song into the history of the people who came from West Africa, bringing with them the knowledge of rice cultivation. Enslaved, separated from the rest of the country, they spoke Gullah, cooked dishes like the jollof rice eaten along the west coast of Africa, and had no hope of freedom. Long after legal emancipation, they remained in the rice paddies, as if on an unreachable island. For all that Gullah enchanted anthropologists, there was nothing given to the Gullah speakers in return. They lived behind rice paddy barriers; they were among the last descendants of the West Africans to leave the plantations. The people who oversaw their work were known as rice drivers. "Amazing Grace," sang Fouche, the bearer of the history. As some Gullah speakers saw their way out through festivals and shows for whites along the east coast of the Southern states, Fouche had come to see her way in the humanities. In the café that was not a café, she was the star.

Mary Ann went on seeking funds for the course, struggling against the established world. The bureaucracy of the college gave her no financial support; the bureaucrats continued to insist that she give a part of everything she begged or earned for the course to the coffers of the college.[1] She had moments when she wondered if she could go on. The problems with the college were difficult, but the bureaucracy, which thought of a dozen ways to make life difficult for the Clemente Course, never said Mary Ann would have to abandon the course. There was always the suspicion, however faint, that the college administration took pride in the work. And then there was Mary Thornley. President Thornley would not let the course or Mary Ann flout the rules, but she would never let the rules destroy the course.

Mary Ann pulled money out of concerts, plays, cafés, and art shows. She assembled a talented faculty, and she and they turned

---

1   Trident Tech was not much worse in this than many other colleges.

the course from a classroom conversation to a life in the humanities. Students went to museums, visited the historic houses, traveled out to Fort Sumter for the history section. They saw plays and
presented plays. There was always something to eat for the hungry
and a gentle moment for the wounded. A homeless Lakota Indian
came to class from his place under a bridge. A jazz musician fought
to rid himself of the drug habit and won and lost the battle. When
Mary Lu Redden, who directs the Clemente Course in Halifax,
Nova Scotia, told me about a reading of the *Odyssey* that raised
$20,000, I told Mary Ann about it, and there was a reading to raise
money in Charleston.

She joined civic clubs, appeared on television and radio, connected the course to the South Carolina Humanities Council. If
Mary Ann herself couldn't convince people to support the course,
she brought her students along. When it came time to recruit students for the following year, she asked former Clemente Course
students to help. One of the best recruiters was Felicia Allyn, who
had gone on to become a student at the College of Charleston and
to work full time in the production department of a local network
affiliate television station.

Felicia Allyn was born in Seattle, Washington, to what she calls
"a white supremacist family." Not long before I talked with her,
she had grown heavy, nearly obese. The thick cinnamon-colored
hair piled on her head for a photograph was all that was organized
about her. By the time we talked, she had become slim again. Her
skin was smooth and pale brown. She spoke hurriedly, running
the sentences together. Now and then recalling the academic world
that she had embraced for three years, memories came tumbling

out of her. In the nostalgia that underlay her telling of a wild life there was the sign of the regret that accompanies maturity, the transformation that can never be complete.

She said, "My mom got pregnant with a race child, and she got scared and left Seattle and went down to Portland and gave birth to me and brought me back as a child to Seattle, and I was raised in Seattle. Her family was real racist. She's Irish, and back in 1968 her grandfather was the head of the Ku Klux Klan and all her family were neo-Nazis. And there I was, the black sheep.

"I didn't meet my father until I was twenty-one. My mom raised me by herself in the projects. You know, we were living in the projects in the South Side, and it was black. They were doing the segregation thing. They would ship us off to the white school and the white school didn't want us. The projects were mean, because you were getting stuff stolen, you were getting jumped. There was gangs that were starting to rise there. It was very scary. I remember being a child and being scared all the time, hiding in a linen closet. They were duplexes and the next-door neighbors would be screaming and shooting guns and I would be scared and my mom would be at work as a bartender. My mom was single, so she had to work two jobs. And I would just hide under all the clothes and just hide and cry. It was just real scary."

Felicia grew up into a young woman with straightened hair and smooth skin. She learned to look fetching, sometimes aggressive, but even when she gained weight, she could not hide the history of the child who hid beneath the laundry.

"It was really weird," she said. "I got into so much trouble: I dropped out of high school, started running with a gang, got into some trouble, and the judge said I needed to go into the Job Corps or they were gonna put me in juvenile. So I went in the Job Corps and I got my GED the first time I took the test, turned around and got a high school equivalency diploma. Then I got accepted to Boise

State University, was there one semester, ended up going to a club one night, and this band was playing and they were from Portland, Oregon, and I asked if they knew Allyn and [through that chance encounter] I met my father for the first time.

"I graduated from Job Corps and moved to Portland, Oregon, and that's when it really got bad. I ended up hooking up with a guy. Tupac Shakur the rapper, he sold his drugs for him. He was always on his records with him. His name was Big Kato, and I started dating him, and he showed me how to rock coke and rob people and shoot a gun and all this crazy stuff. He's the one that Tupac sings about on all his records and stuff. It's funny because he was a Crip and Tupac gave him money to sell dope. And Tupac was known to be a Blood. Kato was an OG[2] in a Crip gang. He was older than I was at the time. I think I may have been like twenty-two, twenty-three. He was thirty.

"Through all of this I belonged to the Roller Sixties gang. We had cousin Crip gangs that were like cousins to our one gang. And one of the Crips was going away to do a two-year bit and we gave him a big barbecue. And my sister[3] kept pressuring me to go over to this guy's house that was an OG of the gang. What ended up happening was I got shot through my hip, through my uterus, and through my bladder. I was in the hospital for like eight hours—the same hospital I was born in. They saved my life. I was going under and I asked the anesthesiologist, 'Are you guys going to let me live?' "

The shooting happened during a wild melee. When it began, Felicia was putting food for the barbecue in the refrigerator. Felicia and several other people were smoking marijuana when more people arrived. Felicia said they were dressed like members of the

---

2 Original gangster.

3 She avoided using her sister's name, and I did not press her about it.

fearsome Richmond Bloods,[4] who had come to Portland to rob the local Crips of their money and dope. Heavily armed, they had demanded all the money in the house. She thinks they expected the money would be turned over without a struggle, but one of the owners of the house pulled his gun and started shooting. In the gun battle Felicia was wounded, and while she lay bleeding, she witnessed the killing of two men. Her partner for the evening was shot to death and another man, a member of the Crips, was also killed.

She said, "My sister came to see me when I woke up—out of surgery—and she said she was moving to North Carolina. She moved the next day. She was scared, because she was caught up in the gun battles. One of the people ended up robbing a dope man and shooting a seven-year-old in the head. He's dead now, but he did the killing. There is a short film about him. He's been in the papers so many times for shooting and killing and stuff like that in Portland, Oregon. He was a very popular gang member. I think he passed away in 1999.

"After I healed—about a year and a half—I got real scared. So I moved to Charlotte with my sister."

She found work in a toy store. A woman she met there convinced her to leave that job to become a salesperson for a company that made outdoor electrical signs. She completed the company training program, moved to Charleston, and began a nomadic life, traveling and selling signs. But she found the business community closed to outsiders: "If you don't know somebody that knows somebody, you can't get in the door." She ended up going into business with the only person who bought a sign from her, the manager of a nightclub. The business was doing well, then there was a shooting at the club, and it soon closed.

---

4   From Richmond, California.

An acquaintance suggested that she apply for disability, and soon "the disability check came—right on time. So then someone told me about housing and . . . I was just on disability, in housing, still selling just a little bit of weed and stuff, because that was all I've ever known was how to sell drugs and stuff.

"Was just laying low and I get a call: my father died. And I fall apart. One morning I wake up and there's a weed pipe on top of the fridge and it had rock in it. I hit it and I actually felt like myself, and that's when my drug addiction started. I didn't go up the food chain of drugs to get on crack. I just went straight to crack. And I stopped having the will to live and I started living on the streets. I started selling crack and running prostitutes and turning tricks and living in and out of hotels and crack houses."

She moved in with her mother, was arrested for possession of cocaine. She was sentenced to four years—ninety days in jail and the rest on probation. As soon as she was released from jail she went back to using drugs, was arrested again, and sent back to court. The judge was lenient again, releasing her to a rehabilitation program but threatening to put her in prison to serve out the whole four-year term. "That scared me," Felicia said. "And I decided I was going to do the right thing. Nobody in the history of the Charleston Center Rehab ever finished the rehab, and I finished the program in twelve weeks. My counselor told me either I'm the greatest manipulator in the world or I've got this and I'm gonna excel."

In that conversation with the drug counselor, her life began to change. "I don't know where it came from," she said. "I just blurted out, 'I want to go to school.' And she pulled out a flyer and said, 'There's a Clemente program and it's geared exactly for people like you. And you know, you'll be in school at Trident Technical College.'

"And I was like, Oh my goodness, I have not been in school since '86. And by the grace of God I did pass the GED test the first time, and I don't know how that happened, but it did. So all of my life people have told me that God saved me for a special purpose and that's why I didn't die when I got shot.

"And the next thing you know, I get in Clemente. I had to go to the college—I had to take the college test, and I scored low. I was like right on the borderline, so Dr. Kohli sat me down and said, 'Do you really want this?'

"Like I knew I didn't want to go back out in the street. I knew I didn't want to do drugs. At this time I was real clean. And I was like, 'Yes, I want this.' So she said okay. I ended up getting a B in that class. And it proved to myself that, yes, I can go back to school.

"In the class it was never 'No, that's not the right answer.' It was always, 'Let me think. I know where you got that from.' It was always like that, with all the instructors. I was so thankful for Clemente that I volunteered. And that was when it was first starting up. Dr. Kohli was trying to pull people to actually be in the Clemente Course, and I just went full-fledged. I went to all the neighborhoods I used to be in. I knocked on doors. I handed out flyers. I was telling people on the corners selling drugs: 'Look, if you're on probation, come do this, because it shows you're green.'

"And they're like, 'Wow, you were really messed up.' And they're like, 'What do you need?' " And then she started having a waiting list.

"As much as I believed in Clemente, I ended up reading the booklet [the Trident Technical College guide for prospective students] to go to school, and I just prayed before I opened it, and I opened it up and put my hand on it and it was Radio and Television Broadcasting. And I did it. I hit the dean's list two or three times. I graduated[5] with a three point something grade point average.

---

5   Felicia attended Trident Technical College for two years to earn an associate's degree. The Charleston Clemente Course is taught on the Trident Technical College campus.

"I was a mentor to the Clemente class. You know, when we started getting into Shakespeare you're on a whole 'nother language, and it's just so surprising—how the students just grasp what's going on. They were talking about Othello. I'm looking at them, like, Wow, this is just remarkable, studying it, understanding it, having conversations. Those students were just so sharp!

"I mean the way they [the instructors] handled us, it was just like a family, and now I go to the College of Charleston and through that I got hired at ABC News 4, and if you were to come and talk to the managers and the directors and anybody here they would say—and I'm not bragging on myself—that we're very grateful that we have Felicia here.

"My life is just totally changed around. I never believed I could go to school, because I didn't do good in school, because I wasn't interested in school back when society said, 'You have to be interested in school, because you have to go to college and then you do something for the world.' I just wanted to do my thing. I was just chasing around. I was raised a scaredy child and I promised I was never going to get scared, so I started getting tough, I started getting mean, walked around with a gun. I think that's where I went wrong.

"I have an associate's degree from Trident Tech. So now I go to the College of Charleston, studying media, for my BA. I want to be a reporter. And I'm married and life is great.

"When Dr. Kohli met me, I was scared. I was fragile. I didn't believe in myself. I had no self-esteem. The best thing about Clemente was afterwards, getting my Clemente certificate, seeing that grade, knowing I accomplished it. And the love. I always tell Dr. Kohli she is like an angel to me."

Mary Ann and I sometimes exchanged e-mails daily, sometimes I did not hear from her for several weeks, and whenever that happened, I grew concerned and wrote to her. I don't know how she found the time to write letters that were both graceful and gracious. They contained revelations about the character of the people who taught the Clemente Course and the students whom my wife had taken to describing as the real heroes, the ones who came from out of the miasma of poverty to sit with Cézanne and Shelley and dream of what is possible.

In Charleston, a man who had served two sentences in prison sat with his young children on either side and read *Othello* with them. A television station came to film his reading and to hear his testimony. Mary Ann was in the film too, but only for a few seconds, deferring to the students. She understood what walls they had burst through to come to her classes. She embraced them with hard questions and no nonsense. They came with AIDS and memories of the vortex of alcohol-filled days to read Shakespeare's histories and the histories of the city of Charleston. They spoke of "the wall." Felicia said that, in Charleston, "the whites sit on one side of the room and we sit on the other side, even if now we sit in the same room." In the Clemente Course, people sit together.

On December 17, 2010, as I was writing this chapter, the following letter arrived from Mary Ann Kohli:

Hi, Earl,

Miracles on Columbus Street [Palmer Campus of TTC] just keep happening. If you don't believe in a Higher Power or Santa Claus, you really should reconsider. Your Clemente

Course here keeps getting saved over and over by events and people who appear out of nowhere just in the St. Nick of Time. It is the damnedest thing I've ever seen. It's worth it just to stick around and see what will happen next. Here is the latest.

I put donation envelopes in the programs for graduation this year with "To and From" Christmas stickers on them. We received $1,100 in donations.

Dr. Thornley has a big black tie dinner and silent auction fund-raiser for the Trident Technical College (TTC) Foundation each year in January. Carrie called me up and asked if I would get a signed print from Jonathan Green for the auction. She said the money would go to Clemente. I asked him and received a print valued at $4,000. I paid for the framing myself as a personal contribution to the cause. I am also working as a volunteer at that event as a waitress or whatever they need.

As a result of the newspaper release about Jonathan Green's participation in the graduation, I heard from my old boss at USC [University of South Carolina]. Carolyn Matalene was in charge of the entire freshman English program at USC when I was a teaching assistant/graduate student there. She and her husband have retired in Charleston. She wants to help teach writing to my students. Her husband, who was a professor of classical literature, wants to teach the Shakespeare play. Both want to help with fundraising.

Carolyn knows the retired playwright in residence at USC—also now residing in Charleston. He came to the graduation and may be willing to write the Poe monologue. He wants to work with the Clemente students about writing and producing their own play.

Chad's mentors—two professors from College of Charleston—are meeting with Dr. Thornley about possibly connecting Clemente with Drug Court here in Charleston, and having people sent to Clemente instead of jail.

Now how is that for some powerful stocking stuffers?

I wound up the graduation program last night with two quotes: "Truth without love is cruelty and love without truth is sentimentality." My point was that the Clemente Course is not about sloppy sentimentality. My students live on the razor's edge of truth—so much so that if they fall over backwards, they die. If they balance on the sharp edge of truth, however, they will discover the validity of this proverb: "Since my house burned down, I now own a better view of the rising moon." It has been as true for me as for my students. Truth can kill, but it also can redeem.

And I have been,

Mary Ann

CHAPTER 12

Kukulkan and Quetzalcoatl[1]

Little Russy

It was by chance that my eye had fallen on a copy of John Lloyd Stephens's famous book about his travels in the Yucatán when I was nine years old, wandering deep in the stacks of the El Paso Public Library. The book had fascinated me then, and I had never abandoned my interest in Mesoamerica. A second chance encounter led to the establishment of the Curso en alta cultura Maya–Hunab Ku in a cement-block structure a few feet off the road in the tiny village of San Antonio Sihó, not far from the ruins of Kalkiní on the border of the states of Yucatán and Campeche. I was on a small plane heading southeast out of Mexico City bound for Merida, when I began talking with the young man sitting next to me. He suggested that when I got settled in Merida, I ought to telephone his father, Raúl Murguía Rosete, who headed the office of the United Nations Development Program (UNDP) on the peninsula. I wrote down the name and telephone number. When we

---

1 A description of the founding of the Clemente Course in Yucatán (*Curso en alta cultura Maya–Hunab Ku*) appears in *Riches for the Poor*, and an interview with José Chim Ku appears as an appendix to *The Life and Times of Mexico* (New York: W. W. Norton & Company, 2004). Ma. Russy Chay Tucuch does not appear by name, although she can be seen standing on the far right in a photograph published in *The Life and Times of Mexico*. Kukulkan and Quetzalcoatl are the Maya and Náhuatl names for the culture bearer—both can be translated as "plumed serpent."

landed, the boy and I shook hands and went our separate ways. Two days later, I phoned. Murguía was gruff but polite. He asked how long I was planning to stay in Merida, and set a date for a day well before my planned departure.

I expected a UN bureaucrat and instead encountered a tall, lean man, with a carefully trimmed beard just going gray and a laugh in which I heard a hint of bitterness. He reminded me of Jorge Valls, a Cuban Catholic Socialist writer who had spent twenty years and forty days in prison, because he disagreed with the methods of his "friend" and fellow revolutionary Fidel Castro. Murguía could not utter more than a few sentences without some amusing irony coming to play. He laughed at the ironies even as he spoke them. Unlike Valls, whose seriousness dominated all conversation, Murguía was charming. And tough. We became friends almost immediately.

We talked for a while about the Clemente Course, which was then in only its second year in New York. He wasted no time with pleasantries about the work. As with everything else in his life, he moved toward implementation; he appeared to be utterly incapable of that great human failing which I think of as dithering. He moved, propelled it seemed by a great laugh that sounded like a deep masculine *ha! ha!* We set a date to meet Jorge Cocom Pech in Valladolid. Cocom Pech was a descendant of a great Maya family, a man of influence. The plan was to enlist Cocom Pech in the search for a place and a group of twenty to thirty students. We would assemble the faculty.

In the course of our conversations, Murguía and I agreed that we would teach the Maya humanities to Maya students. I would help in the creation of the curriculum. Most of it would be based on the famed "Maya Bible," the Popol Vuh or Pop Wuj. There were other important works, but the Popul Vuh was foundational: literature, moral philosophy, and history, in a form that was nothing less than spellbinding.

Several days later, Murguía and I set out for Valladolid, a lovely town very close to Xocen, which the Maya say is the center of the world.[2] We parked and went into a hotel bar where we expected Cocom Pech. A light rain that had followed us on the road from Merida turned into an immense downpour. The streets flooded. I soon saw why the sidewalks were raised several feet above street level. While the rain continued, Murguía and I talked and drank tequila. We drank tequila and waited for Cocom Pech. And waited. And became angry at having to wait. And drank tequila. Hours after the appointed time Cocom Pech and two young fellows, attendants of a sort, arrived. We drank tequila. The conversation did not go well.

Instead of working with Cocom Pech, we turned to the tiny village of San Antonio Sihó, where UNDP had a small project on growing medicinal herbs. Murguía gathered a group of young men and women to listen to my proposal for a course in the Maya humanities. It was there, while explaining the Socratic method and the concept of midwifery, that I told the students I would be their *partera* (midwife). The young women drew back, horrified, as if some sort of monster had appeared in my stead. Murguía leapt into the conversation, explaining that I meant *dialogo maieutico* and did not really intend to deliver their babies. We all laughed, but it was a long time before the young women in the course were really sure of my intentions.

Back in Merida, we had to organize a faculty. Raúl began with the *presidenta*. For that vital part, which corresponded to site direc-tor in the U.S. courses, he invited Alejandra García Quintanilla to his office. She was a historian who had received her doctorate from the University of North Carolina. She spoke perfect, unaccented English. Although my wife and I have come to love her like a sister,

---

2   The navel of the world, similar to the Nahua (Aztec) Anahuac.

she was very serious and very wary when she came into Murguía's office. I saw a full-figured woman with curly black hair wearing a *huipil* (Maya dress—a white embroidered shift). While I described the course in what she came to call my "*cervantino, impecable*, broken Spanish," she listened carefully, without comment. Her face was formed for laughter and tears of compassion, but the intensity in her eyes led Murguía to refer to her with his usual irony as the *chichimeca* (fierce people of the arid north of Mexico, precursors of the Aztecs, the last to resist conquest by Spain).

She agreed to the role of site director. We needed several other people to complete the faculty: someone who could work with the relation of the humanities to the *milpa*, the small farm where the *tres santos* (corn, beans, and squash) were raised, and to the forest, where one finds chaya and other food growing wild, as well as an occasional bird, small animal, or even, illegally, a small deer. Silvia Terán, the much honored ethnobotanist and ethnologist, was perfectly suited for the part.

The key to the faculty—the person without whom neither Alejandra nor Silvia Terán nor Raúl would agree to go ahead with the project—came to the office the next day. Miguel Angel May May was younger than the rest of us, casual in dress in a way we were unable to effect, Maya, born in the Yucatán, and more comfortable in the heat and humidity. He appeared to be in his early thirties, although his hair was touched with gray. He wore his Maya identity very proudly, almost defiantly. Miguel May was skeptical, but willing to work with the idea. In a deep voice, speaking very deliberately, in professorial tones, he offered to teach the Maya language and acquaint the students with Maya literature, both ancient and contemporary. I liked him, even his uneasy smile.

Murguía and I went out to Sihó the next day. It was there that I committed the gaffe that has brought head-shaking, knee-slapping laughter from people in Mexico for more than a decade. Raúl had assembled a group of twenty young people from the village to listen to our proposal. Some of them worked in a UNDP project there, others still lived with their families. The building in which we met was made of concrete blocks. It was small, perhaps ten by twenty feet, and unfinished. The electricity was of the wavering kind that would not support electronic equipment because it failed to deliver the steady amperage required by the devices; the windows were holes in the wall that could be secured with crude wooden shutters; and the long table I had said we would need was not one but many small wooden tables arranged in a row. The potential students sat on a variety of chairs, each one apparently connected in some arcane way to one of the small tables. Raúl introduced me, and I began my description of the course, this time in the Maya humanities. I knew a bit about the subject, having been engaged with it since my childhood experience in the El Paso Public Library.

Before we could begin, however, the concrete-block structure had to be turned into a classroom. The row of small tables were not part of a classroom; the students had carried them and the chairs from their houses. They were dining-room tables. The students were bringing the heart of their households to the one-room structure so that we could hold class there. That evening, I phoned my wife in New York to tell her about the day. When she heard about the tables, she said that she had some money in a personal account, not very much, but enough to buy some inexpensive chairs and perhaps a table. Murguía and I went to Sam's Club, which had just opened in Merida, and bought plastic chairs, composition-board tables, a blackboard that we could hang on a wall—everything we needed to produce the midwifery of the Socratic method.

Several days later, the faculty and I arrived in Raúl's big white passenger van. It was one of the hottest days I can remember. The tiny building was so hot that several of the people who lived in Merida said they felt faint. Each member of the faculty soggier with sweat than the next took his or her place to speak, and they all spoke well. Silvia, the ethnobotanist, was careful to display her knowledge of local flora in a manner that did not bruise the feelings of the students, and Alejandra spoke with great eloquence as if she were reading from a prepared text rather than introducing the students to their own history. And then it came Miguel May's turn. He wore a white *guayabera* that had remained perfectly pressed and appeared ice-cool against his deep brown skin. When he spoke, it was in perfect Maya, with the tones and accents the students had heard in the voices of distant ancestors. He brought them from the drowsing afternoon heat to the cool memory of who they had been before the invasion, before the corruption, to the time when hardwoods grew tall in the forest, and Mayab (land of the Maya) was theirs.

Until that time, I had put up a very mild resistance to the call by Raúl and Alejandra to dedicate one fifth of the course to teaching Maya to the Maya. There was a tinge of absurdity about it. Teaching English, of course, to English speakers had always made perfect sense to me. The intricacies of the language, the beauty of expression, the likelihood that an entire civilization and all the thoughts that had ever been said by mind or mouth within that civilization were contained in the language—these had been my dearest friends for as long as I could remember. English was the most intimate creature in my life; I was said (in what was undoubtedly a serious exaggeration) to have spoken before I could maintain a sitting position in my cradle bed. It was my most profound belief, perhaps the only certainty in my life, that man is born of words, and that the true marriage of male and female in the collective man is the vow of humanity that language makes. Although I knew some Latin, a smattering of Greek, and quite a lot of Spanish, I could not find the whole of history in those languages, only some singing, much weeping over history, arguments and ideas, but not the whole. English was my world.

One of the students had asked me quietly, as if it were a crime of betrayal, if I would teach him to speak English. Before Miguel May spoke and I saw the students' love of their own true existence in the words and the music of their making the words aloud, I would have agreed with the boy who wanted to learn English, a language he admired as an accountant or a shopkeeper might—I would have agreed to the teaching of English, welcomed it, because I could do it for them, and this other language, this foreign language, dying as it were, meant very little to me. Only after I saw the faces of the Maya students in the presence of their own language did I fully comprehend what Raúl and Alejandra knew: every language is a world, even if the world no longer exists except as it is contained in language.

Not long afterward, I was at Palenque, the grand Maya city in Chiapas that had been the home of Lord Pacal (Shield), whom some scholars describe as the Caesar of the Maya world for his ability to lead armies and wage war, leaving behind wreckage and eventually a string of conquered cities. This time, after climbing the great flights of stairs leading to the important buildings and tombs, I wandered off into the jungle along the tiny stream that fed fresh water into the city, and saw a butterfly of a shade of blue such as I had never before seen or imagined. Months later, looking up the word in the Barrera Vasquez Dictionary of the Maya language, I saw that there were nine different definitions in Maya for the color blue, whereas the Porrua Spanish dictionary offered only three, meaning that without the Maya language, six butterflies disappeared from the world.

What happened in the tiny classroom in the heat of the late

summer afternoon in the small village of Sihó, where flies dined by the thousands on the discarded juices of the *henequen* (sisal) cactus as it was squeezed and shredded into rough strands of rope, made sense of the world for me. There, and in the jungle surrounding the monumental city of the Great Lord Shield, I learned truly what it is to be human.

Unlike the classes in the United States, the Maya course lasted for three years. Raúl Murguía was a demanding funder. He permitted no laggards, no waste, and no deviation from the rigorous curriculum he had approved. He was like that in every small UNDP project across the Mexican south. Compared to the vast, lackadaisical bureaucracy in New York, the Mexican operation under Murguía was crisp and impatient. If a small NGO run by a personal friend of his did not perform, he withdrew its funding. His aim was to improve the lives of the people, and whoever failed to do that was warned, warned again, and then dropped. He was as devoted as the Cuban Valls, but tough where Valls was religious; where Valls prayed, Murguía acted. Like Valls, Murguía had suffered under a corrupt government, although not so terribly and not for so many years. Both men had taught the poorest illiterates of the world to read and write. Both were fearless. One depended on the mercy of God and the other spoke of the ironies of life and laughed.

Nearly ten years after the first class met in Sihó, an organization was formed in Merida to provide open education to the poor of the peninsula. It was headed operationally by José (Pepe) Sanchez of the Secretariat of Education, and its organization and operations were to be overseen by a board of founders, which included two former Mexican ambassadors, leading scientists from the National

Autonomous University of Mexico (UNAM) and the University of Yucatán, and me. Although Murguía was one of the moving forces behind ASEA (Asociación para educativa abierta), he was not a member of the board. Luz Elena Buena, former Mexican ambassador to countries in the Caribbean, was the chair. My dear friend Dra. García Quintanilla was one of the key figures. After being invited, I explained to her via e-mail that I would not accept the invitation unless some of the people at the first meeting were Maya. I suggested Miguel May and perhaps two of our former students from Sihó. Alejandra spoke with Luz Elena and Pepe Sanchez and Raúl, and said that I could go ahead and buy my airline ticket: it was done.

The evening before the meeting, we gathered at Embajadora Buena's house for a late supper, which was an opportunity for me to get to know some of the other board members before the formal meeting at the university. The next morning, Miguel May and one of my students from the Curso en alta cultura Maya–Hunab Ku, Russy Chay, were already seated at the conference table when I arrived. Miguel and I had an abrazo and then Little Russy stood up. I had not seen her for some years and was delighted to find her there. We had a great abrazo and laughed with pleasure at seeing each other again. She gave me a tiny alligator made of beads. "We sell these in the plaza," she said, and laughed. I remembered her as the smallest of the students, even shorter than her sister, who was also in the class. She was very shy then. Drawing her into the dialogue had been difficult, especially in light of the willingness of one of the other young women, and several of the young men, including one of the leaders of the village. To find Russy, the granddaughter of a *h-meen*,[3] sitting at the table among ambassadors, department heads from the universities, and the man from the Secretariat of

---

3   Literally, a "doer"; a traditional medicine man.

Education was astonishing and disconcerting. What if she had to speak?

I took my seat at the far end of the table, next to Embajadora Buena, the chairperson. The head of the Psychology Department stood next to the Embajadora. He had brought a videocamera and set it up on a tripod. He told the group that he wanted to record this meeting of the founders. Since I had been so insistent about the Maya having a place at the table, Luz Elena gave first place to Miguel May, who said a little prayer in Maya to bless the project and then read one of his stories that had not yet been published. He read it in Spanish, and then because we were in the place that was called Mayab (the land of the Maya), I asked if he would read part of it, at the very least, in Maya. He read, and it captivated the listeners, for he said the words, as always, carefully, slowly, as if admiring the sounds as he made them. There was applause for the story and the reading. Then la Embajadora called on Little Russy.

She had spoken Spanish with a heavy Mayan accent when she came to the course in Sihó. It is a curious sound, almost as if the person had a German accent in Spanish. Sometimes this is difficult for people who are not familiar with the accent, or the Maya words that come into a person's speech in a local form of code-switching. Intellectuals in Mexico City do cruel imitations of Maya speakers having trouble with Spanish pronunciation. And there was Russy, in a room filled with people who might be imitating her accent over a glass of wine at dinner that night. I was concerned, for I knew something about the racism that the Maya suffer.

Little Russy stood up. She was not much taller standing than sitting. She had gained some weight since I had last seen her. Her face was full and very wide: it appeared not so much innocent as incapable of guile. No one in the class had been as shy or lovable. She hesitated for a moment before speaking. I wanted somehow to rescue her. I had brought her to this moment.

She began, in clear, correct Spanish, "I have a PowerPoint presentation. . . ."

The people sitting around the table were dumbfounded. No one had imagined that a tiny woman from a village at the end of an impossible road could make a PowerPoint presentation and speak so well. As she spoke, describing the organization that had arisen out of the will of several women in the village, their search for gender equality, their growing demand for this new role, and especially an end to the physical and verbal abuse of women, the listeners became a part of her effort. The psychologist who was operating the videocamera suddenly began blowing kisses to her, and when she finished, I thanked her and said that I had been fond of her for many years, but now I was in love. And everyone laughed at the effusive congratulations and applauded Little Russy for a long time. At a luncheon in the university garden following the meeting, everyone vied for the chance to sit at Russy's table.

Because of her talk and the efforts of José Sanchez and Alejandra García Quintanilla, the ASEA organization, which had begun as a course in Occidental studies for Spanish speakers, became a course in which the Maya were the most successful students. Several courses were taught to the Maya in Maya language and culture. They were not standard Clemente courses, but cousins or children of Clemente courses: riches for the poor. At this writing, there is an ongoing course at the University of Yucatán taught by Alejandra Quintanilla to educate Maya teachers in villages across the state to teach Maya language, history, literature, and philosophy. And another set of courses in the state of Quintana Roo is being assembled.

The metamorphosis of Little Russy into the leader of a women's group working for gender equality in a society that has never recognized women as equals remains the most astonishing change wrought by the Clemente Course in Mexico. Twelve years after her experience, she described her life and work. How much of the strength and clarity of her vision came from the course is not something I can say. I had asked her to speak about her life, and in a clear, strong voice, speaking in Spanish, the tiny woman from the tiny village found words that first taught me to treasure the self-critical nature of the humanities.

"My name is Maria Russy Rosalba Chay Tucuch. I was born in San Antonio Sihó, Halacho, in Yucatán, on September 9, 1975. I attended primary school in Sihó until the fourth grade. Then I had to leave school because there were problems at home. My mother was sick. I had to help her and take care of my younger brother. It hurt me to leave, because I loved school. I really wanted to study, but I had to learn to be a housewife: to know what went on in the kitchen and how to embroider, that kind of thing. I was very unhappy, but I did what I had to do. Pretty soon, I was selling my embroidered dresses and earning some money for my things and for the household. It wasn't much, but it helped.

"When I was fifteen years old, I heard about a program for adults from INAH [Instituto Nacional de Antropologia e Historia]—but it was for illiterates. I was still itching to learn, but I didn't want to go back to primary school. I was part of a group of fourteen women, *Coox Baxa Ha* ["Let's go, girls!" is a loose translation], who built houses and worked with children. Then, when I was twenty-two years old, I heard about the School of High Maya Culture [the Clemente Course]. When they started to talk about the school it caught my attention, and once again I wanted to study. But when I got close to the school I thought that I couldn't do it, because of what they presented to us, all the subjects we were going to study—at that time, I had not been reading or writing; I had put my studies aside.

"There were four women in our group who were ready for the school, and three of us, including my sister and me, who also wanted to attend but were not prepared. I felt less able than my friends, because some of them had received their diplomas; they had completed high school or middle school or grade school. And I had abandoned my studies in the fourth grade! [Nonetheless, she and her sister attended the meetings where Raúl and I explained the course, and they decided to go to at least a few classes.]

"When I started learning the history of the Maya and all in the course in High Maya Culture, studying in the school led me to go back to complete grade school and middle school, but in a school for adults. When I began to know a little about the Maya culture, I became anxious to learn more, especially because of the classes that Alejandra [García Quintanilla] taught. As I learned history, the Maya calendar, the glyphs, I realized the importance of regaining the knowledge that had been lost during our history. They did not teach it in the formal schools of the government; they did not speak of these things. There was history, but it was another history. And there was nothing about our role or the material that we learned from Miguel May—Maya reading and writing. This had the greatest impact on me.

"The parts that interested me most were the history of the Maya and Maya reading and writing. And so it gave me to understand many things in the history of the Maya, that we had been marginalized, that we were, as persons, at the bottom, that those who speak Spanish know everything and have the rights to everything; all the possibilities belong to them. After I learned the history of the Maya, I knew it was not the truth. Our history, our culture, our language, and the traditions we have are on a par with those of the people who speak Castellano; we are not from the bottom and we are not going to be that way. I became proud of my Maya roots. I knew that I had to find my own identity. I was speaking Maya. I became a Maya person.

"In fact, when I spoke Spanish, I spoke with a Maya accent. I personally was proud to be a Maya woman, one who had the ability to fight for the rights of other women, helping to be sure that there are equal rights for everyone, equality between men and women.

"This is some of what happens when you find your origins again, because then you know the things that you are given by nature and you take those things that are good for you. It was in the [Clemente] school that I learned this about the basics of my culture; it came from reading the Popol Vuh and all. And immediately after I knew about my own culture I moved into it, the culture that I loved. It's different from the other culture [Spanish/Occidental], where I am the object of the society. In my culture I am the subject."

"Our group, *Coox Baxa Ha*, works with children. We think they are the future. To raise the children as persons of action, to do things, to be able to do things was our aim. To produce a well-rounded person, we think they must not only learn how to use their heads but how to feel, and how to speak. There are questions of the heart as well as the head.

"We were working with the children, but we realized that when they got home, the things we had spoken of did not exist—having a name, being sent to school, being treated well. We said they have rights, but in the home they did not have these rights. What we taught in the school was like lying to the children. We realized that we had to work with everyone involved, in this case the mothers and fathers. That led us to begin working with the women. We had a meeting to talk with them about their children. It was then that we realized the women didn't respect the rights of the children, but not because they didn't know or didn't care. The circumstances didn't allow them to accept the rights of the children. This upset us very much, because we saw that we weren't doing what we needed to advance our work. So, I believe it was in 2005, we made a diagnosis in our town, and this was the finding: we were speaking of the rights of children, but these rights applied to women as well. And when we became aware of this, we saw that the principal deficiency was that the women had no work.

"We suggested participation in the society, because at that time it was only for men. The women did not take part in decisions; that was left to the men. So we began to take up certain subjects. There was no health center in the communities. Now and then we had a nurse or sometimes a public health person and sometimes a doctor or medical assistant. To get medical care, you had to leave the community. This was a major need.

"In the same year, 2005, we organized a forum with the women and found out what was most important to them. They wanted a space where they could go, a place where they could talk with someone who listened to them, a person who understood the situation in which they lived. And then we started to work on other questions, about leadership, about helping them economically, advising them about starting profitable organizations, each of which had groups of five to eight women. Some made hammocks, others embroidered by hand, others by machine.

"When these groups get together to make their embroidery, they talk about their rights, their health. At the moment, there are seven groups: five in Sihó, one in Maní which is close by Merida, and the other is in Tecoh, a group of Mayas from forty to sixty years old. They have their profitable activities. They raise chickens, and when we get together we talk about these things with them. We work with them to give them the tools so they can move in the public world of society. We talk about questions of gender, of equality, how they must see that their groups make quality products, how to sell their products, what to do with their husbands, how to raise their children. So we deal with many things with them, political participation, the kinds of things they must do as women. We enable them to engage in traditional crafts and also to participate in the community, how to speak in public, and so on. We do not ask them to memorize what we tell them. We give them the tools to use what is theirs. That's the work we do with the women."

Santa Ana Tlacotenco

To find the house of Librado Silva Galeana in Mexico City requires genius far beyond anything yet mapped by a global positioning system. It had been possible before the Mexican government built a soccer stadium in 1968, disrupting the streets and directions in the hills above the stadium. After 1968, no taxi driver could find the street where Librado lived. "Here are the instructions," I would tell the driver, handing him careful notes. And still we were lost. A trip that should have taken no more than half an hour required more than an hour and countless stops not to ask how to get to Librado's house, but how to get to the street that led to the street that crossed the street that led . . .

Whoever visited Librado had to want very much to see him. I did, for I had promised the preceding day to accompany him and his wife Elpidia Elena to Milpa Alta, far to the south and high above the rest of Mexico City, where the air was clear and cold, and the language spoken in the streets was the classical Náhuatl spoken by the Aztecs before the Spanish invasion. We stayed for a while in Librado and Elena's house. She was disquieted by prospects for the evening. We were going up to the community center in Milpa Alta, where Elena was to present her newly published cookbook (*Recetario nahua de Milpa Alta, D.F.*). While we waited for someone to come and pick us up to go to the presentation, we talked about the work Librado was doing with Miguel León-Portilla, the famed historian and translator from Náhuatl. Librado and Francisco Morales Baranda, both of whom had been born and raised in Santa Ana Tlacotenco, worked together to translate the arcane writings of the Nahuas in the early sixteen century as they had been written out in Roman script by Fray Bernardino de Sahagún.

I had sat now and then with Miguel and Librado and sometimes Francisco as they struggled to bring the deepest sense of the Náhuatl into Spanish. They were an interesting trio: Miguel, the most famous living Mexican scholar, was a short, robust man, filled with ideas, histories, quotations, and languages (Greek, Latin, French, German, English, Náhuatl, and elegant Spanish). He spoke with the academic breathlessness of a man who could not wait to tell all that he knew. Librado was a larger man, somewhat younger than Miguel's nearly eighty years, but not well. He sat with one leg wrapped in a blanket and propped up on a chair, the result of an automobile accident. Librado was a stickler for close, almost interlinear translation. Francisco was a dark, very handsome man, who wore wide pinstripe suits in the British style when he was at the National Autonomous University of Mexico (UNAM) and work clothes on the large farm where he raised *nopal* (prickly pear). He was the moderating force. During the few times I had been there, I argued for a more graceful translation. It was, after all, a work in Spanish that they were seeking to produce. The three of them were to be the intellectual core of the Clemente Course for Náhuatl Speakers.

To translate the *Cantares Mexicanos,* the great Nahua (Aztec) songs and prayers, was exceedingly difficult. The problems were always the metaphors. It was difficult work and it produced contentious arguments, as did almost everything about Aztec and Maya culture. I had witnessed a ferocious debate between Librado and another Náhuatl speaker at a celebration in a tiny village high in the mountains of Morelos. Even so, I was not prepared for the reception to Elena's book or for the fierce arguments a few days later when we prepared the curriculum for the Náhuatl Clemente Course.

At the community center, Elena, Librado, the widely published poet Xochime, and I sat at a table on a slightly raised platform above a small audience. We each spoke for a moment before Librado paraphrased a story from his introduction to the recipes. Although she was not Nahua, Elena had been married to Librado for many years and had learned to cook from his mother and sisters and other women in Santa Ana Tlacotenco. After the presentation, Librado said he would take questions. A man in the audience complained that the recipes were not truly Nahua. Many of the ingredients, according to the man in the audience, had never been used by Nahuas before the conquest. A terrible argument ensued over the use of corn and corn husks. Librado responded in defense of his wife, but the man in the audience refused to concede his point. Soon he was joined by another man and another until it appeared that Elena's cookbook was sunk. Finally it was my turn to speak, and I did what I thought León-Portilla might have done in defense of his friend. I told how Quetzalcoatl, the Nahua culture-bearer, had enlisted the ants to bring corn up from the land of the dead to save the Nahuas from starvation. The idea of a gringo telling the Nahuas of Milpa Alta about their own god was more than the argument could tolerate. To prevent a riot, Francisco Morales Baranda, who was as always in the company of a beautiful young woman, invited everyone to enjoy a kind of spaghetti dinner made of long, thin strips of *nopales* (prickly pear denuded of its thorns) cooked in tomato sauce.

The argument over Elena's recipes was mild compared to the gathering at the UNAM two days later. We had been teaching a Clemente Course in Occidental culture in Cuernavaca for several years, but this was to be our first venture into Náhuatl. Dra. Herlinda Suarez Zozaya, a professor at the UNAM, had organized the course and recruited the faculty for the Cuernavaca courses, and she and León-Portilla had put together a Náhuatl faculty. The course to be taught to the Náhuatl speakers was to last for two years. The first year would be taught in Santa Ana Tlacotenco, the small town in Milpa Alta; would be devoted to Aztec language and culture. The second year would be devoted to world culture and would be taught in a classroom at the National University.

We had described the course to a group of first-rate Nahua scholars, converting the vision of Petrarch into the language and culture of the classical Aztecs. The scholars were asked to bring their reading lists to a meeting at the UNAM. It was to be a brief meeting to acquaint each of the scholars with the work of the others. We assembled in a small room at the university. The argument began almost immediately.

Who would teach agriculture?

I said there was no agriculture section. One person was lost to the meeting.

Astonishingly, Librado Silva became enraged over who would teach Náhuatl, and my friend whom I had defended in Milpa Alta and in the mountains of Morelos decided not to teach. Fortunately, the head of the academy of the Náhuatl language was at the meeting, and he took Librado's place. Then there was a debate with the art history teacher, who wanted to teach contemporary art criticism rather than the classical art, which I thought should begin with the Olmecs, who made the giant basalt heads on the east coast of Mexico and were among the most ancient peoples in Mesoamerica. The art historian held to his list of Derrida, Foucault, Habermas, Greenberg, and Barthès, none of whom had ever written about Mesoamerican art. To ask a group of Nahuas in the town of Santa Ana Tlacotenco to discuss the wars between Clement Greenberg and Harold Rosenberg or Derrida and Habermas was insane. Having already lost Librado and the corn planter, I bowed to the superior learning of the assembled scholars and in a whisper of contrition reminded the young art historian that Clive Bell, the great British critic, had cited the Olmec work as among the most outstanding examples of "significant form."

Could we just come forward from the Olmecs to the great sculpture of the Eagle Knight or the giant figure of Coatlicue with her serpent heads and her necklace of hearts in the Anthropological Museum?

I don't know if it was Bell or the Coatlicue that convinced the young art historian; he did not speak to me again, but he nodded once and put away his reading list. Then came philosophy.

Francisco Morales Baranda had produced an interesting reading list, but I did not think his notes on the readings were entirely correct. Fortunately, Miguel León-Portilla had given me a copy of the new Spanish edition of *Aztec Thought and Culture (Filosofía Náhuatl)* the preceding day, and I still had it in my briefcase. By citing the work of the master, I was able to win Francisco over to the ideas I had learned from León-Portilla, whose work we both admired. We ended by discussing the need for integration of the disciplines, the teachers meeting regularly to marry the philosophy to the literature to the history and art. I did not think those meetings would ever take place. The news of the classes would have to be carried from one professor to the other by Herlinda Suarez Zozaya.

The next day, we went up to Milpa Alta. The city fathers had gathered all the candidates to enter the course in the main room of the library. There were perhaps seventy-five chairs set up in precise order. One lonely and patrician chair faced all the others. When I entered the room accompanied by Herlinda Suarez and the president of the Academy of the Náhautl Language, the students took their places. Herlinda made the introduction.

"We are going to learn the Socratic method," I said. "To do so, we cannot sit this way. We must sit in a circle so that we are all equal. Then we can enter into a dialogue."

There were men and women of all ages, far too many to make a proper circle. They assembled in layers, perhaps fifty in the circle and the others gathered behind. I could not imagine how it was possible to conduct a Socratic dialogue with so many students. I discussed the problem with Herlinda. "Don't worry," she said. "Not all of them will come to the course. You'll see." Since she was a tenured professor of education as well as mathematics, I shrugged and went over to my lonely chair and dragged it into a small space in the circle. "Are you all Nahuas?" I asked.

There were no dissenters.

"I am not Nahua. But I work with don Miguel León-Portilla."

As always in Mexico, Miguel's name worked magic. The students arranged themselves more formally in their chairs. To begin, I asked about the origin of the *nopales* that grew in such profusion in Milpa Alta. There was silence.

Did anyone know about a wizard?

Was the *nopal* his magic?

Finally, someone sitting in a group of chairs at the farthest reaches of the circle raised a hand. "Copil?"

Yes, the wizard's name was Copil. What happened to Copil?

Slowly, they began to tell the story of Copil, how he threatened the people, and they killed him, and tore out his heart, and buried it in the place that came to be called Tenochtitlan (the Aztec capital).

And what of his heart? Is it still there?

No, sir, the *nopal* grew from the place where his heart was buried.

And what else do you know about that *nopal*?

They saw an eagle standing on it with a snake in its beak. Our flag!

Yes, yes, and now there is a good wizard who plants many *nopales*: Francisco Morales Baranda, who will be your professor of philosophy. And he is standing right there! I pointed to Francisco, who had entered the library very quietly and stood with Herlinda beyond the circle of chairs. He and the students laughed, for everyone knew Francisco and his fields of *nopales*.

We talked some more. The professors-to-be observed the questioning with care. The students grew more comfortable with the method. There was more laughter. When I asked how many knew the work of the Great Speakers,[4] a young man stood up. He was sturdy and handsome and he stood as if he were a Nahua of that time before the Spanish invasion of Mexico. His bearing was regal, although his clothing was poor. He said he would speak in Náhuatl. His voice rose in the room. The words came slowly, clearly, each one declaimed in the ancient Náhuatl spoken in Santa Ana Tlacotenco. His voice grew louder. It became the voice of the surviving royalty of Tenochtitlan, those few who had escaped the steel of the Spaniards and the obsidian blades of their Tlaxcalan allies. It was as if the warrior/poet voice of the Great Speakers of the Aztecs had returned. He spoke with great vehemence until he came to these words, and as he spoke them, he wept. He did not lose his bearing, he did not lose the strength of his voice, yet he wept:

> *What is it then that our friends know?*
> *Suffer your unhappy heart.*
> *We are not born twice,*
> *one is not a child on this earth twice;*
> *we only depart this earth.*
>
> . . . .
>
> *Where does my heart live?*
> *Where can I make my home?*
> *Where will my house remain?*
>
> . . . .
>
> *Suffer, my heart.*

---

4   There were no Aztec kings; the ruler was known as the Great Speaker. Unlike most other indigenous groups in the Americas, the Nahuas did not call themselves "the people." *Nahua* means "clear speaker," which makes it quite reasonable for the ruler to be known as the Great Speaker.

Do not be saddened here on earth.
Perhaps this shall be my destiny.
He knows.
Perhaps I have deserved no more
than to have been born this way?
It would be good if it were so.
One does not live anywhere,
so speaks my heart.[5]

He spoke as if his words, said in the ancient way, enabled him to recall the time, the glory, the life and death and terrible existential sadness of a warrior world. He was a big man, in the full, magisterial moment of youth. It was as if by some rule of custom that he stood and all the others surrounding him sat in silence. He spoke, and they listened. The room, the seated throng, belonged to him.

In the early afternoon of that day, in the town square, hundreds of chairs were filled with students and families. There was a stage, where chairs had been placed for the dignitaries. "I cannot sit here above the people," I said to the organizer of the afternoon festivities. The others who were to sit on the stage agreed. We sat in front of the stage on the same level as the people in the audience. There were speeches and music and singing and dancing and eating and drinking, and the Clemente Course for Náhuatl Speakers was launched in Santa Ana Tlacotenco.

---

5   *Cantares Mexicanos*, fols. 31v–36r; Spanish translation, Miguel León-Portilla; English version, Sylvia and Earl Shorris, from Miguel León-Portilla. See the Song of Orphanhood in *In the Language of Kings*, pp. 173–78, quote at p. 174.

CHAPTER 13

The Block

The phone rang at three o'clock in the morning. "It's Denys Goggin calling from Sydney. Good morning to you."

"It's three o'clock in the morning; call back in six hours," I said, sure that it was a madman or a dream.

At breakfast, I told my wife about the call. She agreed that it must have been a dream. At nine o'clock the telephone rang, and there was Denys Goggin. He wanted to know when I was coming to Sydney, and for how long. He said that he had read about the Clemente Course, and he and his friends wanted to start courses in Australia. I had to be there to launch the project. The leadership of the Society of St. Vincent DePaul had been recruited to the cause of the course as part of their mission to the poor. Yet more people had to be informed, and there were funds to be raised. It was imperative that I appear in Sydney.

I told Denys that I had no talent for fund-raising, but that did not deter him. As I began to learn something about the Australian character, I realized that my promise of failure only whetted his appetite for the struggle to come. We set a date for a flight out of New York to Sydney via Los Angeles. Going to Australia on the basis of a telephone call from a man who could not figure out the time change suggested that one of us was crazy. I assured my wife that it was him. Sylvia replied that if I knew Goggin was mad and I still planned to go to Australia, I must be mad too. I conceded her point and made preparations for the trip.

Goggin said that two men, Bernard Cronin, manager of a homeless shelter, and Colin Robinson, a social scientist, would meet me at the airport upon my arrival in Sydney. They weren't there. Not at the gate and not at the baggage area. I was trying to decide whether to catch the next plane back to New York via Los Angeles or spend a few days having a look at Sydney when two men approached me. One said, "Earl?"

I nodded. Colin grabbed my suitcase, and off we went. Apparently infected by Denys Goggin's understanding of time zones, I thought I had arrived in Australia at two in the morning in New York. Since I didn't want to awaken my wife in the middle of the night, I did not phone to say that the plane had landed safely in Sydney. Instead, Cronin, Robinson, and I went directly to Charles O'Neill House, a residential shelter for homeless men.

On the way to Charles O'Neill House in Surry Hills, I tried to learn something about my partners in this venture. Bernard Cronin had been a Roman Catholic priest working in a mission in Africa, when he traveled south to Capetown on a brief holiday. Africa was a long way from his native Ireland, and Capetown was yet another journey from West Africa, where he had been working. While in Capetown, he fell in love with Dorothy, a fair and lovely woman from Botswana. Bernard left the priesthood, married Dorothy, and the two of them fled to a distant continent where they believed a mixed-race couple, a divorced woman of East Africa and a defrocked Irish Catholic priest, could find happiness. Unlike the many tales of poverty, prison, and orphanhood that characterize the Australian settlement, this one had a happy beginning. Dorothy found work using her skills and Bernard found a job using his: he became the head of a homeless shelter.

When last I saw them, Bernard said that they were leaving in a few weeks for Ireland and then on to Botswana. His parents had never met Dorothy and Dorothy's parents had not met Bernard Cronin. He did not know how the middle-class families in Ireland or Botswana would react. Although it was never easy to read Bernard's feelings, I think he was looking forward to the surprise.

Colin Robinson had been one of the tens of thousands of "home children"—orphans, street urchins, or simply poor children unwanted by their parents—who were sent out from England and Scotland to Australia to provide "white stock" to settle the continent. Many of these migrant children had been abused or turned into slave labor.[1] If I recall correctly, Colin was ten years old when he arrived in Australia. He was a handsome man when I met him, with rounded features and a more gentle and compassionate air than Cronin, who approached suffering in a stern and businesslike manner. Colin could speak easily in the Australian style, glad to say good on ya or call someone mate, but the language of England, pronounced with a wellborn accent, was his comfort. Bernard had the diction of a religious touched with just enough Irish to make it capable of forgiveness. As we drove out to the shelter, they outlined an agenda for my stay and explained the nature of O'Neill House, which was a very special kind of shelter. The men who stayed there, often straight out of prison, were expected to quickly find work and be integrated into society.

There was another, much larger men's shelter we would visit later in the week that did not boast such hope. This other shelter resembled nothing so much as drawings of Bedlam at its worst. I did not think there was anything I could do there. The Clemente

---

1   The practice began in the seventeenth century and continued until the 1960s. Children were sent in large numbers to Canada, South Africa, and other British colonies, as well as Australia. British prime minister Gordon Brown finally apologized for the practice in 2010. It had begun in 1618 with one hundred children shipped to the Virginia Colony.

Course required some minimum of order. Many of the men in the large shelter were unwilling or unable to sit through a half-hour television program. I asked Bernard if we could arrange brief lectures or round table discussions for groups of the men, and the man who could be as stern as ice looked at me with Miltonian sweetness. I soon began to think that he and Peter Howard and many of the other people I came to know in Sydney truly believed that Paradise can be regained.

I am less convinced of the fall of angels than they are, and even more dubious about the existence of Paradise, but there are places like Charles O'Neill House that give rise to hopes. The four-story building in a quiet, middle-class neighborhood housed about forty men in three stages of rehabilitation and a final stage of preparation for work and life outside the shelter. The rules were mainly the rules of reason: cleanliness, order, sobriety, and a modicum of hope in the future. Outward signs of racism, which is a powerful aspect of Australian life, were not evident. One of the men who worked and taught in Charles O'Neill House was Clarence Slockee, who is a member of the Mindjingbal clan of the Bundjalung tribe of Aboriginals. Clarence could play the Aboriginal instrument, the *didjeridu*,[2] sing Aboriginal songs, and perform Aboriginal dances. By working as a member of the staff at O'Neill House, he changed the character of the shelter, made it Australia and a part of the people. He is a strong and very graceful man, married to a pretty blond woman and the father of a beautiful child, then an infant girl, who came to O'Neill House with her mother, providing a streak of normalcy as well as a glow of physical beauty that I had never seen in larger shelters.

---

2   The hollowed-out trunk of a small tree, usually eucalyptus, fitted with a beeswax mouthpiece. Instruments are often two feet long—the longer the instrument the lower the pitch of the sound. The *didjeridu* has been in use for more than a thousand years by indigenous people in Australia.

I agreed to spend much of my time in Australia at O'Neill House. I liked Bernard and Colin, and I found Clarence both charming and talented. A Clemente Course would be formed by these men; I had no doubt of that. They had read a piece of *New American Blues* in *Harper's* magazine and the mainly theoretical *Riches for the Poor*, but were lacking the sense of belief that comes of seeing the uneducated but literate adult poor in dialogue about the foundational works of culture. We talked to some of the men about the course and asked them to read the Allegory of the Cave in preparation for the first class, which was to be held the following day. Some of the men volunteered to join the class, but not all; it was not compulsory.

On the way back to the hotel where I was to stay, we talked about O'Neill House, the Vincentians, the course, faculty, and the always present weight upon teaching the poor: money. Australia was like Indiana or Connecticut or Cuernavaca in that respect; the people who wanted to start a Clemente Course had no quarrel with the idea of paying teachers. They understood it as a way to distinguish education from charity: when the teachers were paid, we could make demands on the faculty and even replace them if it became necessary. Besides that, we believed that good teachers deserved to be paid for their work. They would raise the money if I would agree to be the show.

When I checked into the hotel, I was surprised to find that my understanding of time on the far side of the international date line was no better than Denys Goggin's. I had miscounted by eight hours. My wife was in a panic; Qantas confirmed that the flight had landed, but would not say who was on board. The hotel had no record of anyone by my name. My wife knew the family tale of her husband having been listed as MIA and his father responding to the news with something less than alarm: "He'll turn up." This time, she was sure I was dead. The message she left at the hotel, in the event

I "turned up," began with the word "Urgent." I thought something terrible must have happened to her. She had returned the favor.

A few days later, I met Denys Goggin at Vincentian House. We shook hands, and he apologized again for having awakened me at three in the morning. "I don't see how anyone could make such an error," I said, and told him why my wife was not speaking to me.

The schedule, which had seemed daunting at first, grew hourly. We were to drive through the scorched miles of blackened scrub forest on the journey from Sydney to a Campbelltown housing project for the poor, to meet with the people who ran the project in the hope that they would start a Clemente Course. Clarence had arranged a meeting with leaders of the Aboriginal community and a visit to "The Block," an area within sight of the center of Sydney that had been occupied by the poorest Aborigines since they had first contended with the invaders for control of the continent. Most of the slum housing had been torn down, and the government was building a community center in the area. All that remained to be cleared was the small patch known as The Block.

On my second day in Sydney, we went back to Charles O'Neill House, where Bernard had been teaching an abbreviated version of the Clemente Course; really, something of his own devising. Students had been studying art, and they had read a few stories, but the more demanding curriculum of a "full" Clemente Course—history, philosophy, logic, and a more rigorous reading of literature—had not been attempted. I had hoped to teach a first philosophy class, but it had been put off for a day; instead, I was given some time to wander through the facility on my own, talking with men who were not yet out in the community learning the skills required to rejoin the workforce. On an upper floor of the building, where the men lived in rows of cubicles, I saw two sturdy figures in identical dark blue trousers and white shirts engaged in an intense conversation, not standing face to face but talking around a thick piece of wood that anchored the common wall of two cubicles. The dark blue trousers and white shirts were part of the standard issue to men leaving Australian prisons. The strange positioning of the discussants around a thick wooden post came of a house rule: the men were not allowed to enter each other's cubicles.

I stopped to eavesdrop, perhaps to join the conversation. When I drew closer to the men, I saw the swollen darkness of exhaustion around their eyes. Perhaps they had just come out of prison or had worked all through the night at some difficult job. Bernard had told me that some came out of prison in their blue trousers and white shirts and went directly to work, or spent their first days and nights walking the streets of the city, enjoying even the weariness after months or years in prison.

As I stood there, the argument went round and round and came back again and again to the role of a son when his father could well have caused the death of an innocent man. I thought it must have involved a well-known Australian murder case and that the men were interested because of their recent stay in prison. Nonetheless, the case seemed strangely familiar. The man had died in captivity after being accused of murder himself.

"That's not what it said," one of the men argued.

"You know that a man will say anything in his own defense."

"But the gods . . ."

I interrupted to ask what they had been reading, who had said what to whom.

"Plato," the younger and apparently stronger of the two men answered.

"Nah," said the other, who was taller and had a shock of pale brown hair that fell off one ear when he shook his head. "Plato never said a thing. It was Socrates did the talking."

I asked if they had been reading a dialogue with Euthyphro. They said they had read it early on the previous night.

"Weren't you supposed to be reading the Allegory of the Cave? And if you had time, weren't you just to have a look at the *Apology*?"

"Can't do it that way, mate," said the taller one. "It's the murder that it's about in the beginning."

They had been reading and arguing all night. After they downloaded the first dialogue from the Internet and printed it out with the O'Neill House machine, they read it quickly, and went on to the next. At breakfast, they continued their dialogue. Once satisfied with their understanding of coming out of the cave into the light, they had gone on to the trial of Socrates, then backtracked to read the dialogue on the porch of King Archon.

"Did you decide that you are pious men?" I asked.

"Because we love Jesus," said the shorter one.

"Because Jesus loves us," said the other.

I laughed, and they followed with louder laughter, and began talking at the same time in Australian accents so thick I would have had trouble understanding them if they had been speaking singly. They had not only read the dialogue, they had read commentaries on it, and they had picked up enough from their reading to be able to translate the dilemma into contemporary terms. I told them that they were already excellent students, and the shorter of the two looked at me with the countinghouse eyes of a man who had spent years in prison and called me "mate," and for some reason I felt deeply uncomfortable, as if something very bad was about to happen. And it was, but it would not be the fault of the man with the countinghouse glance.

Clarence Slockee arranged a meeting with a group of Aboriginal people at which he played the *didjeridu* and Sue Green, a young professor at New South Wales University, spoke of her Aboriginal ancestry and the suffering she had endured because she was a mixed-race child. We sat in a large circle. I spoke briefly about the Clemente Course and then listened as one Aborigine after another spoke of the racism that had been inflicted upon him or her. At the time, the Sydney police were still using photographs of Aborigines for target practice, and the school system was geared to maintain urban Aborigines in poverty.

I was anxious to teach Aboriginal people in the towns and out in the countryside. When I asked Clarence about teaching on The Block, he said we would go there the following day. "Maintaining indigenous languages is an important part of the Clemente Course," I said, referring him to an essay I had written about the loss to human culture with the disappearance of languages. It would be vital in Australia, where languages were disappearing at an astonishing rate.[3]

The next day, Clarence took me to Eveleigh Street on the east side of The Block,[4] where his aged aunt still lived in a small tenement row house. There were plans to tear down all the houses on the street, which faced the railroad tracks, but Clarence's aunt refused to move out of her house. The old woman was not welcoming, but she was willing to talk for a while, assured by Clarence's presence that I was no danger to her continued residence on The Block. I asked her about teaching in the neighborhood. She thought it would be a good idea, but when I inquired about which language to teach, the woman—who was very old and had dark brown wizened skin—said there were so many languages spoken on The Block that people could only speak to one another in English.

Then we were quiet for a while, until a car passed in the open area beside the tracks, moving at high speed, throwing a cloud of

---

3   When whites settled in Australia, there were at least 500 distinct languages spoken on the continent, perhaps as many as 700. About 120 remain, and 100 of those have so few speakers they are unlikely to survive for more than another generation.

4   The Block is not one block but an entire neighborhood in the Redfern section of Sydney. The land has become valuable because of its proximity to the center of the city.

dust into the dry air behind it. We stood in the shade thrown by her house, chatting aimlessly again. I looked past her, through the open door into her rooms. Hers was a Christian house, distinguished from the original world by a cross on the wall, and separated from the naked scrub country of the outback by a small couch that sat low and legless on the floor, once of many colors, many shades, now faded with age, like her dress, like the light that had once been in her skin. The old woman had come from another millennium and settled on The Block, which had become a dangerous slum and now a prize to be taken by the real estate developers. She and I spoke across many centuries while small trains passed in the background and more cars threw dust into the air as they passed, bumping and bouncing high on the holes in Eveleigh Street.

Two young Aboriginal women came along to talk about a community center they were building in the interior of The Block. A large area had already been leveled in preparation. These were the ladies of urban renewal, and the old woman who refused to move from her house only tolerated them because of Clarence and Colin Robinson and me. After a time, we had no more to say to the old lady, and we walked up the slight hill on Eveleigh Street to the junction with the main road at the top. Two very large people sat on beach chairs in the shade of a row of great and leafy trees. They were slightly drunk. The woman's blouse was unbuttoned, exposing her breasts. The man leaned his great weight forward and began asking questions. I had already been warned about people like them on The Block. They were mean and liked to fight, especially with strangers. And they carried knives.

When I first stood in front of them, the man and woman raised their beer cans, which were wrapped in brown paper bags, and made ferocious grimaces. The man stuck out his tongue, like a Maori warrior. I considered sticking out my tongue in return, but refrained, thinking it might be some form of accepting a challenge.

He and the woman asked a few gentle questions of our little group, then he focused on me, and his questions were aggressive: Where was I from? What was I doing there? Did I have connections to the police? Why did I want to teach Aborigines? Or any poor people? What business was it of mine? Didn't I know they already had a school on The Block?

He insisted that they were not drinking alcohol as they lifted the cans of beer to their mouths. I said that I would buy them each a can of something non-alcoholic if they would tell me something about The Block. They produced three cans of beer from under the low bench where they sat. I said that I did not drink while I was working, but that I would drink one later in their honor. My sense was that if we were ever to have a course on The Block, it would have to meet with the approval of this huge pair, bloated and half drunk by the middle of the day. One of the urban renewal ladies later confirmed the role of the guardians of The Block. I told the urban renewal women it would be best to wait until the community center was built; The Block, at least for the moment, was not the best place to begin.

Classes began at Charles O'Neill House. I visited along with Christine Crimmins at a shelter for women suffering from mild dementia in their old age. The women, who wore pale print housedresses and had pale, puffy faces, smiled when they were not drifting. We talked about poetry and philosophy. I do not know what they understood, but they seemed pleased, and Christine and I were both happy. She and I visited later that day at a food kitchen for homeless men, and it was not quite so pleasant. One man taunted the others in a threatening way. A German had harsh words for a timid fellow who said he had been to college but seemed unable to explain why he preferred to live on the street. The German was wiry and just entering middle age, the college man was very pale and trembled. While we were talking, the German reached over and took a piece of meat from the college man's plate. I told the German that was bad behavior, and he looked at me out of the coldest eyes and offered to pull the meat out of his mouth. I looked at Christine, who is a slim and very delicate woman, and feared for her safety, but she seemed unafraid.

We visited with the leadership of the St. Vincent DePaul Society the following day. I told them about the Clemente Course, and they were polite and full of questions. I thought there was no doubt that we would have a full Clemente Course the very next year in Australia, but the problem—the very bad thing I had sensed was coming—happened soon after I left Australia. The management of the Society of St. Vincent DePaul changed, and the decision was made to end the brief versions of the Clemente Course Bernard Cronin had been teaching at Charles O'Neill House. Bernard left O'Neill House. Colin Robinson and his son made a film about homeless men in Sydney, and without steady work, he and his wife and son left for England.

While in Australia, I had agreed to do what I could to help secure funding for the Clemente Course in Australia, including an interview by Sky television, the network partially owned by Rupert Murdoch. We arranged for the interview to take place at Charles O'Neill House. The network said that one of its leading interviewers would be talking with me. I expected someone who might have been on Public Broadcasting in the United States, which is not what Mr. Murdoch has in mind when he programs television in Australia. A youngish woman in severe blouse and pants, every bit a match for her dark and intent look, came into the room, followed by a cameraman. Were it not for the fact that the woman was wearing no makeup and needed to comb her hair, which was long and straight yet fell in tangles, I would have thought she was the interviewer. Moments later, another woman entered the room. She walked carefully on high heels, not mincing as models do, but graceful, with a full stride. I told her my name. She did not catch it. She told me her name. I was not interested.

The first woman, apparently the producer and director, reached into her case and took out a mirror, a brush, a small makeup kit, and handed them to the star, who took pains to enhance what I had thought was perfection. When she had finished, she handed everything back to the producer and took a seat on a chair no more than a foot from my knee. She smiled. Everything about her was perfect, but not in the way the *Venus de Milo* is perfect. The perfection that smiled at me was not made of divine marble. It was proximate and perfumed and made of glass.

The cameraman adjusted a light, stepped back, spoke to the producer, who signaled to the interviewer who had been studying notes on a yellow pad the producer handed to her. She said my name, and the name of the shelter, then asked why I had come to Australia. When I had finished my answer, careful to keep it brief, the cameraman stopped, and the producer wrote out the next question and handed it to the interviewer, who read it very slowly, put the yellow pad on her lap; the cameraman nodded to the producer, who signaled the interviewer, who read the question, asking me something or other about the Clemente Course. Again, I answered as briefly as I could, the camera stopped, the interviewer handed the pad to the producer, who wrote out the next question, and handed it to the interviewer, who read it slowly, laid the pad on her lap, and asked the question.

After my answer, the cameraman changed positions so that he was now filming the interviewer. Meanwhile, the interviewer handed the pad to the producer, who wrote out the next question and handed it to the interviewer. The sequence was repeated again and again. Not once did the great beauty ask a question that the producer had not written on a yellow pad. I was dumbfounded, stumbling over my words as I engaged in conversation with a ventriloquist's dummy. At the end of the interview the producer handed the pad to the dummy, who read something about thank you, her name, and the name of the program. The producer thanked me, the cameraman turned off the camera, and while he packed up the equipment, the woman of glass stood up, smiled, and walked out of O'Neill House.

I asked the producer why she had not done the interview herself. She told me she had been an on-camera interviewer and news reader for a long time, but now she was a producer. "Is this the way the network treats women?" I asked.

She looked away, across the room, to the cameraman who was packing up the last of the equipment. When she turned back to me, I saw the resignation of a woman who had crossed a boundary line into another kind of life. She said, "I like being a producer."

On the way back to the United States I told my seat mate, a pilot who flew a personal jet for a Hong Kong businessman, about the strange encounter with the Sky Network interviewer. He told me that everyone in Australia knew her; she was a national joke. I wondered how I would have behaved had I been let in on the joke. Would I have let slip a cruel word or made an expression of sarcasm that harmed the chances to start a Clemente Course? I turned to thinking of the touch of resignation in the face of the producer. I had already passed that time in life; I could be compassionate.

On my next to last day in Australia, I gave a talk at Sydney Grammar, which is a fine private school, with a huge auditorium, in the very heart of the city. Several hundred people showed up, making their way through a crowd of pickets who were opposed to the war in Iraq. Instead of beginning the talk with a joke or even thanks to the people who had been so kind to me, I talked about my opposition to the American bombing and invasion of Iraq. If there was anyone among the hundreds of people in the auditorium who disagreed, that person gave no sign. Afterward, there was the usual wine and cheese, and one of the men who had been up all night reading Plato—the sturdier one—came up to me and said that he had been to the art museum before coming to Sydney Grammar. "I was afraid to go in there before, because I saw those women in their fine clothes, and I thought it was only for them, but now I'm studying the humanities and I can go in anywhere, even with the best of them."

I knew by then that Colin and Bernard were not going to be the founders of the Clemente Course in Australia, which left me feeling that I had wasted time and money in pursuit of something too difficult and too distant. I remained fond of them despite my unhappiness. We had a grand farewell dinner in a lovely restaurant across Darling Harbour, and promised to stay in touch. The next morning, I gathered up my *didjeridu*, clapsticks, and boomerangs, and headed home. It was over.

The persons who were missing at the dinner were Jude Butcher, who headed the School of Education, and Peter Howard, a professor at Australian Catholic University (ACU),[5] and the organizations that were missing were the Society of St. Vincent DePaul, which had decided that short versions of the Clemente Course were not useful, and Mission Australia, which has been serving the urban and rural poor of the country for more than 150 years.

Peter and Jude Butcher, a Christian Brother, began the Australian Clemente Courses at Vincentian Village a year after I left the country. They were able to secure funding from the Sisters of Charity and the Sydney City Council. Both Peter and Jude insisted that

---

5   Australian Catholic University is a public university funded by the government and open to students of all religions.

the classes be small and the teaching rigorous. Peter has become the center of the course in Australia, and he has proved to have a great talent both for disseminating the idea and for keeping the rigor of the original intent. It takes several years for a student to complete the course of study in Australia. Each subject is taught intensively in turn. There are now two courses in Surry Hills, where it began at O'Neill House, and one each in Brisbane, Newcastle, Campbell-town, Canberra, Melbourne, Ballarat, Adelaide, and Perth. Edith Cowan University, Ballarat University, and Flinders University have joined ACU in teaching, and United Way and a dozen other organizations are involved in the work.

Jude and I had a brief visit when he passed through San Francisco on his way to work in Arizona. I have never met Peter, although we work together via e-mail, and speak occasionally by phone when I can figure out what time it is in Sydney. Much of our communication is about Aborigines, because both Peter and I think it is vital to begin teaching out in those parts of Australia far from the cities and towns. People who work out there speak of the "grog problem," but I think it is perhaps a matter of prudishness as well as alcoholism. Peter, who has a genius for organization and a deep commitment to the positive effect of the humanities on the poor, will start courses for the Aborigines, I'm sure. He is a scholarly and gentle man, and I have come to think of him as a friend. It is a long time since I have been to Australia, and I would like to go back, to see old friends and get to know some of the people who have gone on from Clemente Australia to university. One day, perhaps. I have not heard from Bernard or Colin for a long time. It is difficult to know what work they are doing now, even with the ability of Internet search engines to locate people. Bernard Cronin is the name of several people well known in Australia and in Australian history. There are 265,000 entries for Colin Robinson on Google. He and Bernard are lost to me.

CHAPTER 14

The Happiest Person
Living in Poverty

This was a conversation in 2011 among graduates of the course in Salt Lake City, Utah.

We were organized around a small table in one part of a large room. I put a small tape recorder in the center of the table, explaining that I was no longer able to make notes very quickly as I could when I was young. The women did not object.

As I listened to them, I thought how they all lived under one roof in different houses, and the idea of the binding by the humanities occupied me so deeply that I lost my concentration and was only awakened to the moment by the intensity of the stare of the women who sat across from me. Although I am a writer of fiction as well as making attempts to understand the world through essays and reportage, it is impossible to write here about the inner lives of these women except as they tell it. If this were fiction, I could tell you everything you want to know. It is not. You and I will have to make do with what the women said. Some of them want to tell their thoughts and find that there is a barrier to making them public. Others hold closely all that simmers and sometimes boils below the surface. It will be for you as it is for me to think with them about their lives and how they were affected by the humanities. If there is too little said here, it may be that I do not think it is my place to probe. The women came to talk about the Clemente Course, which is called Venture in Oregon. They came to talk because the course succeeded for them, and because Jean Cheney, who founded the courses in Utah, asked them to come. Their trust in her and affection for her is well placed. They know.

Amy began. She is a straightforward woman, who puts away her own life in a safe place. It is an academic discussion for her: she is careful to tell me what she thinks I want to hear; that is, she answers the question I pose—"Can you tell me about your experience in the course?" Whenever she feels the momentary lack of a name or an idea, she asks the others, drawing them into her conversation, socializing, bonding, winning them over to her. The first of the women to speak, she opened the dialogue for all the others.

"I've been out of school for a very long time and I was intimidated to go back," she said. "I know I'm not that old [thirty-seven], but I was intimidated and I kind of wanted to try out my wings and see where I was as far as school. This was a self-help thing for me. It gave me the confidence to know that I can read and be analytical about things, that I can write papers, that I'm right on course with everything, that I have a pretty good voice. The professors were so wonderful—the beauty that we saw in art history, Jeff [Metcalf]'s literature class, books read in a different way—his sense of humor is amazing. The process of looking at others' writing and being critical of it first, and then looking at your own, breaking down what you read. . . . And Jack—you can't say enough about Professor Newell. I'm in love with the man—he's so beautiful: he just gives you the other side for history and how you look at the humanity of everything, not just rote memorization of date after date after date. And Bridget [Newell] with philosophy, that was a course I had a little trouble with, because—I don't know. I love looking at things. I love analyzing them, but that took me a longer time than the other classes to find my footing.

"It wasn't Socrates, it wasn't Plato. I can't remember the first one we read. 'What makes the good life?' And I can't remember who wrote that. It was an interesting piece that I connect with the end piece: the happiness piece by Keats [?Ode to a Nightingale] was a lot more meaningful to me, perhaps the discussions in the class. It took me a while to like that class, but that class taught a way to look at things differently. It was life-altering for me. And I have a full sense of confidence now."

A second woman, Greta, was released from the strictures of sitting with a stranger by Amy's request for help. Greta is very blond, and slim. She looks more like a high school cheerleader than a woman who is raising two children. There was a sense of regret in the sound of her voice and in the way she spoke. If there was also bitterness, it came only when she spoke of love. Then her speech was clipped, as is often the case when people speak of a world that could have been otherwise.

It was difficult to understand her name, which she strangled when she pronounced it. "I just divorced my last name," she said. "Just barely. I've kept it for my children." And that seemed calming for her. "I've always wanted to go to college," she said. "I always thought that was right for me, and the course was just the first step back in. Straight out of high school I met a guy who was on drugs. For a couple of years I tried to help him. For a couple of years. I tried to help him, and I joined in. I got off drugs and he stayed on drugs, and it was just not feasible. "I was really, really weak."

The other women would not accept her opinion of herself. "I think she's strong," they said to me, speaking in almost perfect unison.

"I was never hooked on 'em," Greta said. "I was hooked on him, not on the drugs, but it's far worse."

Dacia arrived then. There was some banter, and then Greta went on, talking about her children, "I think it was great that they

saw me doing something for me. They saw how much I value education. [The children] are three and five, and my five-year-old loves
my art books. And he loves going to the art museums now, loves it.

"I hashed out a lot of my past, writing. I got a lot of stuff out
of me that I just held in forever. It was writing and the literature.
I think it was the combination of both that brought it out. I have
a favorite poet: Langston Hughes. There's a piece, 'Mother to Son.'
That's just been my poem for a long time."

The women began a general discussion of poetry, speaking
about Shelley and Wordsworth. Abruptly, they moved to [Sandra
Cisneros's] *The House on Mango Street*, a book they liked but found
simplistic. Hilda, a Latina, said that her Cuban mother objected
to the book because of the poor quality of the Spanish. "I remember going to the library, and the books smelled so good, the old
books. We used to save up Coca-Cola bottles and buy a paperback
for seventy-five cents. I always loved books."

Dacia said that she is Navaho. She said that Dacia is not a
Navaho name and she does not know Diné, the Navaho language.
"I'm a poet," she said in the flat, unaccented tones of the mountain
West. "I do it [poetry] all the time. I'm a full-time student at the
University of Utah. I graduated from high school. When I started
in college, I flunked out. I wanted to study social work, and it trig-
gered a lot of things. And nobody told me that would be natural, so
I fell into depression and flunked out, and never went back. I tried
to go back after my son was born, and no college would take me
back." Dacia speaks precisely, tightly. She is precise about herself:
she carries notebooks, her hair is tied into neat, tight corn rows.
Her gaze is unwavering; she tests people with her gaze, challenging
them to leave an opening for her angers. She is offputting, aggressive, and yet very winning.

"They said, 'You need to rectify this (all of my Fs from that
one semester) somehow.' And nobody helped me out. I was really

ashamed. They sent me to the school counselor, and she asked me a question: 'If you could have anything right now, what would you do?'

"And I said, 'I'm goin' to school.'

"And she said, 'I don't know what's going to happen, because there are plenty of colleges that won't take you.'

"And I said, 'Well, I'm goin' to school.' So I went to the city library and there was a poster there for the Venture [Clemente] Program, and it was like a week before the deadline and I submitted my application. I remember being at the Post Office, and I kissed it, and I sent it, and as soon as Jean [Cheney] got it, she called me—it was three o'clock the next day that I got the call, and she said, 'I'd like to interview you. Will you come in?'

"So that was how I got in. And from there, everybody was 'You need to go to college, you need to go to college.'

"I don't know if I can, because the course was at Westminster [we were meeting in a room at Westminster College], and it's a small campus. And I thought, 'I won't get lost there. And if I do, somebody will notice.' So I got here, applied here, all my scholarships were coming here. And Jeff had prompted me to apply for women's research at the university [University of Utah], and I did, just to make him happy, because I really liked this a lot. And I got a scholarship, and I called the man and said, 'I'm not goin' to the university; give it to somebody else.' It was summer 2007, just before school started, and the director of the women's research center, whom I know, called me and said, 'We've got money for you.'

" 'And I'm not goin' there. I'm gonna drown; nobody will know, nobody will care.'

"She said, 'Just come talk to me.' And I love her, respect her, so I go, 'I'll come talk to you.' I got up there; she goes, 'You know, we have child care.' Because my son was like two. And my schedule here was like everybody else's schedule, and it was really hard. And she said, 'Here at the university, you can create your own community.' And I was intrigued, because I never had a community before, and she sold me on that. So I jumped ship at Westminster and went to the university for the past four years.

"I'll graduate—hopefully, next year, or the year after that. My degree is a question. I thought college was going to be like this, like here, in the [Clemente] program. And it's not. It's really hard. I'm a brown body in a white institution. It's written into policy, it's written into everything. There's a lot of racism in this state. I had to drop from a couple of semesters because of depression."

I asked if they gave her trouble because they thought she was an immigrant. For a moment, she was puzzled, then she laughed.

The women encouraged her. Every one of them was either in college or starting the next year. Hilda, one of the last women to speak, said that she was going to a tech school to learn to be a computer programmer. "I had always wanted to go to school, but then from 2002 on my husband fell ill, and he just started going downhill, and I just totally lost hope, really, and a friend of mine at church introduced me to the Venture Program. She says, 'Hilda, you know that you should go back to school,' and I go *bababa*, you know me around young kids and all. I just totally lost hope, and I did as she did: I went over there, and I had seen some pictures of past students and I said, 'Wow, I'd really love to be around the school and learning again.'

"And I did the application over the Internet, which was very long, like two hours long, and I forgot about it and Jennifer [Bauman] called me in for an interview. I came in, and I was like, 'Wow! You considered me.' I came in, and she said right away, 'You're the type of person we need in our program.' And from that day, it's like something awoke in me. I was so energetic that day. I cleaned everything. I just started to dream and hope again, and when I started classes, I found myself crying all the time and having difficulty. The assignment was to make something artful and I could just sit there, and nothing was coming, and I was, like, 'What is wrong with me? My mother was a painter, I used to paint with her. I was a musician. What's wrong with me?' And I discovered that I was dead. I was dead inside and I had to find somehow just to get out of there and break through.

"And what she says is, 'Hilda, start doing something. Just do anything. Doodles, cut out things in magazines and put them together.' And that's what I did. And as time went on . . . I remember when we got into the modern art, I remember crying because we have got to the limits in art, there's no new movement, nothing. And I felt like, 'Wow! This can't be. What else is there to do?' and I remember that hit me strong. And in the critical writing class, I cried a lot too. At one instant I had to walk out."

She looked over at Greta, the thin blond woman who had talked about getting off drugs. Hilda said, "You brought back part of my life, too. I was involved in drugs when I was in the military and he was in the military. And I didn't know he was on drugs for like three years. And he was shooting up, and when you said that, I could transcend from like here to there. When I was young, right out of college, my grandfather committed suicide right on the street in San Francisco. . . .

"I had a boyfriend I could not get away from. I worked at Lerner's downtown, and I had to have my friends [keep him away from me] when I went out and got on a bus. He would climb up three-story windows and into my apartment, crazy, and I just completely broke down in college. I thought something was wrong with me. I went into an emergency room, and they thought I was drinking and they tested me for drugs. And finally, this nice intern came in and asked what was happening. And I was hyperventilating. I had like panic attacks.

"I tried to go to school and I couldn't. I was so embarrassed, I would talk about it in class, talk about all these issues. It was a traumatic experience for me. And then when I tried to go back, it was buried under this non-confidence. I can't do it.

"I really shut down. I was really close to my grandfather, but I really shut down for four or five years, and I had my kids at the end of that depression. It took me a long time. This program was great for me, because I got to look into other people's stories, and I saw that my ship is not alone on the ocean. You don't get that in a regular college course. You're not close to people in a regular college course, you're one among hundreds and hundreds. You're like a tiny little minnow in a big pond, and I just wasn't ready for that experience. That was really daunting for me. This was a course in humanities."

There was a silence, and then Dacia read a poem.

Dear Judith,
I know you emailed me cuz I need some mentoring
I need some mentoring from a brown girl
Grown into a brown woman
With brown feet to match
Brown feet that have danced and walked and dragged a brown
    body through institution after institution
Searching for that PhD at the end of the undergrad and
    Master's tunnel

Dear Dr. Flores,
I need some mentoring
Woman to woman
brown speaking brown
calloused hand with matching calloused heart
Reaching out for me

Today I do not require mentoring on my CV or Personal
    Statement
Today I need to know how you did it

Dr. Judith Flores Carmona,
How did you do it?
I need to know
follow that trail
so that I too can earn the
P
H
muthafuckin **D**
after my name
add accreditation to my game
have a semblance of validity when I begin to spout
the same truth that walked and stalked this brown girl down
    the halls of

                    preschool
                    elementary
                    jr high and
                    high schools
                    and Here
                    and Here
                    and Here

Body twisting as I
Braid the power of fear, rage and pain so I can
Break the halls of brick and glass that litter my academic
    assimilation

Dr. Judith Flores Carmona,
I need some mentoring

How did you make it?
How did you get up everyday and walk into an institution that
     tried to spit you out?
that tried to bleed your tongue
that never held its tongue
never passed up an opportunity to knock you off balance and
     into a spin

Please Judith
Don't tell me
"Oh, that never happened to me."
Don't resort to the pat response of
"Well, the Academy does things differently . . . dot, dot, dot"
Please don't tell me that my wounds aren't real
that someday it won't hurt as much
Or that I should grow thicker skin
Or that I'm too emotional
Or that I am not really wounded
Or that the Academy isn't really out for my blood

Yes yes yes
I know
there *are* safe spaces
                    Sparse
                     and
          f a r   b e t w e e n

How did you pick yourself up when you realized those
bootstraps weren't real?
Pick yourself up enough to seek the heat of another body
Whose arms were open to you

and would shield you
> soft and warm
while you tended to those wounds
or
did you find those arms?

Please, Doctor,
I need your expertise,
and please,

don't tease me.

In the weeks before I went to Utah, Barbra had sent me a letter telling about her experience in the course and something about herself. It was a well-written letter, interesting to read, and I thought it would suffice to reproduce all or part of it here. Nonetheless, I pushed the tape recorder to the end of the table where Barbra sat, for it would have been unkind to leave her out of the conversation after she had made the effort to come to talk with me. Had I not given her the chance to speak, the most astonishing story of a life in Utah would have remained unspoken and I would not have come to admire a woman's courage in terrifying circumstances.

Barbra is a big woman who gives the impression of great physical strength. She carries her weight around her hips, and when she sits, she sits very straight so that she seems taller than she is. Her clothes were loose-fitting, and they had a wholesome look about them: big prints, bright colors, American agricultural women's clothing. She was a handsome twentieth-century woman in nineteenth-century clothing in 2011. She had made up her face, rouged her cheeks, and accentuated her features. She had dressed for company.

"I like to say that my life started ten years ago. What an amazing adventure! I'm so so fortunate. You know, I'm probably the happiest woman living in poverty. I don't know if Jean [Cheney] told you, but I was raised in a polygamous cult. I wasn't a pretty girl so I wasn't wanted for marriage. At least not right away, so I was given in payment for a dental debt, and the dentist did what he wanted to me to pay for the debt of drilling other people's teeth, and so I had to suffer through teeth that rotted and fell out, because I was a throwaway child, not one of the ones that was wanted for marriage.

"Eventually, I was married off to someone who needed a dishwasher, and I kept thinking, at least I'm wanted for something. But I didn't think I was worth a whole lot, [thought] that there was something wrong with me because I was born with a giant question mark in my head. God put it there and it got me into nothing but trouble. I would ask my dad why he hit my mom. What did she do wrong? And then he would quit hurting her and hurt me instead for defying his Christian authority, because you're not supposed to ask questions of your father. That's against the rules. That's not respecting him.

"I lived in this very odd world where there wasn't a United States. There wasn't freedom. And the best you could hope for if you weren't one of the favorite kids was that when you died, maybe you could make it up to heaven where your workload would be lighter. If you made it to heaven, you probably wouldn't be punished as much, you wouldn't be beaten as much. Maybe life would be happy in heaven, but it was absolutely acceptable that you would be miserable your entire life. That was called 'enduring to the end.' So it was normal to be unhappy. In fact, if you were laughing, people would wonder why, that you weren't addressing your duties, you weren't being faithful, you weren't working hard. And I worked as hard

as anybody, but man, I had this question mark in my head. There
were so many things that didn't make sense.

"It didn't make sense that when friends of mine turned fifteen
or sixteen and noticed a girl and would smile at her that they would
be punished by being taken to the desert, and they never came
back. And we all knew that they probably died out there, but boys
weren't allowed to compete with the Prophet for women. And if
they dared to compete with the Prophet for women or smile at a
girl, that was punishable by death. It wasn't real death, it was sort of
death. They would take the boys out to the middle of the desert and
take off their shoes and not give 'em food or water and leave them
there. And if they managed to get out alive, they were allowed to
live and maybe to marry someone like me. And if they died, it was
God's will. And I've heard excuses always to why life didn't matter.
It was always under God's will.

"I found I didn't like God very much and I found I hated men a
whole lot, because they were so mean and I didn't see why they had
to be. If someone just asked me nicely, I would do anything. And
there was one incredible day when my dad was . . . I thought he was
gonna kill my mom. I had been married once and the man was so
drunk I was allowed to be disassociated with him and assigned to a
different husband. I was so tired of hurting, and when I saw my dad
trying to hurt my mom again I was in his face about it: 'You *will* not
hurt her; she's hurt enough.' And maybe part of me was screaming
that I deserved to not have pain for one day too, but of course he
just replaced me again for her until she begged him not to kill me.

"This fight took place in the commons so everyone saw him
beat me. I guess he was mean enough that finally elders asked him
about his punishment style. Leaving bruises is one thing, but nearly
killing someone is something else. And my dad decided that I was
the reason for all of the discontent. I kept asking him questions. So
he decided the best thing to do was to make me have a broken heart

and a contrite spirit. If you can break the will of someone, then they're teachable to do what they're commanded to do. So they decided to kill my son in front of me.

"And in this God was hilariously kind to me. It was the middle of winter, and they have to make some things look like accidents otherwise the police get a little bit too inquisitive. So they had two people holding his arms [her son's] outstretched and my uncle was in the van that was racing down the street to run him over. Everybody would witness: oh, what a tragic accident. But they decided that if they killed one of my children, then I would do anything to save the others, and they would finally have me quiet.

"My uncle was a little arrogant. He drives a more sporty car, he's not used to a van. And bless his heart, he gunned that sucker, hit some ice, spun it around, crashed it. It went on its side, and everybody ran to save him, to see if he was all right. I grabbed my kids, jumped into a car that had been left idling so it would be warm, stole the car, and drove away. And my kids and I began an adventure.

"For ten years I had been told that anything outside of this compound was hell. I was leaving heaven and forfeiting my entire eternal salvation. And at that moment I didn't care, because I thought it will only be me that dies in the eternity, but not my kids. I thought that I had no value, but they must. The minute I held them, they were miracles to me. I had to save them.

"I drove until I saw a policeman who had pulled someone over, and whoever he pulled over owes me big time, because the guy never got a ticket. But I pulled in front of the police car and I'm shakin' and I'm crying and I *ping pinged* on his window, and he rolled it down, and I said, 'I just committed a felony, but you have to help me.'

"O-o-kay, he's wondering, we got a crazy. He goes, 'What are you talking about?'

"And I said, 'You have to help me, please. I committed a felony, you have to take me to jail, but you have to save my children.' I told him I had just stolen a car and why, and he said, 'Gee, look, there's an abandoned car right on the side of the freeway. Why don't you guys come in and get warm?' And we talked for a little while longer, and he decided that he was gonna take me away from southern Utah and get me to Salt Lake City where I would be more safe.

"I told him that I had a car that was in my name that I had worked hard to earn, and I wanted it back. So I gave him the keys, and he went to the compound and said, 'There's a car that has an illegal license plate on it, and I'm impounding it.' So he impounded my car and brought it to me, and I followed him to Salt Lake, and we stayed in that secure shelter for one month while he took statements and things, and after that we were turned loose. And I didn't know how to shop in a grocery store. You know, I didn't know how to do anything. My children didn't have records of education. We didn't have birth certificates. The problems we had to solve were so huge! But I had to save them.

"For the first five years, we dealt with being homeless. We got into a shelter program, got help through Interfaith Hospitality, which is now Family Promise. And they got us into more secured housing. And then my pastor one day said, 'I had this flyer for college.'

"I said, 'I don't know how to go to college. I'm barely paying rent. And I'm too stupid for college; and I really don't know how to do this.'

"And he said, 'You talk with a passion, and when you write letters, they're complete sentences. And you love words.'

"I said, 'Well, words were all I had except for these questions inside of me. All I could do was observe the world; that was my only way to save them.'

"He goes, 'You're gonna go to college.' And I was terrified, because I thought, what place do I have in college? By now, they had talked me into tutoring, getting a GED, realizing that I could do some things. And that terrified me. I had never factored a polynomial in my life. I don't know what kind of crazy, evil, torturous man decided to invent that kind of mathematics, but I'll never date him. I was so afraid after getting this GED that gave me permission to go to college. And that about killed me alive, and I thought, I can't do this. You know, this other high school GED thing was so hard I can't do more than that, and my pastor said, 'You're going to college.' And I did.

"It was so amazing! Jennifer is this bouncy ball of energy; she just makes you want to eat up art alive. And I'm always on a diet so this is no calories. It's just that people could use paint to write as passionately with visuals as I tried to do with words. And one of my favorite classes was history, because of Jack Newell, who loves freedom. And he loves teaching people that you're part of a country, and you can make a difference in that country. And until then I didn't make a difference to anybody, all I did was survive.

"And more than that, I didn't think I had life left, because by then I was doing chemo [Barbra has lupus] every Friday. We didn't even know if I would survive any more than a few weeks, but I was in college: I had to see this sucker through. What an adventure! I'm still not dead.

"One of my physicians asked, 'Why aren't you dead?' because they wanted to know how I had survived chemo for so long when others don't. And I said, 'You never told me I was supposed to fall over dead. You have to tell me these things.'

"I said that I'm all that my children have. I'm curious, I'm full of questions, I have to see how they turn out. I have to get them past this awkwardness that they're in and into being their own sentient self. They're still carrying scars of all that's happened. I need to see them be complete people.

"And I'm learning that college is my ticket to become somebody so that I can provide better for them so that they can become even more. And over the past semester . . . I had to survive to get this stupid associate's degree. You know, I just had to.

"This last semester I started thinking, 'This isn't enough,' because only in this last semester did the courses start to get interesting. Not 1010 [the number of a course], that should only happen to people on death row! And 1050 should be against the law entirely. And some of these prerequisite courses were so intensive and pressure! They weren't the nurturing Venture. What your heart had to say was more important than a spelling error. The workload was not tenfold of Venture, but tenfold in pressure because no one is telling you anymore that you could do it; you had to tell yourself. This cocoon you were in now let you free to be braver. So now I'm trying to be braver, and now I'm thinking, I want my bachelor's. How the heck am I gonna afford that? But I'm putting my three kids through college with me. I mean, we eat Ramen on china, because if this is what dinner is, it's gonna be festive.

"I know that all the questions inside of me are freedom, and I get permission to just . . . be free!"

Not long after our conversation, Jean Cheney said to me that Barbra and five other graduates of the course went together to see the admissions counselor at the University of Utah, who had agreed to guide them through their applications for scholarships. Jean said in her note that we ought to try to learn how our students affected the colleges and universities they entered. A professor in Porto Alegre, Brazil, had said something similar. The Clemente students were not part of a grassroots movement, like those whose DNA was so interesting to the academy, they were academicians of the modern agora, argumentative, excited, democratic, and dangerous.

Because I am forever, it seems, talking to students to find out what works best for them, I asked the women in Salt Lake to turn to the academic part of the course. As always, it was Socrates, whom they admired, who led them into thinking. They understood that he spoke truth to power long before 1955, when the Quakers coined the phrase. The idea of questioning the world came to them from Plato. They read the Allegory of the Cave as if it were the story of their own experience before they came to the course. I had by then heard it in much of the world. Niecie Walker had been right. The students were pleased to be in the light, but they did not want to go back down into the cave to speak to those who remained behind in the darkness. *Antigone* pleased them too, if the tragic confrontation of love and order is pleasing. Perhaps cathartic, Aristotle's word, tells better what it meant to them.

CHAPTER 15

Ahn-neong hah-seh-yo

The ancient backstreets of Seoul rise and curl and twist down again into impenetrable paths that no vehicle can negotiate. We could not see people or bicycles in the sharpness of the curves. The driver stopped, backed down a curved street, started up another. I could not speak to him. He sat next to me, muttering and complaining in Korean, then suddenly laughing at an escape from disaster. Ko, Byung-hun had not explained why we were going up into this ancient darkness. There had been fighting in these streets. What was saved and what had risen again was not clear in the darkness.

"We cannot go up," the translator said. "Walk." The driver pulled the four-wheel-drive van up over a curb, and we climbed out. We had been to the temporary shelter down below, but now we had to climb. The hill was too steep to walk up. Centuries ago, the Koreans had cut deep stone risers into the hill, steps for a giant, each one more than two feet high. In the moonless night the stone risers and the steps looked black. Shapes of buildings, dwellings or storehouses, rose on either side of the great steps. We climbed upward. There was little talking. I could make out the shapes of the first of us to mount the steps. Someone took my arm and lifted and dragged me up the steep step. I was confused by the darkness and the flow of Korean conversation around me. I heard the woman who was translating say my name. As we rounded a curve, a light showed the lead climbers in silhouette and I saw that the translator was the tallest of us, and that she was in the form of a well-built man.

The man who had been directing the group stepped up to a doorway, which opened immediately, and he stepped into the yellow light of a room beyond. I heard him speaking with a woman in Korean. Apparently, the woman would not permit all of us to enter, just the translator, the man who had entered first, and me; the others had to hang back in the doorway. I looked around to Byung-hun and the architect. Byung-hun smiled. The architect pressed forward, seeking a better vantage. In the room, a fat woman in what looked like a huge jumpsuit made of a deep lavender material was playing on a small scarred spinet piano. The music was a melancholy tune that I did not recognize. When she was introduced to me, she did not look up, and the only sign she gave of having seen me was a shift in the tune and tempo to what might have been jazz.

The woman in charge said through the translator, "The Americans used her. She was their whore."

"She must have been a child," I said to the translator. She nodded, but did not translate what I said.

A woman with a small girl came out of a back room. The woman wore many dresses of cottons and other fabrics and a final overlay of some diaphanous cloth. The little girl wore a dress over a dress, like the woman. I knew the meaning of people who wore all their clothing all the time. The girl smiled. This was a long-term facility of some kind; I did not know exactly what. I felt in my pockets for something to give the child—a sweet, a coin, anything. There was a mint still wrapped in cellophane that I had picked up somewhere. I held it out to the little girl. As my hand moved toward her, the little girl fled to her mother's side, and the two of them ran back into the darkness. I looked to the woman in charge. She said nothing, gave no indication that anything unusual had happened. No sooner had the woman and child fled than they were replaced by a youngish woman, perhaps thirty or forty years old, with hair dyed dark red and spiked with some kind of gel. *"Ahn-neong hah-seh-yo,"* I said. And she answered in English, "Hello."

"Do you speak English?" I asked.

She gave me a fetching smile. It was clearly the opening of some kind of negotiation. She had very delicate features, like a toy person. She wore lipstick and rouge, and her eyebrows and lashes were black and heavy and made her hair seem more garish. "Yes, speak English," she said.

"I came here to teach the humanities. If I brought a book of poems here for you to read and discuss, would you do that?"

She looked puzzled. The translator spoke to her in Korean. The red-haired woman addressed her answer to me, "Yes."

"Can you say something more to me in English?"

She smiled seductively. " 'Fourscore and seven years ago our fathers brought forth, on this continent, a new nation, conceived, in Liberty, and dedicated to the proposition that all men are created equal.'"

I nodded to indicate that she should go on. And she did: "'Now we are engaged in a great civil war, testing whether that nation, or any nation so conceived, and so dedicated, can long endure. We are met on a great battle-field . . .'"

There was no sense asking her to continue. I interrupted to ask, "Do you like poetry?"

She offered the seductive look, but said nothing.

The next day, the translator and I bought a book of poems at a small store near my hotel, and she promised that it would get to the shelter. It was the beginning of the first Clemente Course in Asia, not counting the Gettysburg Address.

The work in Korea had begun when I was asked to give a lecture to a joint conference of UNESCO and the International Philosophical Society at the new Women's University in Seoul. The subject was American thought, which I saw as a chance to spread the gospel of the Clemente Course. I gave the talk via teleconference since I had other work to do at the time and could not go to Korea. The lecture went well enough until the two respondents took their turns. They both devoted their time to excoriating me over a sentence in the talk in which I said that the capitalist system in the United States created poverty as well as great wealth.

The organizers of the conference sent along some stories about my lecture that appeared in the Korean newspapers, but I don't know a word of Korean. The only thing I could recognize in the stories was my face, and I was not smiling.

A year later, an e-mail arrived from a fellow at the Gyeonggi Lifelong Learning Center. It was followed by another e-mail from a Mr. Dong-Deok, Park, "Documentarist," who wanted to make a television documentary about the Clement (sic). I said that he would do best to shoot it in Chicago, where Amy Thomas-Elder could help him, and in Madison, Wisconsin, which was nearby. In Madison, he could film the work of Emily Auerbach. Emily is a professor of English at the university there, the host of a radio program, the co-founder and director of the Clemente (known as Odyssey) Course in Madison, and the author of several books. I promised to ask both site directors for permission, and to let him know if he could contact them. Both Emily and Amy agreed. I attempted to explain that Emily had created her own variation on the Clemente Course, and that it was very successful. I have no Korean and Mr. Park has very little English. I have no idea what passed for dialogue between us, but everyone was agreeable to Mr. Park's journey. Before very long, Mr. Park, cameras, and assistant arrived in New York. I asked where he was during the war. "Not born," he said. I shrugged, smiled for his camera, bowed, and sent him off to the Midwest.

Perhaps the symposium had not been the disaster I recalled. Why else had Mr. Park journeyed halfway around the world?

Mr. Park was a demon videographer. Emily reported that he took pictures of everyone and everything. He had even tried to follow her into the bathroom. It all seemed slightly comical until a videotape arrived with an edited version of Mr. Park's work. The comedy of languages and cultures fell away. Park had made the first video of an Odyssey/Clemente Course class. He had filmed students, with their permission, in their homes and neighborhoods, and he had captured the warmth and genius for teaching of Emily Auerbach. For the first time, we had our work in sound and pictures, even if it had subtitles in Korean. Park had broken through the language barrier to understand what we were doing and to find a way to bring it to interesting, comprehensible life on film.

The next time I saw Mr. Park was at the arrival gate in Seoul. He met me there with his large videocamera on his shoulder and the eyepiece tight against his face. The flight from California had lasted for more than eleven hours, and despite the comforts of the Korean airline, I was dazed. Several other people were gathered in a knot behind Mr. Park. As we introduced ourselves, Mr. Park stepped away and kept recording what seemed to me an entirely uninteresting event: a weary old man greeted by strangers who persisted in bowing and smiling although the old man just stood there as if he had died and didn't have the grace to fall.

We walked through the airport to a room where three people waited for us. They were seated at a small rectangular table. There were greetings, bows, much inane conversation in Korean, English, and the language of imperfect translation. Through the babble and bows, I found that I was to sit at the table along with interviewers from two newspapers, a translator, and Lim, Jung-Ahn, a very important dean from Sunghonghoe, a university I had never heard of. The man from the Lifelong Learning Center translated. I looked for a face I could remember, a smile I could understand. My search ended with one of the people who had met me at the gate. Withheld laughter is an endearing sight: the cheek muscles dance and the eyes shine with tears of restraint. And he had a round nose that belonged on the face of a Polish peasant or a bust of Socrates. His nose wrinkled, he lost control of his laughter as the absurdity of the situation struck him. I do not think I have ever seen a more open and trustworthy face.

When I saw him laughing, I laughed too, and we were friends. I asked if he wanted to sit with us at the table. He understood my English question, and declined politely. One of the newspaper reporters interrupted our new friendship. She told me that she was working against a tight deadline. He confirmed her request with a nod. Apparently, my new friend Ko, Byung-hun was in charge of the operation. I wondered if I had been wrong about the withheld laughter. Perhaps it was not friendship, merely the Korean managerial style.

The interview began. The questions were gently phrased in excellent English. It all seemed to me like a great error, that the Koreans had mistaken me for someone else. I was tired and dry. I asked for water, and water, ice, and a soft drink arrived immediately. The Koreans were gracious and interested. I soon realized that the people seated at the table and standing in a small crowd around it were not interested in me: they wanted to know about educating the poor. I had been right to make the trip. It was going to be interesting and useful. The conversation became more animated. Now I had questions for the interviewer and the others in the group. Was there a large population of underprivileged people in Korea? How could that have happened in the midst of what the West believed was a Korean economic miracle?

They talked about the economic crisis of 1997 and the suffering caused by the International Monetary Fund. We were still in Incheon, but they said that when we got to Seoul we would pass by the park where ten thousand people had lived in tents in the center of the city because the IMF policies had pushed them into unemployment and homelessness. I would not see people sleeping in the center of the city, but there were still many, thousands, uneducated, in the midst of plenty. I told them we had similar problems in the United States, that it was the discrepancy between life for the rich and the poor in the United States that had given rise to the Clemente Course.

There were questions about the theory behind the course. We talked about democracy and its rise in ancient Athens. Since I had been preparing for the visit it was possible to talk about Korean philosophy and the idea of constant movement, using the metaphor of heaven and earth in the stillness of perfectly balanced opposition until humans were created to live between the two, leading to constant motion. Therefore, we could expect the poor and uneducated to rise up to better, more beautiful lives. We compared the ancient Korean idea to the hierarchical Confucianism that had dominated the country for so many years.

From the airport we gathered in several cars. Byung-hun had by then taken full charge of my trip. He carefully explained who each of the people were and how they were related to education and democracy. One of the men in the group, Kim, Min-gi, older than the others, was the author of the song that was used as the anthem of the Gwanju uprising that overthrew the dictatorship and established the market (as opposed to Socialist) democracy in South Korea in 1980. Mr. Kim, Min-gi spoke no English, but we were able to talk through the efforts of Byung-hun and others. I congratulated him, and explained that the *telos* of the Clemente Course was democracy. He knew the Greek word for end or purpose. To use the Socratic method in a gentle way to teach the humanities, I explained, is the art of freedom. He said that the *telos* of his art had also been freedom. Byung-hun explained that the songwriter had risked a great deal, even his life, to overthrow the dictatorial government.

I took the songwriter's hand and shook it in admiration. We all laughed with happiness and comfort. The man from the Lifelong Learning Center asked if I liked jazz, and when I said I liked it very much and had many friends who were jazz musicians, he was pleased. I promised to send him a CD autographed by a drummer who had recorded with Cal Tjader. He asked if I wanted to go to a jazz club while I was in Seoul. "If there is time," I said, but I had come a long way and I hoped there would be more productive work.

The Koreana Hotel was even more Americanized than the people who had met me at the airport and conducted the interview. In my room, which was furnished in Western style, I unpacked a few things, tried to wash some of the long trip out of my face, phoned my wife in San Francisco, and went to bed. As usual, I could not quite figure out what time it was in my head. I phoned the hotel desk, then set the alarm on the little clock I carried with me. I lay there in the darkness for what seemed like hours, wondering if I had come to Korea to bring yet more Western ideas to the East. And my friend Byung-hun—could I have read his face accurately? Was it goodness I doubted? Had I lost the ability to trust real laughter? Why had I come there? I went to sleep with thoughts of cultural imperialism dancing in my head.

Morning brought the Reverend Simon Lim, an Anglican priest who had already taken the idea of the Clemente Course and begun teaching homeless men. Simon, a slim and sincere man, who nonetheless could laugh, although not like Byung-hun, was building a different kind of shelter for homeless men. We visited a clinic run by the Anglican Church under Simon's direction. He introduced me to the doctor in charge. The doctor and I exchanged a few words in English, then the doctor took me into the clinic, where homeless men who had come off the streets sick, hungry, and dirty looked up from their lethargy and disease. The doctor told them something in Korean, then he left to go back to work in his examining room while I walked down the long row, shaking the hand of each man and saying something inane that was immediately translated into Korean by a tall young woman whom Simon had brought along for that purpose.

After I had finished my round, Simon led us outside to the shelter under construction. He was anxious to explain how the shelter, which had not progressed beyond the standing plywood walls and some inner partitions, would permit each man to have the privacy of a cubicle of his own. Through the translator we exchanged the word "dignity." Byung-hun was with us. He and I exchanged comments that were meant to be witticisms, but were no more than excuses to laugh. We both understood that only laughter could release the tension of one English speaker among a group of people who had to rely on a translator. It was very much like a classroom where laughter opens the minds of students to dialogue.

The previous day, stories about the Clemente Course had run in several of the major dailies and the electric sign that ran around the exterior at the top of one of the tallest buildings in Seoul announced that the man from the Clemente Course had come to Seoul to teach the poor. The electric headlines and the newspaper stories had made me uncomfortable. I was glad to be in the shelter among the homeless men, asking them if they would come to a course that taught the humanities.

The next afternoon I gave a lecture to a very large crowd in a university auditorium. There were preliminary talks, much polite applause, and headphones with a simultaneous translation into English. The man seated next to me was the governor of the province and an announced candidate for the presidency. Next to him was a woman of such perfect features that she would have been considered beautiful by the standards of any culture, not just the West. I was astonished by her. The governor introduced her as HyeKyung Lee, chairperson of the Presidential Commission on Social Inclusion. He said that she would be very influential in starting Clemente Courses in Korea. I asked the governor if he would also help us, and he nodded toward the woman on his right. I leaned over toward Byung-hun, who sat close by, and asked if he could arrange a meeting with the chairperson. He spoke to her briefly, and she responded to me in unaccented English that her schedule was full. I told her that I was very sorry, for I thought that many Korean people could benefit from our work. If she could find fifteen minutes, I would not waste her time. She shook her head and smiled politely.

The translators had sent word that they would appreciate it if I would not deviate from the written text I had provided, and I was sorry that I had agreed, for I would have liked to ask the chair of the Commission on Social Inclusion for her help, explaining what was needed to teach the poor of Korea. While the governor made his introduction in Korean, I debated the value of good manners versus the chance to start the courses. In the end, it was timidity rather than good manners that kept me to the text. I had learned from Byung-hun how to pronounce "Lao-tse" and to say "Confucius" in the Korean way. It had been interesting to give myself a crash course in Korean history and culture before writing the lecture. The hierarchical character of the Confucians who came from China to rule the Korean Peninsula for many centuries had surprised me. I had found Lao-tse a powerful force in opposition to Confucianism, and the sense of serenity in the *Tao*, the perfect opposition of heaven and earth, very different from the Korean idea of man coming between heaven and earth and creating constant motion.

The next day, we went to lunch in a Buddhist restaurant. I was seated next to Byung-Hun's daughter, Jae Young, who was in her early teens. I had taken her and her brother to a press conference with me so they could see how silly it all was. Both children sat in the room with me, stifling their laughter. I was amazed at the children's ability to speak English, and charmed by them. During lunch, which was served by monks wearing traditional garb, I enjoyed the general conversation, but found the children, who had by then become my pals, more interesting. I noticed, however, that Jae Young ate with no interest in the best vegetarian meal I have ever eaten. Finally, I leaned over and asked her, "Do you like this restaurant?" She wrinkled up her nose, and said, "Rabbit food."

I laughed aloud. It was tasty, but it was, to my palate, rabbit food. Everyone at the table turned to look at me and the children.

Jae Young took the moment as the formation of a bond. From then on, I was her "American grandfather." We exchanged e-mails through her high school years when she spent a few unhappy years at a boarding school. Now, she lives in Paris and attends the Sorbonne. Her English has begun to pale a bit, crowded out by French. Recently, Byung-Hun sent me photographs of the children. They are beginning to look more like their mother, who is very beautiful—a professional singer—and a bit less like the Socrates of South Korea.

The following evening, instead of a brief visit at her office, the chairperson of the commission arranged a dinner at a Japanese restaurant in the center of the city. It was, like many Korean restaurants, on the second floor of a building in a busy commercial center. Byung-hun and I walked there from the hotel, passing street stands selling various kinds of pickled food, and then down a curving street away from the broad avenues of central Seoul. It was cold, and we walked quickly. There was no time to be a good tourist, although the stores were fascinating to the glance; Byung-hun said that HyeKyung Lee had invited several other people to the dinner. I asked if my Korean granddaughter, the gourmet, was going to join us. He laughed, for he knew about the rabbit food comment.

We climbed the stairs, still laughing, but once we entered the room, the atmosphere became formal; there were distances. The chairperson was already there, seated at the center of a long table, surrounded by men and several women dressed in dark Western suits. It could have been a meeting of bankers, but these were all government officials; two directors of the Presidential Commission on Social Inclusion, Young-Tae Kim and Dong-Se Min, sat on either side of the chairperson. There were a few pleasantries; HyeKyung Lee introduced the others at the table, and we went to work. She had reported the gist of my talk to them, they had read about the course in the newspapers, but now they wanted to talk about it in more detail: How did it fit into resolving the Korean problem left over from the disaster caused by the IMF?

The Commission on Social Inclusion was divided up into distinct areas, only two of which were directly connected to the Clemente Course: housing and education. It was clear that the national government could help to fund the provincial and city courses. The director of the education section made no promises, but he said that he would try. The conversation then turned to housing, which interested me, because the Koreans were clearly far more advanced than the Americans in thinking about housing for the poor; they saw it as an opportunity for social inclusion rather than for the social exclusion that had long been one of the unspoken aims of the American system. I asked the man in charge of designing the housing if there was something like a day room or a community room in the housing he was designing. When he said that there was space, I asked what he thought about converting the day room space into a humanities room: "It would require hiring a coordinator for the humanities room and a budget to bring poets, musicians, and teachers to the room. At the same time it would build intellectual and social community among the poor, connecting them to the rest of society. That is the goal of social inclusion, isn't it?" We all agreed. But then I realized that the woman who looked like a movie star managed her commission in hierarchical fashion. The directors looked at her before they ventured an opinion and kept looking over at her with each statement of interest or intent.

Meanwhile, the dinner was served. Although I did not recognize many of the things that had been plucked from the seas around Korea, I chewed or simply swallowed most of them. Then came the fish course, which was a whole fish, small, cleaned and cooked. Fresh chopsticks were served along with it.

"Do you know how to use chopsticks?" the chairperson asked.

"Yes, a little."

We smiled at each other across the table, and went to work with our chopsticks. The chairperson, who had received a doctorate from the University of California at Berkeley and spoke English without accent, took the skin off her fish and picked a piece of meat from between the tiny rib bones. I followed her example. The skin came off easily, and the flesh was firm and not the least bit oily. I glanced around the table and saw that everyone was stealing little glances of their own, not at the chairperson now, but at the American, expecting him, I imagined, to fail at eating the fish with chopsticks. The chairperson watched me most intently, and I, in turn, looked across the table at her. Frankly, she was not very adept with her chopsticks. What Jae Young had told me in the Buddhist restaurant was apparently true: Koreans used forks rather than chopsticks.

The fish was proving more difficult for her than for me, since I had lived in San Francisco for many years and often ate with Chinese friends in restaurants where one was expected to use chopsticks. The fish course had turned into something of a cultural competition between the chairperson and the American. We both picked away, neither of us smiling now as the exposed flesh was eaten and it became necessary to wriggle the chopsticks between the delicate bones of the ribs. Who would be the first to have to reach into his or her mouth to pull a tiny fish rib off the tongue? I vowed to myself to chew up any bone I found in my mouth and swallow the pieces. If I choked, it would be in a good cause, for I had come to believe that we were in a tournament to find out if my "Western" idea of education would be implemented for the Korean poor.

The chairperson and I ate ferociously, delicately, meticulously. I do not know what kind of fish it was that had been set before us, but I will always think of it as a contest fish. And near the end of it I could not raise my eyes from the minute pieces of white flesh that still hung to the bones here and there. Finally, exhausted by the effort, I looked up from my fish, which appeared to have been attacked by a school of piranha so naked were the bones, and saw that the chairperson had conceded the game to me. Her fish, shreds of flesh still adhering to the bones here and there, sat sadly on her plate. I gave a great sigh of victory, and everyone laughed, for the contest had existed only in my mind. No other fish was so naked, no other bones so bare.

There soon emerged a debate with the probable faculty of the Clemente courses in Korea. Two young professors accused me of cultural imperialism, saying that the curriculum I proposed had no Korean or other Asian material in it. My answer was to claim innocence: "If I knew Korean literature and philosophy, I would have included it. Surely, you must not think that I would want to teach a purely Western course here in Korea. In fact, I've told Byung-Hun that I think Korea is entirely too Western as it is."

Byung-Hun nodded and produced the gentle laugh that won over everyone he met. The debate ended as soon as it had begun.

One problem remained: How was the teaching in the Clemente Course different from other teaching? Socrates was my answer, and suddenly, without my participation, the Reverend Simon Lim and Byung-Hun and others had arranged for a demonstration of the teaching method the next day. They proposed that I teach the Socratic method to a group of homeless men from Simon's shelter. I agreed on the condition that the men read a good translation of the *Apology*. If it was the Socratic method they wanted to see, then it should be Socrates who does the teaching. There was much discussion in Korean, and then the Reverend Simon said it was agreed.

Two days later, in midafternoon, Byung-Hun and I entered a room filled with press people, the omnipresent videocameras, and assorted academics. At one end of the large, rectangular room a square had been made of long tables and chairs had been placed around it. At the farthest table a man and a young woman had already taken their places. They indicated that they were seated at the head table and gestured for me to join them there while the homeless men would sit at the other three tables that completed the square. I declined, explaining to the translator that I would be better able to practice the Socratic method if I sat along the side, among the people. The translator and the man whom I did not know, but who was presumably in charge of the demonstration, appeared to be very unhappy with my choice of seats. We had a brief conversation about it. They said that I could see everyone best from there, but I insisted that it gave the impression of a lecture, and worse, a hierarchical situation when I wanted to establish a dialogue in which the people had both their political and personal freedom and still chose to enjoy these in an orderly way. "It's very Greek, don't you think?"

He answered with a shrug.

The homeless men came into the room through a door near the back and took their places at the tables. Each man had a small packet of papers in his hand: the *Apology* of Socrates in Korean. I asked how many had read the material. The translator repeated the question and most of the hands went up. Then I asked how many had read all of it, the translator spoke, and fewer hands were raised.

"What was this story about?"

The answers came back slowly.

"What was he accused of?"

Some curious responses came back. I asked if everyone agreed with the responses. "Was he a Christian?"

"Did he believe in Jesus?"

It took a very long time and a great many questions to get to the crime of corrupting the youth, but we got there. Speaking through a translator, waiting for each question and each answer to be translated, was tedious and strangely tiring. The homeless men and I looked at one another. They were all clean and neatly dressed in Western-style clothing. Simon had done a good job of preparing them.

While we talked, I could hear the sound of the shutters from the back and sides of the room. The videographer moved people about as he changed angles and lenses. As the discussion went on, it became clear that something was amiss in the translation they had been given. They thought Socrates was a judge himself, and they did not believe he had children. One man said Socrates was very rich, and all the others agreed. At last we got around to the question of virtue, and one of the men sitting next to me raised his hand. He said something in Korean, and everyone laughed. When I heard the translation, I laughed too. He had said, "I don't want to talk about virtue. I want to talk about money."

More than a few of the others agreed, and the conversation veered away from Socrates to the problem of having no money. These were homeless men, all of them living in a shelter; I could hardly blame them for being concerned with money. It took a long while and many questions to bring the conversation back to virtue and happiness, and I had to stipulate that it was important to have enough money for food and shelter before we could get back to the subject of the *Apology*. Later, I thought I might have saved a lot of time by simply telling them what they had read, but I was determined to hew to my belief in dialogue rather than lecturing.

Near the end of the time I asked them if they thought Lao-tse would agree with Socrates, and I was surprised to find that they did not know much more about Lao-tse than they knew about Socrates. Afterward, I talked with several of the professors who had been worried about cultural imperialism, and we agreed that it would be necessary to teach Eastern as well as Western culture. At the end of the time, after the reporters had talked with the students, I made sure to exchange polite bows with all the students and to shake the hand of the man who was more concerned with money than virtue.

Before I went to the airport at Incheon, we had lunch—Byung-Hun, the jazz fan from the Geonggi Learning Center, Min-Gi, the Reverend Simon Lim, and I—at SamcheongGak (House of Three Purities), which is a traditional Korean palace originally built to serve the interests of the government, but now in private hands. The gate was opened by a woman wearing traditional dress standing very tall on low stilts. It was a pleasant but somber meal. There was a sense of the end of the war again, the end of the overthrow of the dictatorship again. Min-Gi sang a bit of his famous composition very softly. I said I was sorry that my Korean granddaughter, Jae Young, was not there to lighten the occasion with laughter, and we surely needed her younger brother, whose English limited him to wishing for a limousine. We ended with bows and embraces and headed for the airport. We could not then gauge the result of our work. Farewells were sad and anxious.

I needn't have feared. The Koreans have understood the idea of the Clemente Course like no other people, including Americans. Byung-Hun translated *Riches for the Poor* into Korean, and within a year visitors from Korea began coming to the United States to talk about the course. I soon realized that the "Koreanization" of Asia, as many people referred to the vast political and economic changes the continent was undergoing, came of having fought recently for the many aspects of freedom. A strong adherence to the rules of custom served to limit some personal freedoms; democracy had been won here and there, and with it greater political freedom; among personal freedoms, the role of women was still insecure, especially in rural areas. But it was all changing, and the change upward toward a better life had given astonishing energy to Korea. It became my role, in long essays sent to Byung-Hun, to urge the place of laughter and dialogue in education. But my role was barely noticeable; it was people like Byung-Hun, and the whole crew of the President's Commission on Social Inclusion and the civil government of Seoul, who were effecting change. Compared to our old but not yet exhausted democracy, the Koreans were exciting. The mayor of Seoul, Oh Se-Boon, had recognized what the Clemente Course could do for his people. He employed five universities to teach the course to the urban poor. Over four succeeding years, more than 1,200 people a year were taught in the mayor's courses alone, and there were other courses in other Korean cities and towns. Sunghonghoe University, the one I had never heard of when I got off the plane, was the lead university, and the person in charge of the vast project there was Ko, Byung-Hun.

The Reverend Simon Lim has left Korea now, posted elsewhere by the Anglican hierarchy. I recall visiting the Seoul cathedral with him. It is a curious building, British, with a Korean tile roof. After we had toured the interior of the structure, admiring the paintings, climbing many long flights of stairs, we went out into the garden and Simon opened the door to a tiny room furnished with a board for a bed. It was the place where he went on retreat, sleeping on the board, taking nothing but plain rice and water for nourishment. He said that when I came back to Korea, he would arrange for me to stay there. "It would be a good place to write a book," he said.

CHAPTER 16

On Puget Sound

The Clemente Course in the Humanities is a peculiarly American idea. It has Greek origins and there are often more students in other parts of the world, speaking other languages and following other cultural patterns, but it never ceases to be American and it is never more American than in the strip of land between the rain forest and the Sound called Jefferson County, Washington. Around the small towns and worn-out farms and fished-out, fouled streams; in the local branch of the state college and in the alternative high school; and even among the well-kept houses around Centrum, which calls itself Washington's center for the creative arts, there is a sense of community that is born of the humanities.

At the center of the center of Jefferson County is Lela Hilton. In a dozen years of organizing the Clemente Course, of funding it and feeding it and taking it in her arms as if it were the child of the people, she has gathered the disparate worlds of Jefferson County into a community. She lives in a house in Chimacum, built not many years ago on land she had owned for a long time, almost since she came to the Northwest to finish her degree. The house is, as she said, off the grid, a place on a hill in the woods. Her husband, Jake Jacob, envisioned the structure, and together Lela and Jake set it on the land so they could see from the windows down deep through the trees. They did not build it all themselves, although Jake could have done it. He is a builder of treehouses, famous in his field as the consultant at TreehouseARTZ after climbing a thousand trees and building a hundred houses.

Lela's academic life is a marriage of literature and the environment, and it comes through in her speech and the sudden turns she can make in conversation when a bird passes or there is a bear cub in the woods. Jefferson County is a good place for someone who knows the natural world and can walk in it. Much of the county is national park land, mountainous and still sharpened from birth. Mt. Baldy is there, and it looks down to the west on rain forest and to the east to the towns, most of which have names beginning with the word "Port," as in Port Hadlock and Port Ludlow, and the largest city in the county, Port Townsend. The tiny communities often carry names beginning with the word "Fort," which tells some of the history of this place named for Thomas Jefferson, Most of the Native Americans have moved out or been driven out or found ways to live in the western part of the county, avoiding the census, just as the poverty rate (about 14 percent in 2010) does not give an accurate picture of life in Jefferson County. Lela Hilton says that "it takes two jobs and a small business" for people to survive in Jefferson County, unless they are part of the population in the wealthy resort area around Port Ludlow or Centrum.

Local wisdom has it that the one real city in the county, Port Townsend, is rapidly becoming a home to the unemployed. And it is not the only area with severe economic and educational problems. Quilcene has also seen difficult times. How there are so many struggling so mightily to survive in a county where the poverty rate is officially 14 percent is one of the anomalies of rural America. Numbers don't describe the place, Lela Hilton does, and she does it by the way she looks upon her work with the Clemente Course.

"Most programs that work with poor people are about deficits," she says. "This program is about assets."

Lela's work has been used as a model by the National Endowment for the Humanities, and I have used it as a starting place for other Clemente courses in rural areas of the United States, Mexico, Argentina, and Africa. Yet I do not think of this modeling as cultural imperialism, for it is almost entirely the hope that democratic society at the most basic level, the American sinew, can be translated into other cultures. Jefferson County was good ground, although it had been battered by the wounding of its natural wealth, and it has always been difficult to raise the small amount of money required to maintain the course there. Like Mary Ann Kohli in Charleston, South Carolina, and Claudia Paladino and Patricio Grehan in Argentina, Lela Hilton turns the struggle for money into yet another way to embrace the idea of community.

One afternoon in Jefferson County, Lela and I drove out into the old farmland to pick up one of her students on the way to a party for funders and students and friends of the local Clemente Course. The land did not have the rich look of farmland in Illinois or California. There was a gray tone in the earth, and at that time in that season nothing was growing. I had been across the mountains from Seattle to the farmland on the east and seen the graying of the long months of drought and walked through the emptied towns. Water had saved most of Jefferson County, but not the farms. The young man who waited for us at the side of the road lived and worked on the ungiving land. He did not have running water in the house where he and his partner practiced the life of anarchists, separate from the state in every way they could manage, even the water supply and the food stores. They ate what they could grow on the unwelcoming land.

He was thin, and his beard was thin, almost black on his pallid cheeks. He climbed into the backseat and closed the door. I thought he would stink of the lack of water or of patchouli oil, but he had only the odor of a man and earth. His name was Justin. I asked if he truly was an anarchist, and he said that he was. And then I asked about the limits of anarchy as he understood it, not as in some British rock bands, and he did not say anything. "Do you believe that all private property is theft?" I asked, expecting him to have a lot to say on the subject. But he only agreed, and fell silent.

After a few minutes, he and Lela began to talk about food. She had been supplying him and the young woman he lived with the little they needed to supplement what they could grow in return for the work they did around the farm. I did not ask him how his anarchism fit with coming to the Clemente Course, which received some money from the National Endowment for the Humanities. He did not want to talk much, preferring to sit back in the car wrapped in his coat, just letting it happen.

He is a handsome young man, a farm worker and a hunter. He lives on what he kills and what he is allowed to plant and harvest. At the party, he was very much at ease in the crowd in the house Meredith and Peter Wagner had built around a totem pole nearly twenty feet high that they had commissioned to be carved to fit their tastes and the room Peter had designed. Meredith Wagner, who sits on the board of Washington Humanities and is director of the Jefferson County Library, had been part of the Clemente Course almost from its inception in the county. She was the connection to the more affluent side of the county and to the sense of civic engagement on that side.

At her party, amid canapés and white wine, Justin the anarchist circulated easily. He delivered the casual chatter expected of guests at a party in a house made of fine Northwest Coast wood, and he paused, as everyone did, to look up into the highest face of the totem pole or out onto the wooded land that seemed to flow from the great windows of the house. In a videotape made not much later, he said, "The Socratic method that the teachers use made me feel very empowered and self-motivated to learn. Having the teachers be really interested in what I was getting out of the different subjects and different assignments was so different than my experience throughout public school.

"Once I tried looking at U.S. history, especially the history of art, it wasn't so easy to say it was just the government's fault as that it's the fault of everything. There's a much bigger picture going on and it's helping me to be not so stuck in my 'ism' and it's helped me to relate to others who have a different experience of life."

Justin has not strayed so far from what he believed when he came to the Clemente Course, but he has become a citizen now, a political man in the Periclean sense rather than in the way of Proudhon or Kropotkin. He votes. He is a licensed driver. Justin's partner, whom he does not call his wife although they have been together for some years now, gave birth on the floor of the bedroom of Lela Hilton's newly built house in the woods. A few years ago, the family left the farm where they had lived without running water and went home to Michigan. Justin entered a formal program for wildlife study and protection. His child, a girl, is almost three years old now. He stays in touch with Lela Hilton, although he is far away. He tells her that he is teaching his daughter about the woods, showing her how to become a tracker. When he teaches her, he does not tell her about the creatures and plants and markings they see, he asks her to tell him. He says he is raising her by the Socratic method.

Lela makes no political or social judgment about Justin and the Clemente Course. What it gave him was the freedom to choose how to live, which is more American than Greek, more Jeffersonian than Periclean. Justin has not made many concessions to the kind of world that drove him away from it into the woods. He is still a woodsman, a man who finds his happiness in the natural life, but it is clear that he is no longer a creature of reaction; Justin has become a reflective man in the woods. One thinks of Thoreau.

The American character of the course, the connection to the culture native to the Pacific Northwest, the will to be free and to be part of some order, the dynamic of democracy, was evident in Justin and in the Wagner house, in the design and in the people who were there that late afternoon. Sydney Keegan was among them. Perhaps she was the most American of them all, the one whose life had become an arc across the poles of work in the county. No one was a more unlikely professor of philosophy than Sydney Keegan, although she looked the part, with her white hair and rimless eyeglasses. When she smiled, which was often, it was not an academic smile, for it lacked any hint of restraint. She could pound her desk for emphasis or ask her questions with authority and gusto. In her class, Socrates was a hoplite once again, a brave soldier who could laugh. Before Sydney began teaching in the Clemente Course twelve years ago, she worked in the back room of the local hardware store. When Lela looked for faculty, she met Sydney, and hired her immediately. Lela said she saw in Sydney Keegan, a woman with advanced degrees in music and philosophy, one who knew the less erudite side of Jefferson County. With Sydney on the faculty, philosophy was a path to the real world, not away from it. She was a good teacher, but not easy; she gave no answers, she elicited them.

The faculty has been the same for ten years. They are all part of the fabric of the county, and they weave the course into it. One professor, Eugene Taylor, thinks history should be taught in a tavern. It is an old American idea. One evening I sat with the Jefferson County faculty and some students drinking and eating fresh salmon. A student sitting at the end of a long table, drinking along with us, said that he worked part time at the local community college in the IT office. After a few more glasses, the talk swirled around to Web sites. The idea took a circuitous route, running through a meeting in Utah, a proposal written in Oregon, a grant made by Carole Watson, acting chairperson of the National Endowment for the Humanities, and finally to a Web site managed by Lela Hilton, who does it on her computer in Jefferson County.

The tavern is only occasionally the hearth of the course. Most often the hearth is the Jefferson County Library or the community college. The course follows the curriculum devised by Petrarch and uses the teaching method practiced by Socrates, but for eight weeks in 2011, Sydney Keegan taught philosophy at the Mar Vista alternative high school in Port Townsend. The class was small and philosophy was a challenge for the students there, but Lela said that they responded to it, and this branch of the Clemente Course will teach more the next year at Mar Vista, working with the faculty of the school to meet state standards. This time, the entire faculty will teach in seminars for the high school. Since then, the juvenile justice system has asked about a connection to the course, because the officers in the system have seen the change in adults who attended, and now there will be seminars for young people who are touched by the system. Camp Jefferson will hold courses for high school students in Chimacum, Port Townsend, and *Girls' Circle,* preparing eighty students to enter the adult course in the following years. United Good Neighbors is involved, and a group that teaches women in poverty skills that will help them to earn a decent living has now asked if the course can be extended to reach these women, because they realize that a decent life requires more than a job. Rotary, Lions, Kiwanis, and Soroptimist International all support the work of the Jefferson County Clemente Course.

Lela Hilton believes that the humanities create community,

that the Socratic method works in the classroom and beyond the classroom into the world. She sees it just as she sees from the window of her house past the near trees down through the branches into the depths of the forest. It is the way she sees the world and touches it. She is the mother of grown children. She stands and walks and speaks in the straight, sturdy way of people who live close to nature. Her hair is still more blond than not, and although it is difficult for her every year to write the proposals and do the asking and cook the salmon and watch over the sales of donated clothes, and she is tired and dreams of a windfall, she will go on. She understands perfectly how it must be. She teaches literature and lives metaphors. Last winter she put on a wet suit and swam upstream among the salmon coming home from the sea.

CHAPTER 17

In the Beginning—2011

*. . . the students started talking about different reasons
that one might do or not do something—trying to get at things
you do for some other purposes and things you do just because
they're right, and one of the girls—a nice, engaged girl—said
that the only reason not to kill someone was that you might
get caught. I thought she was pulling my leg, but she said she
meant it, and the whole rest of the class agreed with her. I am
sure that they don't really believe that, and I'm confident that
they will eventually see that they don't, but. . . . We talk a lot
about what it does to a kid's consciousness growing up in the
neighborhoods they grow up in, and I have always believed
that the Harlan Clemente Lesson Plan Time Line effects are
far-reaching and some difficult to describe, but that conversation caused something of an aspect shift for me.*

—Amy Thomas-Elder

Some things are not planned. Certainly this one was not. I can't
really say how it came about; it just sort of happened, like luck or
magic. Dovetta McKee was the heart of it. Whatever she thought,
we did. A stylish woman, always dressed as if she was going to
her office in one of Chicago's high-powered law firms, she met the
world with a crisp, precise way of entering a conversation, then sud-

denly enriched it with a down-home phrase or musical laughter. We were introduced because I had a theory that underprivileged high school students could benefit from brilliant teaching of the humanities. It had come to me late in the history of the Clemente Course. My view of the surround of force in which the poor lived had evolved slowly over the years. I had been wrong about the need to teach only adults. It had seemed so clear to me when I had first talked with Niecie Walker in the Bedford Hills Prison. But Niecie was right about beginning with the children; I was wrong. After seventeen years, I finally understood that the humanities should also be taught to young people living in the surround of force. High school was not too soon to begin.

I laid out the idea in a lecture in the University of Chicago's Poverty, Promise, and Possibility series. It was an academic exercise, one of those nice-to-think-about propositions that never come to anything. Secretly, however, I thought something might come of this one. But what? How? On the South Side of Chicago? The most decent, liberal man I knew in Chicago had told me that the only way to teach kids in the ghetto was by screaming at them.

"Screaming?" I asked.

"Screaming," he said.

One of the women who had graduated from the Odyssey/Clemente Course told me that school officials had found box cutters and knives in the lockers of middle school girls. "Oh, and one other thing," she said. "Hot sauce."

"Hot sauce?" I asked.

"Hot sauce to pour into the wounds."

My thesis about bringing people out of the surround of force was now seventeen years old. If that worked, why not this? Teach the humanities, as Petrarch had defined them, only not twice a week for a year but this time over four years, one period every day, six hundred hours, in a public high school, in the farthest reaches of the black ghetto. It was like starting the Clemente Course all over again: people said I was nuts. Two members of the board of directors of the Clemente Course in the Humanities, Inc. offered strenuous objections. One said I didn't know anything about high school students, and furthermore I had started the project without consulting the board. The other said not to tell anyone about this or we would not be able to raise money for the course. They were both right, sort of.

They didn't know Dovetta McKee. She was already working with students from four Chicago South Side high schools in a University of Chicago College Prep program. She knew more about the prospective students, the Chicago Public Schools (CPS), and what might be done. It was up to her to decide whether to go ahead. If the Clemente Course for high school students failed or put the University in a difficult position, McKee did not have the protection of tenure.

We looked at five schools from CPS Area 23,[1] where she had worked successfully with Eric Williams, the college prep specialist. It was not a promising list. More than two thirds of the students could not read at grade level, absenteeism was high, graduation rates were low, less than 1 percent of the students met college-readiness standards, more than eighty percent qualified for free meals because they were from low-income families, and the number of students who moved out of the area over four years was staggering: each high school would lose a third of its students. Dovetta said there were a hundred thousand students like that in Chicago. They came from what William Junius Wilson called "the underclass,"[2] and they were destined to continue in that class. Nothing changes

---

1   An administrative designation for an area containing a group of schools.

2   The term, popularized by Ken Auletta, is a cruel misrepresentation of the moral character of the poor. It has done inestimable damage to social justice in America. The Clemente Course is based on a diametrically opposed understanding of the poor. Racism, I think, plays no small part in the concept of an "underclass."

very much on the far South Side of Chicago, although people of good intentions make documentary films and write woeful books and articles about the black ghetto. I had intended to follow that pattern when Starling Lawrence at W. W. Norton insisted upon some solution to the problem of poverty.

The Clemente Course was my answer to his demand, but it had turned my life upside down, and now to face the problem of public education in the inner city, to implement a possible solution, was more than a person of my years should attempt. Every evil that had been engendered by slavery thrived on the far South Side of Chicago. Dovetta knew it, she knew how difficult it would be to make a significant change—one that was repeatable and reproducible, as the scientists say. Yet she went ahead. And Amy Thomas-Elder and I followed.

Choosing among the five best candidates required an act of faith, for there was nothing in the statistical profiles to give hope. There was a clue, however, to solving the puzzle: the principal of John Marshall Community Academy High School, usually known as Harlan Academy High School. Harlan was a difficult, nearly impossible place to manage: everyone feared the gangs, a student had been murdered in the school, parents were dubious about sending their children to Harlan, the faculty was demoralized, and the building was beginning to decay. Reginald Evans had been promoted to principal and sent to Harlan with the hope that he could bring order to the school. Evans moved into the new job with the mantra of failure as his instruction. Every tough kid in Chicago and all across the country knew the words to the inner-city song: Stop the violence. At Harlan, the police were not called to the school; they sat there in their cars or roamed the halls all day every school day waiting for the worst.

Evans soon found an ally at Harlan, a teacher who had been there for many years and was nearing retirement. She kept her hair blond and full and she dressed more formally than the newer teachers, who came to school in sweaters and jeans. Vivian Hapaniewski had spent a career among some of Chicago's most difficult and dangerous students, and she was going to retire without having given up hope that some of the students at Harlan High School would not fail. It was, in a curious way, like the career of the judge for whom the school had been named. When *Plessy v. Ferguson* was decided by the U.S. Supreme Court, only one justice, John Marshall Harlan, dissented from the decision that enshrined segregation in the United States. Hapaniewski and Evans were as stubborn in their beliefs as Harlan had been, when he wrote in his dissent, that the Constitution was "color-blind."

Dovetta McKee offered no details when she made the case for Harlan as the best choice for a Clemente Course. She said that the principal was open to new ideas, nothing more. Like a good lawyer, she gave no details to open the way to argument. Eric Williams of CPS Area 23 arranged a meeting with Evans, Hapaniewski, McKee, and Thomas-Elder. I was to attend via speakerphone, but the speakerphone in the principal's office didn't work. Dovetta solved the problem by holding her cell phone up to the little group. Although I could hear only part of the conversation, it was enough to know that Mr. Evans and Ms. Hapaniewski were formal and distant, curious, noncommittal. Evans's deep and coldly authoritarian voice came through clearly whenever he spoke, which was rarely. Eric Williams and Dovetta McKee did most of the talking.

The needs of the Clemente Course must have seemed exorbitant. We had come out of the ether, invaded the office of a man who had to deal with fifteen hundred students, and made this offer:

We would pay one half of the cost, supply the curriculum, and recruit the faculty. Everything else had to come from Harlan: half the cost of faculty, books, and management, plus a faculty coordinator, recruiting of students, reworking of the Harlan schedule to provide a regular time in the school day, and withal the absolute necessity of meeting CPS and State of Illinois standards over four years. Eugene Robinson, Jr., deputy director of Small Learning Communities, said he could find the necessary funds. Dr. Evans was far from comfortable. He spoke privately with Dovetta McKee about the problems posed by suddenly adding another course to an already full schedule. Evans already had a pre-engineering course and the AVID Program[3] (a system for teaching students how to study) and a business course, and W. E. B DuBois House and Langston Hughes House, and band and sports and the standard CPS high school subjects. "The curriculum is beginning to look like a Christmas tree," he said. "And now you want me to add one more course." It was the polite voice of an overworked and now exasperated man.

Evans would have shut the door on the proposal at that first meeting were it not for his theory of how to improve a school. He rarely spoke about the physical plant or the technology or the number of police cars out front. He could deal with those issues in his spare moments. It was the people he had to fix, and he had to do it within the rules of CPS and the union contract. The Clemente Course promised tenured faculty from the best colleges and universities in the Chicago area. Evans was polite, but he was busy. He had little time for what sounded like another problem. He had to find out how a Clemente Course would benefit Harlan students, and most of all he had to find out who these people were, and why

---

3   Advancement Via Individual Determination.

they thought they knew something about educating disadvantaged students in the city of Chicago.

It was the worst time in many years to start something new. Nobody had any money. School budgets had been cut and would be cut further. The state humanities councils and the National Endowment were suffering. I had presented the idea, thinking that at best it was something to be put away for the years of affluence, if ever those years were to come again. And yet there we were in the principal's office! It was as if Immanuel Kant's essay, *On the Old Saw: That May Be Right in Theory But It Won't Work in Practice*, was being put to the test in a Chicago public school.

I did not think there would be a Clemente Course at Harlan, at least not for that deadened time known as the foreseeable future. After the meetings, I sometimes sat with my head in my hands thinking that the naysayers were right: I was nuts. Solutions to the problem of educating children from the vast American cauldron of poverty had been tried by hustlers and helpers in almost every urban area, and nothing had worked. Even Geoffrey Canada's highly publicized $200 million Harlem Children's Zone had failed: it had become a part of the Bloomberg/Klein catastrophe for New York City children. Chris Whittle's schools for profit had not delivered either profit or education. Sara Stoelinga, the researcher for the Urban Education Institute, which operated four charter schools on the South Side of Chicago, said that test scores in the four schools were at the average for Chicago public schools. This litany of failure or at best holding on to mediocrity while mediocre meant worse every year was not unknown to Reginald Evans. He did not shrink back from the added cost per student of $1,300, slightly more than the cost of supplying a student with a computer. The CPS share was only $650, a little more than a 5 percent increase in the CPS cost per student. At that price, the Harlan/Clemente initiative could be scaled up.

The question Evans had to pose to himself was, Why take the

risk? Harlan had been steadily improving under his management. His drive to staff the school with what he called "good people" was working. He knew Dovetta McKee was in that category and possibly the young woman from the Odyssey/Clemente courses. But who would teach? Would Amy teach? Would the disembodied voice from New York City teach? He had the brief version of the first-year curriculum that I had presented in Bart Schultz's lecture series, and there was a book that was coming to him in the mail, *Riches for the Poor*; nothing more. There was no history to support the idea. It had always been a post-secondary course.

We had begun working on the Harlan project early in the spring of 2011, and now summer was coming, and with it the false starts. Whoever did not think the project was crazy had an expensive idea to improve it: one fellow wanted to do readings of Greek tragedies, continuing a program that had been therapeutic for wounded Iraq War veterans; another thought we needed rock concerts; and then there was the viola, the painter, the potter, and everywhere in every imaginable form, the researcher. I tried them all, especially the readings of Greek plays, which I thought would work very well, but there was a problem of time and the need to pay the actors. The idea was exciting, but I couldn't find a way to make it work. All summer everything seemed to go wrong, be set back. We had formed a committee to support the project, and by midsummer, Dovetta, Amy, and I were the only ones left. Would we start in September? A year from September? Never? I lay awake at night thinking about blame. I recited to myself much of what I learned from the Oxford English Dictionary beginning with the entry for "temerarious," which was used now only in literary context, an idea that pleased an old writer with pretensions. But the entries went all the way down to "temerous" and "temerously," and the lines were filled with words like "rash" and "foolish," "heedless," even "blindness." Yes, they included "boldness," but only when the adjective "excessive" preceded it. There was not a word about courage or bravery. "Temerity" was what I took to bed with me, and as the night went on into morning it turned into the second entry for "temerous," which offered only one word of definition—"timorous."

In the middle of the night never looked like the best time.

It was Vivian Hapaniewski who turned theory into practice. At first, I did not understand why she did it. Of all the people who should have known better, here was a woman who had been a teacher in the school, knew the neighborhood, knew the feeder schools. She was scheduled to retire at the end of the school year, but she told Evans that she would stay on through the first four years of the proposed course as both coordinator and writing teacher. She would help to recruit students, work out schedules, relieve him of the daily burden of managing this new kind of course. It was a long line, from Socrates to Hapaniewski, but it was now nearly complete; only the faculty, students, and the precious period during an already full day were lacking.

Dovetta and I worked on a brochure for prospective students and their parents. It included statements from the former director of admissions at the University of Chicago and the current director at the Illinois Institute of Technology about the consideration our students would receive when they applied to colleges. We also promised faculty from some of the best colleges and universities in the Chicago area. It was a winning promise, but neither Amy nor I had any idea of how or where we would find four associate professors who were willing to come to Harlan every week to teach students who might barely be able to read at grade level and who had rarely, if ever, done homework. Dovetta, Amy, and I confessed that the promised faculty was really no more than a hope, a dream. Perhaps "temerity" was just another word for lying.

Eric Williams spoke for hiring faculty from Chicago State. It was adjacent to Harlan, he had been a student there, Dovetta had done her undergraduate work at Howard and law school at Chicago State. The trouble was that Chicago State had gone through a terrible decline since they had studied there. At one point its accreditation was in question. The graduation rate was 13 percent, among the twenty-five worst universities in the nation. It was on its way back up, but universities do not recover quickly. I said that neither Chicago State nor the nearby community college, Olive-Harvey, were up to the standards of the Clemente Course. We had begun at Bard College and we had tried to maintain that level of excellence everywhere in the world. We would do so at Harlan or it would not be called a Clemente Course.

Since Chicago allows students completing the eighth grade to choose the high school they want to attend, we had to recruit from a long list of junior high schools. We would have liked students from the city's best middle schools with the highest grades and aptitude scores for our first venture in a public high school. We encountered two unexpected filters. The improvements Reginald Evans had made at Harlan had not become widely known; school counselors and parents still thought of it as a school ruled by gangs, with a weary, inept faculty, a decaying physical plant, and a poor record of college admissions. Most good students went elsewhere, and the few good students who chose Harlan were drawn to engineering or business or one of the other small programs. We would get the leftovers.

The recruiting did not go well. Our plan was to recruit fifty students and select twenty-five of those we thought were most likely to benefit from the course. On the day we had set to announce a summer session to prepare the students, we had recruited only a few. And then there were thirteen, and the number stayed between thirteen and seventeen. Based on CPS statistics, we would lose a third of them who would move out of the district during the four years of the course. I asked Vivian Hapaniewski for the names of the school counselors at those schools most likely to send students to Harlan. She sent a list carefully marked to indicate which would be best for me to telephone. Some counselors were unpleasant; several said they had already talked to Ms. Hapaniewski. A few said they had not seen the brochure Dovetta had sent to them. A few counselors said that parents did not want to send their children to Harlan. The telephone calls may have brought one or two more students, if any.

Dovetta McKee and Vivian were in regular contact about the recruiting problem. They were confident of having enough students to begin, but Vivian warned us that the CPS system allowed students to make a final decision within the first few days of the new semester. We would not know how many students were going to Harlan or how many of those would come to the Clemente Course until it was too late to change our plans.

Over the summer, Amy recruited the faculty. The first person who said she would teach was Catherine Weidner, a professor of history at Lake Forest College. Neither Amy nor I had a chance to meet Dr. Weidner before we asked her to teach at Harlan. What we saw and heard was a videotape of Catherine Weidner speaking and then taking questions at a conference. I was so impressed by her ease, her command of the material, and her decency that I feared I might be so anxious to recruit faculty that I had lost my judgment. I asked my wife if she would look at the tape. She thought I had understated the case for Dr. Weidner. Amy agreed. I wrote to Catherine Weidner, and we began.

Audrey Petty, a professor at the University of Illinois, had taught the literature section in a Clemente Course, and Amy said she was an excellent teacher. Dr. Petty was young, interested in working with people who had been deprived of the education they deserved, and she was a published writer, which I thought the students would admire more with each ensuing year. We talked about the curriculum, which she found acceptable for teaching at Harlan. Her academic work was on the Harlem Renaissance, which I thought would be important to the students.

Rebecca Zorach, who teaches art history at the University of Chicago, was on sabbatical, but agreed to teach at Harlan. Dr. Zorach was interested in the work of the younger black artists in Chicago, although her book, *Blood, Milk, Ink, and Gold*, dealt with French Renaissance art. She thought the curriculum I had written was acceptable, but too heavily weighted with classical works. She had a point.

After much coaxing, Amy Thomas-Elder, who taught philosophy at the Graham School at the University of Chicago and was the very soul of the Clemente Course in Illinois, agreed to teach the philosophy section. Amy had a powerful effect in the classroom. Students who had been in her classes in the Odyssey/Clemente Course in Chicago said that Amy was the best teacher they had ever known. They formed attachments to her that continued long after graduation, and Amy grew to care so deeply for them through the year of dialogue that she wept as she gave them their diplomas.

When the first class gathered, the students trickled in, a few just before the 8 a.m. starting time, and others throughout the period. There were twenty-three in all. Fewer than I had hoped for, but still a full complement for a class taught by the Socratic method. They were polite, sleepy after the long summer, mostly girls, a bit surprised by the new routines, but ready for the new class. The first weeks went to developing routines for note taking, homework, and class participation. The Clemente students were asked to read a series of myths: Greek, Navaho, Mayan, African. The idea was to teach the children of the narrow world of the ghetto that other cultures existed. They quickly learned to see patterns in the stories. They did not become young versions of Claude Lévi-Strauss, but they gained some sense of the connectedness of the world and the essential similarities among men.

As they came to their first Clemente classes they had already learned that this course would be different, and they were opened up a bit to what was to come. They may have enjoyed discussing the myths and writing a few sentences about them, but their anticipation of this pleasure did not awaken them all in time for school. Half the students arrived late and some of the others got there just in time for class to end. Dovetta McKee had encountered the problem in her own College Prep classes. She solved it by giving the students orange juice and breakfast bars before class. "You have to cut off serving the juice and breakfast bars at five minutes before the hour; you don't want them eating and drinking during class," she advised. It didn't work.

Half an hour before the first art history class was to begin, Rebecca Zorach arrived at Harlan. The school was still quiet, the grassy area behind the school nearly empty. The police would be there soon. Hall guards were already beginning to take their posts. Secretaries and assistants were at work in the principal's office. On the second floor Vivian Hapaniewski was in the room where the Clemente Course would be taught. She and Rebecca had prepared a slide projector and begun rearranging the desks into a circle to facilitate dialogue.

The first students entered shortly before 8 a.m. and helped to finish arranging the chairs. They were mostly girls, speaking softly, very much like the morning, sunny and slightly cool. Chicago is at its best as summer fades into a gentle autumn; through the windows of the room the field beside the school, now in its darkest green, invited chattering and expectation. The windows were closed, reminders of night. More students came. Miss Hap, as the students called her, met the latecomers with a frown for the time and a smile to welcome them even at the late hour. She was the one who kept order in the room, and she did it easily, for she looked at the students as if she wanted to embrace them.

It was a respectful room. The students set out their name cards, little formalities, every one with a surname so that the teacher might be able to say to them, "Mr." or "Miss." On the board in the front of the room the *Mona Lisa* smiled out at the students. Rebecca Zorach said it was not a painting; she referred to it as a "digital image." She would always make such careful distinctions. This was not an ordinary class and she did not consider them ordinary students. Before the class she confessed to being nervous, for she had never before taught high school students. She was a professor at a great university—had been an undergraduate at Harvard, with a doctorate from the University of Chicago—and she would only be able to teach them as she knew how, for she knew only students from the pool of the best in the country. This morning, she had two things in mind for the Harlan class. First, she passed out a brief page from Vasari's *Lives of the Artists*, and they looked at it together, gaining some idea about the man who had made the painting shown in the digital image on the screen. In the second part of the period, she brought out a bag filled with small packages, each one about twice the size of a fist and perfunctorily wrapped. She asked the students to form groups of three, and she gave one package to each group. This was an exercise in how to see and to speak about what they saw. It was the fundamental work of a class in art history. She asked the students to unwrap the packages and then to talk among themselves for a moment about what they saw. The objects inside were mainly handmade cups for coffee. There was also an *ibrik*, a small metal cup with a long handle used to brew Turkish coffee. She asked each of the trios to describe the object she had given them. One person spoke for each group. She did not have to tell them that only one could speak; they understood. The students felt the cups and studied them. One student said a cup was "frog-colored." Another said she saw a figure in the design of the cup. The one who held the *ibrik* spoke of a golden handle. The imagination of the students calmed the teacher. Dr. Zorach smiled; she and the students had begun to talk; the objects had initiated the art history section, a class was beginning to form.

In the next period, the AVID teacher gave over some of her time to the Clemente Course. Reginald Evans had come quietly into the room and sat in a chair near the back wall. The students, new to the school, did not recognize the man in the blue suit as the principal. His presence caused no anxiety. The class went on. I spoke with the students for a few minutes, and then asked if they would write on a single sheet of paper their name, the date, the name of the college they hoped to attend, and a brief statement about the word "freedom." After they had time to write, I asked the student sitting closest to me if she would read aloud what she had written about freedom. The class had grown restive while waiting for everyone to finish. Vivian and I asked the students to be quiet so that the reader could be heard.

Then the student, a girl, said in a very small, high-pitched voice: "Freedom is being able to do what you please as long as it benefits someone." The class applauded. Surprised and very pleased, I asked if someone else would like to read what she or he had written. Many hands went up. I pointed to one student, he read, and again the others applauded. The statements were not profound. Most had to do with what Isaiah Berlin called "positive freedom"; that is, the freedom to take control of one's life. The following year I would ask them again, and the next year, and the year after that. They gave promise.

I had said good-bye for now to the class when I noticed that someone had written on the blackboard behind me in perfect cursive handwriting: "A student who do not . . ." It was so astonishing that I said in a loud, accusatory tone, "Who wrote that?" The AVID tutor, a slim, handsome young man, perhaps a graduate student somewhere, confessed that he had written it. "Do?" I asked.

The students shouted, "Does!"

While the tutor erased the offending word and replaced it with the correct one, I apologized for the tone of my question.

It was over then. Rebecca, Vivian, and I left the classroom. The morning had been soured by a word. I could taste the connotations: bad grammar led to tardiness, implied truancy, bred violence. The naysayers had been right. The end of temerity is catastrophe. I had made a terrible error. I was dragging other people down with me— teachers, students, everyone. The certainty of failure stayed with me all morning. Only later, on the plane back to New York, when I looked at the names of the colleges the students hoped to attend, did my expectations return. With a few words they defined themselves: Harvard, Spelman, the University of Chicago, Howard, the University of Illinois, Morehouse, Michigan, Juilliard, Duke.

But it was not certain anymore. I wondered if we were all dreamers, only dreamers? This had been one day, a little more than an hour, including the time stolen from AVID. In a few weeks, more would be known. The professors would be able to judge. I waited. None of the faculty had taught high school students before: they knew no tricks, had no old lesson plans in battered binders, no weary lectures wearily to give. This was the Socratic method made gentle, but no less demanding of the midwives.

There were problems. Each teacher had a different view based on her own experience. Rebecca was the anxious one. A student had told her that the art history class was boring. Another student had told me that art history was her favorite class. Rebecca said, "It's going really well in a lot of ways." She spoke of "slotting into a high school situation, having to reinvent the wheel." The students didn't do their assignments, and many of them would not speak up in class. It concerned her, but she said that they were not so different in their work habits from some of her University of Chicago students. She took the class to an art exhibit at Chicago State, because she wanted them to see the real work, not just digital images. Some of the students, she said, did not know the difference between a painting and a photograph.

"When it goes well, it goes really well," she said. "I see them light up about certain things. For the kids who are receptive, it's giving them options. It's connecting them to other things in other classes."

Rebecca Zorach is a gentle woman, very young for a tenured professor, in love with her work, a scholar, but with the sensibility of an artist. The sound of the speaker on the wall in the classroom insisting that some student somewhere in the building respond to its command made her uncomfortable. She worried that high school was geared too much to discipline. "I don't like compulsion," she said, and turned to talking about Kehinde Wiley, a painter whose portraits of hip-hop artists would interest the class. Perhaps it would be possible to bring him and a few of his works to the class? Wiley's adaptation of classical elements to contemporary subjects was, in a way, like the Harlan Clemente Course. One could only hope that Zorach's sensibilities would infect the students.

Audrey Petty remembered her own struggle with not wanting to be smart, and she was aware of the same sense in the Harlan students. Yet Dr. Petty said, "I feel like it's been going well. Starting with the origin stories and folk tales was a good idea. I'm talking about story and narrative in their own lives, trying to invite their investment."

The size of the group was offputting for her. "Fundamental for me is building a conversation," she said. "I try to connect with every person in the room, pushing them, giving them prompts, giving them a question at the beginning of every class—I've done that with my college students.

"Our job is to light some fires. I think they're capable. Every student at some point has shared something with the class." And then she made the comment one expects from the people who teach adult Clemente students, but not yet with high school freshmen: "I'm learning so much from every class with them. I'm trying to be thoughtful at each step. What I sense with this group is tentativeness or shyness. The challenge has been about emotional enlistment." That's when she remembered her own struggle. She said that she could see a shift in some of them, and she gave an example of her method of bringing them together. "One of the first things we did was create a story in the class. Each one contributes a sentence." And she thought it was working. They were reading a García Márquez story and enjoying it. It was easy to understand why she chose to read the story early in the year: for the young, magic realism is the way of the world; they were not surprised that Gárcia Márquez's "Old Man Had Enormous Wings." The class was working: Audrey Petty led them to the dream of art.

At the end of her classes, students invariably went up to Catherine Weidner and thanked her. She was the history teacher, the American, the one who dug deep into the how and where of their lives. They read Locke almost immediately in Dr. Weidner's class. She said, "We had a really good discussion of Locke and the Preamble." She raised the question immediately, "Why do we need a government?" And one of her students said, "Because in a state of nature your mother could beat you."

Weidner's way was to keep returning to the text. It pleased her to see students begin to follow her example. She said, "When we talked about inalienable rights, they went back to Locke. They knew Locke was a powerful influence on Jefferson."

She saw changes coming over the class. "Two weeks ago, we had a class that was a mess. Now, last week was very good, this week better. We talked about the Declaration as a philosophical document, how Jefferson defined these ideas for the country."

The questions she asked in her midwifery came from her own deep understanding, which was the reason why we had looked so hard for teachers with advanced degrees: it is difficult to use the Socratic method if one's own scholarship is shaky. "I never taught high school kids before," Catherine said. "What it forced me to do is to reassess my pedagogy. I can't assume anything. How would I teach the Declaration to people who don't know it?

"If the students continue to participate, they will come away with the founding ideas. They need to understand that there are so many competing voices." She recalled reading a timeline with them, trying to keep them anchored in time and space in the document (the Declaration of Independence). "They are pretty savvy when it comes to the notion of rights," she said.

Catherine had already developed a teacher's affection for her students: "Some are pretty reticent," she said. "There are some really bright kids in this class. They're so polite. They're respectful and grateful." It was the mother as well as the teacher speaking: her older daughter had begun her second year away at college earlier in the autumn. As with Audrey and Rebecca, teaching was a joy. Rebecca took them to painting; Amy asked them to think about ethics; Audrey the writer introduced them to a writer's entry into story; and Catherine took them to their own country—she gave it to them to treasure. Citizenship was beginning, Jeffersonian capabilities were being born.

But there were questions deeper and more perplexing to be put to them, head-spinning questons, ideas that would open their hearts to the great Kantian summary question: "What is man?" Amy Thomas-Elder was the teacher of questions, the philosopher who insisted that their deepest beliefs be placed upon the tables before them and "pinched and poked," as E. E. Cummings had said of the work of "prurient philosophers" taking the world upon their knees to make love to the very locus of being. She said that her students did not do the readings before class; she feared trying to teach the *Apology*; yet she found that some of the responses in the classroom were extraordinary.

Vivian Hapaniewski saw quickly what the problem would be: students would come late for this, their first class. In response to the problem, she and Dr. Evans exchanged the time period with another subject so that the students would all be in school at the beginning of the Clemente Course class. It was a great upheaval in an already settled school day, but Reginald Evans had committed to the Clemente Course; he put the change through.

Vivian gave me the phone numbers of some of the students so that I could call them to talk about their progress. Although I made perhaps a hundred phone calls, only one student answered, a girl who was using a cell phone. She said she was on a bus and asked if I could phone her later. I called for several days, and when finally she answered again, I asked what had happened to her. "I was sleeping," she said.

"But it was still afternoon. And then I phoned again in the evening."

"I was sleeping."

When we did finally speak, she said that she liked the class and that she wanted to go to Columbia, where her sister was studying. I thought it was very ambitious of her to want to attend such a highly selective college. But after some conversation Columbia turned out to be an art and music school in Chicago. She was a very sweet child who lived with her mother and sister. Her mother had great ambitions for both girls.

A man answered at the home of one boy. Perhaps it was the

boy's father; he would not identify himself. He had not heard of the Clemente Course and apparently had no interest in the boy's schooling. The boy would be home on Sunday night, the man said. But he was not.

Vivian and I had a long talk about the children and our hopes for them. We knew each other by then and we could talk freely. The situation was worse than I had imagined. She spoke about low expectations, the demands of the central office, the lack of time, chaos. We tried to comfort each other by sharing what we knew. I found her a loving woman, angry about the system in Chicago. I admired her concern for the students and her frankness about the problem.

In November, we held the first faculty meeting. Reginald Evans had somehow managed to solve the worst of the problems, which was the constant tardiness: he moved the daily class from the first to the second period—the Clemente Course would now start at 8:48 a.m. There were other problems that would take longer to solve: a pair of truants, half the students who would not make comments even when called upon. It was difficult to tell whether they were terrified or recalcitrant or simply overwhelmed. Freshman year is a disorienting time for students, and this was a class unlike any other.

The Harlan faculty admired the college teachers for the depth of the questions they asked, and Vivian said the other teachers were learning from the college professors, but the Clemente Course students were having problems coping with the questions. It was possible that they could not understand what the teachers were asking. No one had ever asked them to consider narrative, recognize the use of perspective, understand natural law, or think of the philosophical questions raised by the myth of Gyges. If they had a ring like the one in the myth used by Plato, and they were invisible, what would they do? Amy brought each student a ring with a lollipop in place of a giant gemstone. They licked their candy Rings of Gyges and talked about what they would do. Slowly, she led them into speaking about power and human nature. She had discovered a way to bring them into physical contact with the questions of philosophy.

It did not satisfy her. Amy still asked herself when they would be ready for the *Apology*. Would it be this year? Were the classes too far apart at once each week? Did they need more continuity? Audrey wanted her students to read *A Midsummer Night's Dream*, but she too worried about the spacing of the classes. Would the schedule have to be different? Two days of philosophy, two of art history, and in the second semester two of history and two of literature? They were learning as the students learned. The teachers were bringing the curriculum into line with the reality of the inner city.

Reginald Evans explained to the college professors that for the students coming to high school was difficult. He said that he had made all Fs during his first weeks in high school. It was a difficult, frightening time, just as this was a difficult time for the faculty who were having their first experience of teaching high school students. We were discovering a new world just as we had done seventeen years earlier on 13th Street on the Lower East Side of New York and in the Bedford Hills Prison. There was much to do at Harlan: many changes to make, different kinds of expectations to harbor, letters to send home with the students, schedules to rethink, curriculums to revise, a culture of the streets to be remade into a culture of learning.

And then in the midst of all the frustrations and worries a boy in the art history class turned in a homework assignment—one paragraph about a picture of the Chicago skyline. He wrote:

When I look at this picture I see a calm, peaceful, and bright city. The city is pretty big and looks like it has plenty to offer.

The town looks safe enough to live in and start a career. Seeing that it's so big it must have some nice attractions and entertainment. Yeah, no matter how you look at it it's one fine place; in fact I just might move there.

The Clemente Course in the Humanities for adults had proved long ago that fine professors could educate a self-selected group of adults living in poverty. The humanities could pierce the structure of the surround of force that held people down and killed them. The Clemente Course for high school students was a different kind of endeavor: it went to the heart of the country and questioned the very idea of freedom and democracy in a diverse nation. Five women and one high school principal were taking the rough idea of a Clemente Course for high school students and giving it life. They were the founders, the Jefferson, Madison, Franklin, Hamilton, Adams, and Locke of this revolution.

At the close of the first faculty meeting in early November, I asked if they would answer two simple questions: Do you think this project will succeed? And will you teach this course again next year?

Yes and yes, was the Joycean loving answer. Yes and yes, they said. Yes and yes. Yes and yes.

Acknowledgments

The Course

The Clemente Course began with a question asked by Starling Lawrence when I first presented the idea to him for a book about poverty in America. He said that he was not interested in a "policy wonk book," nor did he think it was sufficient simply to describe the problems of the poor—it had been done. He insisted upon a book that offered some solution, however small, to the problem. The Clemente Course was a response to his question. He not only accepted the idea, this is the third book he has edited and published about it. Over the years his interest deepened and his involvement increased. He is now the president of the small non-profit corporation that manages the courses, one of its funders, and its chief operating officer.

Leon Botstein has supported the Clemente Course almost since its inception. Today, there are two branches of the Clemente Course involved with Bard College; several courses are operated directly by Bard and managed by Marina Van Zuylen and Max Kenner. Bard also grants college credit to courses operated by the Clemente Course in the Humanities, Inc., through a program managed on a volunteer basis by Dr. Van Zuylen, who wrote the two sections marked A and B in chapter 8, On Revolutionary Ground.

Funding for the courses has come from the state humanities

councils and the National Endowment for the Humanities; Starling Lawrence, W. W. Norton & Company; the AKC Foundation; John Childs, Peter Sourian, Sylvia Shorris, James Shorris, and others. Many colleges and universities have supported courses. Bard College and the University of Chicago have been key.

There are too many courses for all of them to be included in this book. The ones in Oregon, New Jersey, Pennsylvania, Washington, D.C., Texas, California, Connecticut, Florida, Indiana, and many courses in Canada have not found their proper place here. Not all of those courses are currently operating. The worldwide recession has made funding difficult. I regret the lack of space given to the Oregon courses at Reed College and Willamette College, and the role of Peter Steinberger and Jennifer Allen. Similarly for the Kellman Course at Bloomfield Hills College, and the work done there by Cheryl Evan and Bob Deischer over the past ten years. The Los Angeles course is a distant and friendly relative, overseen by Shari Foos and managed by "Doc" Tripp. Notre Dame has been teaching the homeless for many years in South Bend in a course led by Clark Power and Stephen Fallon. The Courses at Trinity College and Franklin and Marshall are now in hiatus for lack of funds, but I am hopeful about their return.

Author and Professor Dr. Zulma Ayes chairs the academic committee for the development and implementation of the Clemente Course in the Humanities at Inter American University of Puerto Rico, Metropolitan Campus. She also offers the introduction to the course in collaboration with Dr. Pablo Navarro. Lyvia Rodríguez and Alejandro Cotté from Proyecto ENLACE del Caño Martín Peña are course coordinators in the community.

The faculty includes Esq. Héctor Luis Acevedo, former mayor of San Juan; Dr. Rafael Aragunde, former secretary of education; philosophy professor Pedro Subirats; history professor Dr. Pedro

González; art professor Dr. Salomón Barrientos; Dean of Humanities Dra. Olga Villamil; and Spanish professors Dr. Luis Mayo and Dr. Dinah Kortright.

The academic committee responds to Chancellor Marilina Lucca Wayland, who was the main force behind the adoption of the Clemente Course at the University.

William Ferris, James Leach, and Bruce Cole, chairmen of the National Endowment for the Humanities, and Vice-Chair Carole Watson and Karen Mittleman of Public Programs, have been supporters of the Clemente Course over the years.

Our faculty, on five continents, have been superb, and I wish I could mention all of them by name. In the end, however, it is the students who are the course. It is to them that I am most grateful.

The Book

Over the last quarter of a century of working together, Starling Lawrence and I have become good friends as well as editor vs. writer. He set this book on the right path in the beginning and he has done all that any editor could for it in the end. No writer could ask for more.

This is the second book of mine that Ann Adelman copyedited. The first one was filled with words and proper names from several original Mesoamerican languages. The current book contains a few words from those languages as well as Korean, Cup'ik, Kiowa, Arabic, Darfuri, and Akan. Ann finds lost words, and overlooked ideas, makes gentle what would have been crude, and gives brio to sentences that are drowsing. I am grateful to her again.

Melody Conroy will be a full-fledged, full-time editor before very long. Writers should look forward to that day.

The last time Francine Kass designed a book that I wrote, she found the most ironic picture of heavenly clouds I had ever seen;

it was part of a nuclear cloud. This time the delicacy of the image on the front of the jacket represents the more winning part of her character.

The Life

Sylvia and I will have been married for fifty-six years by the time this book is published. I never dreamed I could have such good luck.

Appendix: The Clemente Course in the Humanities®, Inc.

Earl Shorris—Chairman
Starling Lawrence—President
Kristin O'Connell—Secretary
Stuart Stritzler-Levine—Treasurer
James S. Shorris—Counsel
Amy Thomas-Elder—Director of Programs
John W. Childs—Finance Committee chair
Grace Glueck—Finance Committee
Jaime Inclán—Research Director
Peter Sourian—Finance Committee
Marina Van Zuylen—Director of Bard College Courses

Web Site
Lela Hilton

Bard College
Leon Botstein—President
Dimitri Papadimitriou—Executive Vice President
Peter Gadsby—Registrar
Marina Van Zuylen—Bard College Clemente Course
    Co-Director
Max Kenner—Bard College Clemente Course Co-Director

The University of Chicago
Bart Schultz—Director, Civic Knowledge Program
Dovetta McKee—Office of Special Programs, College Prep

Chicago Public Schools
Reginald Evans—Principal, Harlan Academy High School
Vivian Hapaniewski—Harlan Academy Clemente Course
    Coordinator
Eric Z. Williams—Office of College and Career Preparation,
    Chicago Public Schools

Resources
Anne Leavitt, President—King's College, Philosophy
Danielle Allen—Institute for Advanced Studies, Political
    Philosophy; Classics
David Bevington—University of Chicago, Medieval Literature;
    Shakespeare
William H. Gass, Emeritus—Washington University,
    Philosophy; Literature
Harper Lee—Literature
Mary Ann Mason—former Dean of Graduate Studies UC
    Berkeley, Law; Social Science
Ismat Mahmoud Ahmed—Chair, Department of Philosophy,
    University of Khartoum
Oupa Lebellem—Director, Teacher Education, UNISA (South
    Africa), African Culture
Bart Schultz—University of Chicago Civic Knowledge Project,
    Philosophy
Ilan Stavans—Amherst College, Spanish Literature
John Van der Zee—History
C. D. Wright—Brown University, Literature (poetry)
Martha Ward—University of Chicago, Art History